P9-ECP-778

PASSING FARMS, ENDURING VALUES

"And God said, let the earth bring forth grass, the herb,
yielding seed, and the fruit tree yielding fruit after his kind,
whose seed is in itself upon the earth: and it was so." Genesis
1:11. "Orchard," 1958, Santa Clara County. *Photograph by and
courtesy of Ansel Adams*

PASSING FARMS, ENDURING VALUES

California's Santa Clara Valley

Yvonne Jacobson

With a Foreword by Wallace Stegner

WILLIAM KAUFMANN, INC.   Los Altos, California
In Cooperation with the California History Center,
De Anza College, Cupertino, California

The endpapers illustrate bing cherries (at twice their actual size), and Blenheim apricots (actual size).

10 9 8 7 6 5 4 3 2 1

First Edition

Library of Congress Cataloging in Publication Data

Jacobson, Yvonne, 1938—

    Passing farms, enduring values. California's Santa Clara Valley.

    Includes index.
    1. Agriculture—California—Santa Clara County—History.
    2. Horticulture—California—Santa Clara County—History.
    3. Santa Clara County (Calif.)—History. 4. Farms—California—
Santa Clara County—History. 5. Jacobson, Yvonne, 1938–
    6. Santa Clara County (Calif.) Biography. 7. Santa Clara County
(Calif.)—Industries—History. I. De Anza College. California
History Center. II. Title.

S451.C2J3 1984   338.1'09794'71   83-19611
ISBN 0-86576-045-4

"There is no secret to farm life. It is work. All I remember all these years is work."

ROSE ZAMAR OLSON (1904—   )

"We have the most fertile land in the world right here. What more could I wish for? We are doing what we want to do, so why should I want to change?"

RUEL CHARLES OLSON (1899—1980)

"I'm interested in pursuing a career in agriculture because its a good way of helping people and not only that; if there were some sort of major disaster, people with knowledge will be needed to help devise ways of supplying food...."

MICHELLE ANN JACOBSON (1963—1982)

All contemporary photographs not otherwise accredited are by the author.

This book was partly funded by a grant given to the California History Center Foundation by the California Council for the Humanities, the state branch of the National Endowment for the Humanities.

Matching funds were provided by:

American Savings & Loan
George Miller Brown Family
Community Foundation of Santa Clara County
FMC Corporation
Stella B. Gross Charitable Trust
Mr. & Mrs. Charles B. Kuhn
Will & Hazel Lester
Mr. & Mrs. Charles John Olson
Pacific Telephone
San Jose Mercury News—Tony Ridder
Seven Springs Ranch—Dorothy Lyddon
Mr. & Mrs. Robert Suhr
Sun Garden Packing Company
Syntex Corporation
Mr. & Mrs. Hart H. Tantau
Nancy P. Weston

The findings, conclusions, and opinions presented herein do not necessarily represent the views of either the California Council for the Humanities or the National Endowment for the Humanities.

CONTENTS

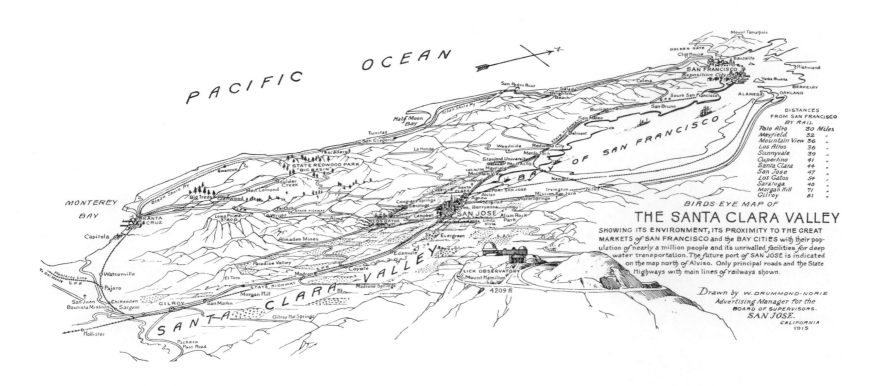

PACIFIC OCEAN

MONTEREY BAY

SANTA CLARA VALLEY

DISTANCES
FROM SAN FRANCISCO
BY RAIL

Palo Alto	30 Miles
Mayfield	32
Mountain View	36
Los Altos	36
Sunnyvale	39
Cupertino	41
Santa Clara	44
San Jose	47
Los Gatos	54
Saratoga	46
Morgan Hill	71
Gilroy	81

BIRDS-EYE MAP OF
THE SANTA CLARA VALLEY
SHOWING ITS ENVIRONMENT, ITS PROXIMITY TO THE GREAT
MARKETS of SAN FRANCISCO and the BAY CITIES with their population of nearly a million people and its unrivalled facilities for deep
water transportation. The future port of SAN JOSE is indicated
on the map north of Alviso. Only principal roads and the State
Highways with main lines of railways shown.

*Drawn by W. DRUMMOND-NORIE
Advertising Manager for the
BOARD OF SUPERVISORS.
SAN JOSE.
CALIFORNIA
1915*

FOREWORD

LOCAL HISTORY IS THE BEST HISTORY, the history with more of ourselves in it than other kinds. It is immediate, intimate, personally apprehended, and at least in America it is by definition recent. It does not have to be split up into categories and kinds, economic, political, military, social. It is the record of human living in its daily complexity, and the sense of place is strong in it. Its actors are our neighbors, our families, ourselves. It is history of a handmade kind, homely and familiar, human lives on their slow way into memory and tradition.

Passing Farms, Enduring Values is that kind of history. An affectionate memorial to the Santa Clara Valley as it was from the late nineteenth century until after World War II, it remembers and evokes a way of life full of the democratic spirit and rich in human satisfactions, now overwhelmed by growth and change.

But as Yvonne Jacobson fully recognizes, her book has more than local application. It is local history that casts a shadow longer than itself. The Santa Clara Valley is a microcosm or representative, it can stand for the once-virgin American continent, and what happened to it can stand for our entire history as a people. The recapture (or more properly, the creation) of the history of this place, even as it is being transformed, is perhaps indulgence of nostalgia, but it is also a move toward a broader understanding of forces peculiarly though not exclusively American.

Like Canadians, Australians, and white South Africans—all invading peoples—Americans suffer from a history deficiency. The immigrants from whom we derive came from many places and diverse cultures, and came relatively recently, and came looking forward, not back. A great cultural fault cuts across our lives and memories, with much fracturing at the fault line and many secondary faults consequent on the first big one. Our traditions, our social bonds, our habits, our affiliations, are broken off, and must later be remade.

Some ancestral cultures, especially those with a religious base, are tough and persistent, as witness the Amish, the Hasidim, and others. Some are constantly reinforced by new immigrations and by continued contact with the old world. Some—and the more they remain stubbornly themselves or the more visible they are because of custom or color or the slant of their eyes the more this is true—are driven inward upon themselves by prejudice and discrimination. For those reasons, some American communities, families, and individuals retain the stamp of their European, Asian, or African origins for generations; and the stability of their social relationships is often accompanied by a geographical stability. They tend to settle in one place and stay there.

They are the exceptions. In general, over time, the old cultures are lost or modified, and are remembered principally at festival times, in proper names, and in ethnic foods. Beliefs and expectations get Americanized, grandchildren forget or never learn the language of their grandparents. Swiftly for some, more gradually for others, new hybrid cultures grow up from the rootstocks of the old. Given time enough, even biological differences ought to be blended into one new hybrid race to match the new hybrid culture.

But in the meantime we have to live with a cut or damaged root system, and what is worse, a root system that is always suffering new transplantings. Also, while races and cultures are naturalizing themselves on new ground, they are profoundly changing the ground itself, often more than once, and that only accelerates the spiral of social and psychological change.

In new country we busy ourselves finding and exploiting the resources that are there, we learn what crops will grow and what will not, we acquire the lore of new weathers, seasons, soils, pests, diseases, opportunities, markets. We cut down forests to create fields, we plant prairies to create orchards. We import domesticated plant and animal species that compete with and often suppress native species, as cattle replaced the buffalo, and as wild oats, mustard, and filaree—Mediterranean weeds brought in by the Spaniards—have all but crowded out California's native grasses. And as our numbers grow and the complexity of industrial civilization forces changes in our living, we urbanize our living space and turn our fields and orchards and vineyards and gardens into subdivisions, factories, parking lots, shopping centers, freeways and cloverleaf interchanges.

Even if we don't urbanize an area as the Santa Clara Valley has been urbanized, our human activities often bring about profound changes. In pragmatically creating a favorable habitat for ourselves in unknown country, we characteristically damage the country and destroy the habitats of native species, including native peoples. Changes that Nature unaided might produce in hundreds of thousands of years come about under our management in less than a century. Some that Nature would never get around to we bring about in a generation. Life in America is more often a becoming than a being.

And all of this speeding, changing front pulls a spiritual vacuum in its wake. Not only are the places we came from left behind, but the past is left behind with them. History and the sense of history are baggage that the American dream loses in transit, and it takes us a good while to realize the enormity of the loss. Sometimes we don't recognize the loss until it is irreplaceable, sometimes we catch on in time.

Often, we feel the absence of history as a simple inability to participate in the love of place that others seem to feel. We have gnawings and cravings for something we cannot name. We are uncertain where we belong, we have doubts about the adequacy of a present that has neither past nor future attached to it. We may be tempted by causes and cults that involve us in communal activities, including some bizarre ones. We may feel an impulse to revisit the place of our childhood, hungering for revelation about who we truly are. The 'Roots' syndrome afflicts more Americans than black ones.

What we are feeling is the displacement of growing up without history, or at least without history that we can recog-

nize and claim as our own. Not everyone who has the history deficiency realizes what it is, but most of us feel it in some degree. The lucky ones not only realize it but try to do something about it as Yvonne Jacobson has done in this book: they begin to gather and assemble and put in order a tradition and a group memory, recognizing that a shared past not only gives us a personal and social identity, but is the basis for pride. It is as necessary for the prevention of cultural anemia and personal *anomie* as Vitamin C is for the prevention of scurvy.

In older parts of America such as New England, well into its fourth century of settlement, the process of de-culturation and re-culturation has come full circle. In New England the Bicentennial was a rich and varied intellectual and emotional sharing. In the West, barely into its second century, it was not. Except among a few enthusiasts, history has not yet been reinvented here, and even where it has, it is likely to be distorted by characteristic myths traceable not to the facts of living but to dime novels and horse opera. In the West, too, change has had a headlong velocity, and that both exacerbates nostalgia and makes retrospection difficult. As fast as a local past is perceived, it has vanished. No sooner is a way of life known and loved than it has to be given up, and may be preserved only in photographs or memory.

And so I understand the feeling, close to desperation, with which Yvonne Jacobson has tried to gather together the available history of the place she was born in, and to evoke, even as it changes into something unrecognizable, the bucolic Santa Clara Valley of her childhood, in the years when it seemed as stable as any American community has ever been, and when it was truly both a Jeffersonian agrarian democracy and the Valley of Heart's Delight.

Mrs. Jacobson (born Yvonne Olson) does not deal in myths, but in the substantial memorabilia of what was once as wholesome, prosperous, and egalitarian a community as the imperfect human race is ever likely to produce. Her book first took form as an exhibit, since made permanent at the San Jose

Historical Museum, of photographs, diaries, letters, machinery, tools, books, clothing, and household gear reflecting the life that the Olsons and their neighbors knew in the Santa Clara Valley for three generations.

Born in the Garden of the World, brought up in it, and still living in it after it has been invaded by the asphalt of Conurbia, she has seen the springs that were Milky Ways of blossom, and the summers rich and over-ripe with fruit. She knows the labors of the several seasons, and the exotic but peaceful melting-pot mixture of breeds and nationalities—Californio, Mexican, Italian, Yugoslav, Yemenite, Scandinavian, French, Japanese, Chinese. She is herself such a mixture, Swedish on one side, Lebanese on the other, and she is married to a South African. Because she grew up at the end of a rich period of horticultural stability when the valley was a fruit bowl, and because her parents and grandparents were wholly involved in what she and her brother still keep alive, she has a living, breathing, sensuous, emotional and intellectual commitment to the valley and its history.

No one could be better placed to report on the Santa Clara Valley past and present. Her parents and grandparents were orchardists, her brother still is, her husband is a computer scientist, immigrant like her grandfather but building the future out of silicon chips instead of the valley's rich soil.

In the process of recording the valley of her girlhood, Mrs. Jacobson tells us a good deal about what it was before white immigrants discovered that there was no place in the world better adapted to the growing of fruit. Once, when the Costanoan Indians lived in it, it was a park-like oak forest reaching southward from a clean bay and cupping up to the enclosing low mountains. The climate was mild and benevolent, the bay full of shellfish. The creekside tangles grew wild berries and the oaks provided the wherewithal for unlimited acorn flour. At least from the nostalgic viewpoint, Eden.

Original sin came with the Spaniards, who forced the hunters and gatherers of the valley tribes into the Santa Clara Mission and co-opted them for farm labor. Spanish cattle and horses increasingly grazed and trampled the grasses of the oak openings, their weeds invaded and took hold, they began to cut the oaks—for lumber, for firewood, for planting space.

The processes begun by the Mission and the adjoining Pueblo of San Jose accelerated swiftly with the first Americans. Within a generation after 1846 the valley was mostly wheat fields. And hardly had wheat begun to form a special pattern of valley life than orchards began to replace it—pear, peach, cherry, prune, forerunners of the golden age.

The valley was never California agriculture as we have historically known it, not the factories in the fields that in the Central Valley and elsewhere have proved so economically potent and so humanly arid. This was down-home farming, three generations of tranquility, beauty, health, and productivity based on family farms of small acreage but bountiful production. The Santa Clara Valley, even when I arrived here in 1945, provided the fresh, canned, and especially dried fruit for half the world. The dried peach pies that my mother baked in Saskatchewan during World War I almost certainly came from here. The smoked prunes that we had for breakfast in Norway in the 1950s probably did. This was *par excellence* a fruit bowl, and it spread its fragrant bounty world-wide.

What has happened to that Eden is made plain in Mrs. Jacobson's text. Change marked time during the Twenties, during the Depression, during the war. But with the end of the war, when enormous new influxes of people began, change speeded up. We heard how many thousands of acres annually were going out of orchards and into subdivisions and shopping centers, we watched the electronics factories spring up like mushrooms from Redwood City to San Jose, and we did not in the least realize or understand the magnitude of the transformation. Then one spring we drove through and the endless froth of blossoms was no more than local patches. One summer we found that there were no longer any orchards where we could pick our own apricots at a pittance a pailful.

The valley was cut by tangles of freeways, we no longer knew the way to anywhere, we got lost going to Saratoga.

That was about the time that Yvonne Olson Jacobson began to feel the loss of what she knew, and began to gather up its history. Much of it is in this book, either in words or in the speaking photographs. The title of the book might be *Paradise Lost.* The moral is that, given a second chance anywhere else, our migratory people might do a little better, save a little more, develop institutions and tax laws that would permit the saving of productive and edenic valleys like that of Santa Clara from what happened here.

Silicon Valley is probably a good, in many ways. The Valley of Heart's Delight was a glory. We should have found ways of keeping the one from destroying the other. We did not, and so the drama of change in this brief Eden could appropriately end with the final stage direction in Chekhov's *The Cherry Orchard:*

A distant sound is heard, coming as if out of the sky, like the sound of a string snapping, slowly and sadly dying away. Silence ensues, broken only by the sound of an ax striking a tree in the orchard far away.

WALLACE STEGNER

PREFACE

THIS BOOK OWES ITS ORIGIN to a shiver that ran down my back in April 1979. My father, my brother, John, and I sat talking about the future of our farm. Once located in the heart of a vast fruit-growing region, the farm is now an island surrounded by high-technology companies and an urban environment. I looked out the window of the office, down the driveway that runs between the vintage barns, toward the antique, hand gas pump, still in use, to the cherry orchard.

The familiar was everywhere. I could see where, as a child, I picked prunes (the prune trees were replaced by cherries), and where I cut apricots in the shed. In the three-story barn I used to jump with my friends from the top floor into the bins of soft, sticky dried prunes a floor below. When he caught us at it, my father would shout, "You kids, get out of there!"

Suddenly, it became clear to me that all this could not last. The idea that I should stop teaching and devote myself to recording our family farm came in the form of a shiver, a premonition. By November 1980, a year and a half later, my father was dead.

As I began the work of photographing our farm and interviewing my father and mother, I realized that our family farm, reaching back to the turn of the century and covering four generations, had significance beyond our family history. Our story symbolized something of the history of the valley, the settlement of the West, and a way of life that is quickly disappearing from the United States.

My grandfather's settlement of these few acres; my father's stewardship over a lifetime with my mother at his side through every harvest; the participation of us three children working alongside our parents until the reins were passed on to us; was this not a pattern repeated a thousand times over in American history? It was certainly an ideal sung by presidents, politicians, philosophers, and poets. The times have changed. Every ten years now, another million family farms disappear through absorption by larger farms, urbanization, or aban-

donment. There are less than 2.3 million farms today. In 1920, 30 percent of the American population still lived on farms. Today, only 2.4 percent can be found there.

Family farms will always survive in one form or another, but the time when America had land enough to fill the dreams of the world's poor is over. The age of the yeoman freeholder is part of history. What is left are remnants of a way of life that characterized America for two hundred years.

Once this became clear to me, our personal story seemed to widen in its significance like ripples in a pond. Determined to set down a record of what we had in the Santa Clara Valley, I approached the California History Center at De Anza College, where I was a teacher in the humanities department. The director, Seonaid McArthur, agreed with my goals. With the backing of the History Center and the Santa Clara County Historical Heritage Commission, who acted as community sponsors, I applied for funds from the National Endowment for the Humanities through the California Council for the Humanities in San Francisco. The first grant financed a photographic exhibit that opened two years later. Response from the community was gratifying. People came forward to offer pieces of family history. Ansel Adams loaned us two photographs that he had taken in Santa Clara County prior to the 1950s. He granted us permission to use these marvelous images in the book as well. Ralph Rambo, county historian, loaned us several of his most prized possessions. There were too many contributions to list individually. The exhibit toured the county and was displayed in the governor's office in Sacramento. Now it is housed permanently in the San Jose Historical Museum, in a restored fruit barn.

I then applied to the National Endowment for the Humanities to use some of our funds, originally intended for a film, for the production of a book. We were given permission to do this and, as with the exhibit, I raised matching funds from the community with the help of Nancy Weston, whose family had lived on the same pear-growing land for nearly a century.

Nancy felt strongly that something should be done to preserve the history of the valley's agricultural past.

What has emerged from a private, individual story is the record of a community. For, added to the photos of our farm, are those of other farms that are still in operation—the remnants of a tradition that once was a whole piece of cloth. Along with the new photographs are those of historical interest, loaned to us by many different sources: farm families, museums, historical societies, archives, and libraries.

In April, 1979, I began a chronicle of my visits to the farm. This journal, which was completed in June, 1980, has served as a resource for the writing of this book, as have the many tapes, photographs, and articles I have collected—now donated to the Michelle Ann Jacobson Memorial Collection at the California History Center, De Anza College, Cupertino, California.

In the job of photo selection George Craven, head of De Anza College's photography department, was of key importance. In fact, without his encouragement, the project might never have come together. I was not a trained photographer, but George gave me the courage to learn this technical skill. He saw the importance of the undertaking since nothing of the type had been done for Santa Clara County. With less than 21,000 acres of fruit, nut, berry, vegetable, and seed farms left on the valley floor, there was no time to lose.

George and I agreed on the nature of the photographs to be included: historical documents that record people and what they do, the landscape in which they live, the fabric and character of their lives. Susan Sontag in her book *On Photography* calls photographs a form of *memento mori* in the tradition of those eighteenth-century painters who captured a scene knowing it would be a memory of what had passed and been lost. In their paintings they included, among the abundance of the harvest, fall leaves, dead game, and—for those who might not catch their meaning—a human skull.

While photographs are testaments to what has passed, they are also affirmations of life. The child captured playing with her dolls, the farmers riding their tractors in the middle of a sea of plants, the weekend company caught in a moment of laughter, the women working in fruit canneries—these are moments whose meaning lies far deeper than nostalgic sentiment, but that partake of that sentiment as well.

Bringing about a project of this kind requires the help of numerous people. I want to thank the California History Center Foundation, the Santa Clara County Historical Heritage Commission, the California Council for the Humanities, and the National Endowment for the Humanities for their help, the Sourisseau Academy for an early grant to aid in photographic costs, our many sponsors and donors, the families who opened their homes and histories to me, and the scholars who aided by sharing their time, especially Dr. Bert Gerow, professor emeritus of anthropology at Stanford University, for materials he has collected on Santa Clara County over thirty-five years.

Wallace Stegner, dean of Western writers, has devoted a lifetime to chronicling American experience through his richly textured fiction and histories of the West. He has spoken with eloquence on behalf of the environment from the Grand Canyon to the foothills of Santa Clara County. Though many regard him as a national treasure and heavy demands are made on his time, he always made himself available as an advisor to this project, reading the manuscript and offering welcome suggestions for which I am very grateful.

Dr. Jeffery Smith (1907–1981), professor of philosophy and humanities at Stanford University, was both friend and mentor. His comment, when I spoke to him about this project, was "What took you so long?" Dr. Thomas A. Bailey (1903–1983), esteemed professor of American history at Stanford, was of particular help because he was born in Santa Clara County and picked fruit for several years as a way to pay for his undergraduate education at Stanford. He read the text for the exhibit and book. Dr. Seonaid McArthur read the text as well and contributed her expertise in California history. Special thanks are due Bruce Strong, a research assistant for the exhibit, who

xv

uncovered many of the fine photographs for it in libraries and archives. He also gave valuable advice at each stage of the book's development.

Other readers contributed their time and special knowledge of Santa Clara County. They include Bob and Audrey Butcher, Nancy Weston, Bob McMann of the Santa Clara County Farm Bureau, my sister Jeanette Gottesman, and Louis Paviso who shared his knowledge of local technology. Thanks are due to Mike Hamilton of William Kaufmann, Inc., who led me through the production phase of the book with uncommon courtesy; and to J. M. B. Edwards, whose skill as copy-editor helped transform the book from a rough text to something more polished. Just as important as those who helped with the manuscript was Yolanda Wuth of Foto-Graphics who copied, developed, and printed most of the black-and-white photographs, often working from faded orig-inals. Her attitude was never, "It can't be done," but rather, "Sure, I'll do it."

Most of all I want to thank my husband, William Jacobson, and our children Mark and Laura for their support and patience during five years of turmoil in our home. To all of these I extend thanks and more thanks.

YVONNE JACOBSON

My father, Ruel Charles Olson (1899–1980) asked me to bring
my camera to photograph his favorite tree, planted in 1906,
which had blown down in a windstorm the night before. The
old giant could not support the 2,000 pounds of fruit my
father estimated to be on the branches. He said about the tree,
"We grew up together."

A family farm in the eastern foothills of the Santa Clara Valley, c. 1900, with orchards established a few years before. Barns and careful fencing suggest it was also a cattle or dairy operation. Note open fields (top left) still in grain production and neatly tended kitchen garden (bottom right). *Courtesy Sourisseau Academy*

Spring plowing in a prune orchard, Santa Clara Valley, c.1910.
Small redwood frame house (center), similar to the one
I grew up in, was typical of valley farms. *Courtesy California
Historical Society, Southern Pacific Photo.*

Nathan L. Lester (bearded man, left rear) with his wife Sarah
and several of his six children, plus neighbors and friends,
c. 1890; all are helping with the apricot cutting. Lester, a
carpenter from Connecticut, bought a 31-acre farm in San
Jose's Willow Glen area in 1883; his grandchildren Ray and
Lee Lester still farm in Coyote today, while great-
grandchildren Stan and Russ, farm in Winters. *Courtesy Lester
Family Collection*

Tank houses like this one, built in 1913 on the Lyons property and later moved to this site on the Olson farm, were once a familiar sight in the valley. *Photo by George M. Craven, 1984*

View from Arastradero Road near the railroad (today's Junipero Serra Boulevard) toward Stanford University's Ryan Laboratory, 1933. Albert Freitas plowed the hay field for his father John M. Freitas, who rented land from the university. The oak tree still stands, but buildings block the view today. *Photo by Dwight Bentel*

The large corrugated iron barn on our farm, built in 1938, stored dried prunes and, on its third floor, housed the grading and sorting devices. From its windows I could see in every direction in the valley.

Los Gatos Creek as seen from east bank, c. 1900, looking
north toward El Monte Sereno in the west. Over the centuries
it was creeks like this one that carried down rich mountain soil
to valleys. Highway 17 crosses the spot today. *Courtesy Los
Gatos Library*

Lunch time for a Mexican worker at the Olson cherry farm, Sunnyvale, 1980.

George Aihara (right), who lived on our farm with his family, visits with Caramie Sayig, my mother's sister, her husband, John, and their five-year-old daughter, Louise, in front of Sayig's Grocery and Delicatessen, c. 1940. On warm sunny days we children would cross El Camino Real to buy an ice cream there for five cents. *Courtesy Louise Sayig Orlando*

My mother and I at the family fruit stand, c. 1946; in the back of the stand is a woman packing cherries. Nothing much has changed here, except that everything else has changed. *Olson Family Collection*

By 1921 Sunnyvale's main street, Murphy Avenue, was lined with cherry trees. The electric sign, installed by subscription, helped to identify the town at night but also indicated Sunnyvale's civic spirit. *Photo from Camera Mart, Sunnyvale*

The same scene—Murphy Avenue, northward from El Camino Real—in 1984. *Photo by George M. Craven*

Andrew Rodriguez, head vaquero or *mayordomo* of the Henry Miller ranch, c. 1895 in Gilroy, holds rawhide *riata* (lasso) in one hand and reins with the other. Note Spanish-style spur on boot, hand-tooled saddle trimmed with silver, and horn to which lassoed cattle were secured. American cowboys learned much from such men. *Courtesy Gilroy Historical Museum*

Local Costanoan Indians in tule boat on San Francisco Bay, 1818, as portrayed by artist Ludivick Choris who visited California with a Russian expedition that year. While the Indians were excellent basket weavers, it was the mission fathers who taught them to weave cloth such as the woman is wearing. *Courtesy California History Center*

California was claimed by the United States when the flag was raised at the Pueblo de San Jose in 1846, as shown in this drawing done long after the event. *Courtesy California State Library*

Two vaqueros roping cattle in front of Mission San Jose (note Indian huts). Lithograph is based on painting by naval officer and artist William C. Smyth, who visited California in winter 1826–27. Cattle introduced from Spain via Mexico took on a wild character in California because they competed with deer and antelope for forage. *Courtesy New York Historical Society*

Vineyard plot of Santa Clara College (now University of Santa Clara), 1911; the plot, though not the vines, dated back to 1819 when Mission Santa Clara was moved to the present site of the university. After 1846 newcomers took cuttings from this vineyard and the orchard across the street to begin the wine and fruit industries in Santa Clara County. The vineyard was replaced by Varsi Library in 1931. *Courtesy Archives University of Santa Clara*

CHAPTER 1
SANTA CLARA VALLEY
AND THE WAY WE WERE

THIS IS A STORY about change and continuity; about what we were before Santa Clara County became "Silicon Valley." It is the story of the family farms, and for me it begins in a tree in our garden—which is to say our farm, for they were one and the same.

The walnut tree stood outside the door to our small redwood house. It was the last of a row that at one time stretched along El Camino Real (The King's Highway), hemming in the apricot orchard, and then turned along the three-hundred-foot driveway to our back door. Before Father Junipero Serra founded the mission trail, El Camino Real existed as an Indian path connecting various villages and tribelets from east to west. Even as a child I could sense that history had passed my door.

There is nothing like a spreading walnut tree for coolness in summer. I spent much of my youth in the orchard trees, especially this walnut, imagining worlds I had vague notions of, creating spaces to fit my fancy. I was a captain coming up the coast of California for the first time, the tree my mast. I was a conquistador, the tree my lookout from which I could survey this vast new territory.

What I was in 1948 was a pigtailed child of ten, a farmer's daughter with a sister and brother, mother and father, and acres and acres of trees—a sea of trees that followed the seasons as regularly as the moon follows the earth.

As I look back now I realize that while I made up worlds, I was living in a real fairy tale. Can you imagine eight million trees—the largest orchard the world has ever seen—blooming in spring? In 1925, one hundred and twenty-five thousand acres of orchards and vineyards were nestled within the protective arms of two mountain ranges. The Diablo Range runs along the eastern edge of the Santa Clara Valley. These mountains appear bone-bare except for the oaks that cling to damp crevices. The Santa Cruz Mountains flank our western side. The Spanish called these the Blue Hills. Some individual mountains were called "black," but in truth these heavily wooded hills that catch the abundant ocean rains are often purple. They block excessive ocean dampness from the valley, but allow enough coolness to produce a perfect growing climate. The Diablo and the Santa Cruz mountains are ribs of the Coast Ranges, which punctuate the coastal topography from Washington State to Mexico. Of the county's 832,256 acres only one-third comprise the famed Santa Clara Valley. As if the mountainous flanks were not enough to render the area beautiful, the valley sits on the southern rim of San Francisco Bay. Santa Clara County was one of the original twenty-seven counties in California.

Fruit flourished from the first plantings of the padres in 1777, and it still does in backyards and pocket farms. The orchard plantings began on a vast scale in the 1880s and orchard trees were the mainstay of the landscape until the 1960s. During that time prunes were the number one crop; Santa Clara Valley controlled the market for prunes in the United States and had a major influence on the world market. Other crops like apricots, pears, and cherries, flourished as well. Juicy, sweet fruit grew not only in quantity but in extraordinary quality: plums plump with sugar, peaches full of color and flavor, cherries so tempting and delicious that overeating was not unusual, and apricots so golden, scrumptious and profitable they were dubbed "California gold" by our neighbor Charlie Lincoln Stowell. Walnuts, almonds, almost any deciduous tree grew here to perfection. The whole effect of such an orchard haven, encircled by mountains and bounded by sparkling San Francisco Bay, prompted the romantic title, "Valley of Heart's Delight." Given early in the century, the title stuck.[1]

The Santa Clara Valley, according to Bayard Taylor, a noted writer and traveller of the nineteenth century, was one of the three most beautiful valleys in the world. No one disputed him. Chauncey M. Depew, a presidential candidate in 1888 and board chairman of the Vanderbilt railway system, which included several major lines, put it this way: "Say for me, as a much traveled man, that this is the richest valley in the world."[2]

18

Unique in agricultural history, we were unique in the state's social and economic history as well. For while much of California followed the Spanish-Mexican tradition of huge land-grant holdings, amounting to thousands of acres in some cases, Santa Clara County was characterized by an adherence to the small family farm tradition. Our own farm never reached 50 acres. At times my father, Ruel Charles Olson, rented land or sharecropped to increase yield and income, just as my brother, Charles John, does today, but the farmland we now own has shrunk to 27 acres. Even twenty years ago, 5- and 10-acre farms were not unusual, while 20- and 30-acre farms were large enough to support a family. Our own family farm still grows cherries and apricots, and despite the change all around us our orchard is itself not much changed. But we are a remnant of an earlier age, almost the last vestige in the Sunnyvale area of a tradition that flourished in this western land of milk and honey for over one hundred years.

El Camino Real, Then and Now

To understand the extent of change in the last thirty years or so one only has to look at the changes along El Camino Real. No longer do orchard trees line what was once a country road from Palo Alto to San Jose and down through Gilroy. No longer does a crossroad like Page Mill, San Antonio, or Lawrence have a roadside gas station with an occasional eatery or saloon, a fruit stand, or a mom-and-pop grocery store.

Just across El Camino Real from us, on its north side, was my aunt's and uncle's business, Sayig's Grocery and Deli, where we children could buy Double Bubble Gum for a penny and an ice cream for five cents. Customers still had charge accounts and fresh milk came in daily from Peninsula Creamery in Palo Alto, which sold milk produced right here in the area.

Now, in the 1980s, El Camino Real is a continuous stretch of development, mostly indistinguishable, from Palo Alto to San Jose. Only when you turn out of San Jose onto the Monterey Highway (still El Camino Real) past the IBM complex do you again see agricultural land. Every time you drive the stretch you are likely to see less and less farmland, for now fewer than 21,000 acres are left on the valley floor. Most of it is south of the Coyote Narrows, so named because the Santa Cruz Mountains at this point are separated from the Diablo mountains by a mere two miles. The open farmlands spread south of this point toward Gilroy, the southernmost town in Santa Clara County.

Our driveway still connects to El Camino Real. While the walnut tree is gone, other signs of the past remain. The tank house with its water tower, a characteristic feature of valley farms, was built in 1913, a time when it was cheaper to combine house and tank into one unit. The redwood came to the port of Redwood City from Eureka, and while both tank house and water tower are weathered, they are still sound. Then there is the three-story barn built in 1938, the year I was born, when my father decided it would be good business to market not only the prunes he raised but those he bought from other growers. John Rose, a local carpenter of Portuguese descent, built the barn from a pattern in his head based on barns that he had seen around the valley and that is, in fact, reminiscent of the Great Barn in New York, a two-tiered shed-roof affair known for its colossal size.

In our valley, barn styles of the Midwest that had been designed for livestock and hay were redesigned or adapted specifically for the fruit industry. While twelve-by-twelve-inch redwood studs were used as support and other woods like fir and pine were used in framing our barn, it is sheathed in corrugated iron.

When I was growing up it was one of my great joys to climb the big barn's steep wooden stairs to what I called "the lookout." Once on the third floor, I could see the tons and tons of dried prunes stored, according to size, in the various bins on the second floor. By climbing to the catwalk on the prune sorter, where the prunes were graded by size before they were stored in the appropriate bins, I could get even higher and look out the windows at my domain. To the south was nothing but trees and, in the distance, the foothills and mountains of the Santa Cruz Range with their lateral ridges, canyons, streams, wildlife, redwoods, and backroads. (Stevens Creek begins from a spring at the top of a ridge where the San Andreas Fault enters Santa Clara County. We live on the flood plain of Stevens Creek and owe the richness of our valley, in part, to the fault.) To the north was the small town of Sunnyvale, just across El Camino Real. Low buildings, mostly houses, stretched to the horizon. Before my time this too was prune and apricot orchard. A photo of the town's main street, taken about 1922, shows it with cherry trees on either side and an electrified sign strung over it with the name Sunnyvale proudly spelled out. While I couldn't see San Francisco Bay from my vantage point, I knew it was there in the distance.

Today, of course, one sees an unending forest of TV antennas, apartment houses, and low buildings in every direction. Now, too, for the first time there is a three-story building of steel, glass, bricks, and concrete directly opposite us on El Camino Real's north side. While the grocery store building and its attached house are still there, the business went out when the supermarkets came in during the 1950s. Now there is a gas station on almost every corner and an eatery every second building. Not far away to the north is Lockheed Missiles & Space Company, while to the south are the numerous high-technology firms that make our county famous. High-tech, Silicon Valley firms are found in almost every direction, whether toward Palo Alto on the west or Santa Clara on the east. Sunnyvale, with over six hundred high-tech firms, likes to think of itself as the hub of the county's new prosperity. Santa Clara and other towns make the same claim. Mingled with the high-tech buildings are shopping centers and housing developments.

It seemed to those of us who were born and raised on the farms of Santa Clara County that they were immutable. The 1920s saw a peak in the number of farm owners at nearly 7,000

and an all-time high in the number of acres planted in just fruits, nuts, and vineyards at 132,000 acres. It was also a time when there were the greatest number of acres in farm production, including graze land: some 80 percent of the county's 835,000 acres. The depression of the 1930s resulted in some decreases, and by 1945 the number of farms had dropped to just under 6,000. Farm acreage, however, was nearly what it had been in the 1920s. Fifteen years later, in 1960, it had declined by a third and farm ownership by nearly two-thirds. Even so, the valley was still agricultural. But it was the beginning of the end. By 1978 only 1,427 (mostly small) farms and 21,000 acres of farmland remained.[3] In the meantime, the county's population had multiplied four times since 1945 to over one and a quarter million. A new economy swept away the old and with it a landscape that had been carefully tended for a hundred years.

Virgin Country

This is not the first time that the valley's way of life has changed. Indians who lived for centuries on these fertile lands, in this benign climate, were confronted after 1777 by Europeans and their Iron Age culture. For present-day San Mateo County to Gilroy was then a majestic oak forest. The valley oak (*Quercus lobata*), the coast live oak (*Quercus agrifolia*), and the black oak (*Quercus kelloggii*) provided the Indians with food in different seasons. Beneath the oaks grew poison oak and the bunch grasses that attracted game: antelope, tule elk, and deer. In turn the feared grizzly would come to feed on animals and man. The Indians, who defined their territory by the streams, including the headwaters, came to the same location to hunt and to gather acorns. For the most part the creeks had no channels but flowed at will over the surface of the plains just as they had done for centuries, bringing down the rich topsoil

from the mountains. In later years this alluvial fill would become the legacy passed on to the industrious family farmers.

The early explorers compared what is now Santa Clara County to an English park. Captain George Vancouver drew this picture of it in 1792:

> For almost twenty miles it could be compared to a park which had originally been planted with the true old English oak; the underwood, that had probably attained its early growth, had the appearance of having been cleared away and had left the stately lords of the forest in complete possession of the soil, which was covered with luxuriant herbage and beautifully diversified with pleasing eminences and valleys, which, with the lofty range of mountains that bounded the prospect, required only to be adorned with neat habitations of an industrious people to produce a scene not inferior to the most studied effect of taste in the disposal of grounds.[4]

A few of the ancient trees survive in Sunnyvale, along with a street named Oak Court.

In its original state our land, at the edge of the oak forest, supported about two oaks per acre, but these were removed between 1906 and 1913, when the orchards were first planted. We would struggle, along with many other farmers, with oak root fungus (*armillaria mellea*, or root rot). Initially, it was caused by the oak roots left in the ground. The fungus grows, lacy and white, between the bark and the wood of the fruit tree, destroying the life-giving cambium layer. Its destructiveness is not limited to fruit trees. Even today our trees are dying from this legacy of the past—at an accelerating rate, since the two wet winters of 1981 and 1982.

Just how rich the soil was is indicated to some extent by the abundant plant life that the Spanish first noted in their journals. The banks of local streams were thick with trees, shrubs, and animal life. The good supply of water, the flat plain, and proximity to the Bay were their reasons for locating the first *pueblo* (city) and a mission here. Little did they know that these obvious advantages overlay a geological treasure house. In 1930 a 10-inch well was drilled to a depth of 425 feet around the corner from our home place, on a piece of property purchased by my grandparents in 1929 from W. E. Jones. The first 4 feet are topsoil, the next 7 gravel and yellow clay, and the next 50 gravel. The pattern is repeated down through 400 feet, indicating that the area was once the site of ancient stream systems. Our land is thus U.S. Department of Agriculture's class I, the best class for deciduous fruits and vegetables. Class I land occupies no less than 156 square miles, or 32 percent of the valley floor![5]

Since our farm is only twenty-two feet above sea level and the bay is just four miles north of us, it is obvious that there is more to the story than meets the eye. Indeed, stream patterns, like a layer cake of gravel, clay, sand, and rocks, reach down a thousand feet or more. Five million years ago the Bay Area was a high-standing trough. The bay in its present form came into existence about a million years ago. Warping and faulting created a valley and violent earth movements the eastern and western hills of Santa Clara County. (The Hayward Fault and

21

the Calaveras Fault in the eastern foothills, and the San Andreas Fault along the Santa Cruz Mountains are still active.) From the first, these high plateaus began to erode. What is today the bay was once a great valley and the Santa Clara Valley its southernmost extension. River systems emerged, cutting the deep, 340-foot channel we know as the Golden Gate. The Guadalupe and Coyote rivers drained Santa Clara County while the Sacramento and the San Joaquin rivers, with their many tributaries, broke through the coastal mountain barriers and drained the great Central Valley.

The gently undulating foothills were shaken loose from the mother mountain but continued to huddle near her like chicks. And the alluvial fill came down little by little. Soil scientists calculate that it takes some five hundred to a thousand years to build an inch of topsoil. Along stream beds Santa Clara County can claim forty feet of such soil, while many parts of the world consider themselves lucky to have half an inch of it. There was more warping and faulting as the valley gradually filled with eroded sediments brought down by torrential rains and winter streams.[6]

If San Francisco Bay was a valley draining the Central and Santa Clara valleys, how did it become filled with salt water? The answer lies in a worldwide change of temperature during an interglacial period. It grew warmer and the great ice packs began to melt, raising the level of the world's oceans at a rapid rate until five or six thousand years ago. At that time, the rate stabilized to about three to six feet per millenium. The bay, known in geology as a drowned valley, is still rising.

It is the bay that helps to maintain a mild climate all year, making it warmer in winter and cooler in summer. When asked why our Bing cherries grew so large and filled with sugar, my father's close friend Dominic DiFiore would offer the bay as an answer: "Every afternoon, the cool breezes come right down Mathilda Avenue from the bay and keep your orchard cool and the cherries firm." The same climate was ideal for people.

So it took about a million years to create these perfect conditions for growing food. This land came as a gift from the ancient past. The Indians, so reviled and looked down upon, left the land intact. They handed over a well-cared-for property to the Spanish. It was a gift that cost the Indians their way of life, but the newcomers gave little thanks in the taking. It has taken just thirty years for this landscape to be covered over with buildings, asphalt, homes, and factories. Thirty years—not even a second in geological time. All across California, as across the United States, prime farm lands are disappearing. In the last ten years, one-and-a-half million acres of farmland in California have been converted to urban or nonfarm land use. The fine soils are forgotten.

If the lands themselves are shrinking, so too are the family farms that embraced a way of life characteristic of America until the 1920s and of our valley until the 1960s. How the family farms came into being here, what they were like, how they fit into history is the focus of the following pages. This book is both a personal story, since I have relied on my own family experience throughout, and a communal story of family farmers like ourselves. It is not an exhaustive study of agriculture or land use in Santa Clara County, but it touches on both these subjects.

Speaking about my family's experience has not come easily, since I had to overcome a lifetime of being taught that, to paraphrase an old Swedish saying, "a person who speaks too much of himself begins to smell bad." There was also the consideration that any one of the thousand or so farm families left in the valley could have been the focal point of such a story. But, in the end, I had to rely on what I know, and I know nothing as well as the experiences of my own family.

I have tried to set our experience in context, to relate our history to what was happening around us and, if possible, to find the universal in the particular, the way in which our lives touched a common thread of American history. In telling our story, I have tried to tell the story of many.

Notes

[1] The title resulted from a competition conducted by a newspaper, the *San Jose Mercury-Herald*, to find an appropriate title for Santa Clara Valley. The earliest promotional piece I have found using the title is Leigh Irvine, *Santa Clara County, California* (San Jose: Board of Supervisors, 1915), which was prepared for the Panama-Pacific International Exposition of 1915.

[2] Ibid., 41.

[3] An excellent account of the crops and conditions of Santa Clara County agriculture can be found in U.S. Department of Agriculture, California Agricultural Experiment Station, *Soil Survey: Santa Clara Area, California*, ser. 1941, no.17 (Washington, D.C.: Government Printing Office, 1958), 31–32, 41 (hereafter cited as *Soil Survey*). The authors of this document evidently assumed that Santa Clara County would continue to be a significant farm area.

[4] Quoted in Frederick Hall, *History of San Jose* (San Francisco: A. C. Bancroft & Co., 1871), 37.

[5] *Soil Survey*, 45. Information on wells and soil composition is drawn from the file of R. C. Olson, which contains documents relating to wells sunk from Feb. 14, 1930, through Mar. 12, 1966. Each well log indicates, from the core sample, the soil composition at the point where the well was being sunk.

[6] No wonder that, in my father's well log, strata of boulders are listed. In early well boring along the bay, even ancient redwood was pulled to the surface by the well-borer's auger.

Other Sources for Chapter 1

Statistics on agriculture have been garnered from many sources including the reports of the State Board of Horticulture (Sacramento, 1886, 1892); Eugene T. Sawyer, *History of Santa Clara County* (Los Angeles: Historic Record Co., 1922); and William F. James, *History of San Jose* (San Jose: A. H. Cawston, 1933). More recent data was collected from U.S. Department of Commerce, *Census of Agriculture, State and County Data*, vol. 1, pt 5, *California* (Washington D.C.: Government Printing Office, 1978).

Information on the geology of the Bay Area is from the excellent collection of essays edited by Olaf P. Jenkins, *Guidebook of the San Francisco Bay Counties: History, Landscape, Geology, Minerals, Industry and Routes to Travel* (San Francisco: California Division of Mines, 1951). Also, Harold B. Goldman, *Geology of San Francisco Bay* (San Francisco: California Division of Mines with San Francisco Bay Conservation and Development Commission, 1967).

Early ecology is treated in depth in David W. Mayfield, "Ecology of the Pre-Spanish San Francisco Bay Area" (Ph.D. diss., San Francisco State University, 1978); John Hunter Thomas, *Flora of the Santa Cruz Mountains of California* (Stanford: Stanford University Press, 1961).

Bayard Taylor's description of Santa Clara County is in his *Eldorado or Adventures in the Path of Empire* (New York: G. P. Putnam, 1850).

CHAPTER 2
BEFORE THE AMERICANS:
1777–1848

IN 1948, SUNNYVALE ELEMENTARY SCHOOL staged a performance in the town's Spanish-styled city hall. I have fond memories of the white-stuccoed building with its arches and red roof tiles. The library was there; recreational activities were held in the basement; all kinds of activities, including tap dancing lessons for children of the Shirley Temple era, took place in the auditorium. The building, which quietly reminded us of the area's Spanish heritage, has since been torn down and replaced by a shopping mall that looks like a combination of prison and fort intended to keep people either in or out. Commenting on the aesthetics of the new structure, my father said, "It's a monument to the concrete industry."

The performance of 1948 commemorated the one hundred years since the American takeover of California. One scene had Indians, padres, and soldiers standing in front of a mission that was constructed of cardboard and held up from behind by supports. I remember being on stage before a full house of parents and public officials when the mission fell down on all of us. If it was not divine judgment on our acting, it may well have been divine disapproval of the history we were being taught in school concerning the Indians, the Spanish, and the Americans.

It would be many years before I questioned what we were taught, but the picture that emerged then was quite different. The Indians, we were told, were willing, happy workers who traded their wild state for the civilization and religion that the Spanish padres had brought to them. What we were never told was that a soldier stood with a gun watching these same Indians work in the fields (not far from the auditorium); that the unmarried Indian women were locked up at night in windowless rooms; and that right here in Santa Clara County an Indian named Yóscolo led a rebellion, stealing two hundred women and several hundred head of cattle, and raiding the mission stores at will until he was caught in 1831. His head was nailed to a post near the church door as an object lesson.

All this at Mission Santa Clara, just six miles from my front door, along the very same road, and about the same distance from the Spanish-styled city hall where the scenery fell down on us.

It somehow failed to come through that the contact between the Europeans and local Costanoan Indians (who numbered roughly two thousand at the time) was so devastating that by 1810 the native Indian culture was disrupted in Santa Clara County forever. European diseases were a major problem: venereal disease, measles, chicken pox, and smallpox, to name a few. As a result the padres had to range farther and farther in order to capture unwilling converts for the agricultural work that the missions required to feed the army and to provide the hides and tallow sold by the king of Spain for his profit.

We did learn that credit for opening Santa Clara Valley, or as the Spanish first called it, Llano de los Robles (Valley of the Oaks), belonged to Captain Juan Bautista de Anza, who led the first colonizers into Alta California in 1776. The main thrust of Spanish colonization was along El Camino Real, the mission trail, and its name reflects that more respect was paid to King Carlos III of Spain than to the King of Heaven.

The specific reason for advancing so far north was the gem of all harbors, San Francisco Bay; whoever controlled it controlled California. In 1770 a presidio and mission were established in Monterey, followed, in 1776, by a presidio and Mission Dolores in what would become San Francisco.

The Beginnings of Agriculture in Santa Clara County

In 1697 Father Juan de Ugarte, a Jesuit, had introduced the first orchards, vineyards, gardens, and grainfields to Baja California. He established herds of cattle, flocks of sheep, and the practice of irrigating the crops. His agriculture set the pattern for the rest of California. But the Jesuits were denied the privilege of settling Alta California because they were suspected of meddling in affairs of state and favoring the pope over the king. The Franciscans took up where they had left off.

The new military garrisons of Alta California required food, and it was quickly seen by the first explorers that the area known as Llano de los Robles was an ideal place to grow it. Hence agriculture began in the Santa Clara Valley. The Santa Clara de Asis mission was established in 1777 on the banks of the Guadalupe River, where wild grapes grew in profusion.[1] Soon after this the fathers discovered that a pueblo was being established across the river at their own back door. It was called El Pueblo de San José de Guadalupé, and was California's first town. If California was to be truly a Spanish enclave, settlers had to be imported, soldiers and their families who would defend the territory while they populated it. The cities were another crucial aspect of colonization along with the missions and the presidios. With them came a political network with which the missions had to contend. The viceroy in Mexico was the head of the system, but there was an appointed governor of California as well. The king, far away in Europe, knew better than to trust his investment to only one group.

The fathers began to complain almost immediately to their superiors in Mexico that the pueblo was taking too much water from the Guadalupe, cutting down too many trees for dams and houses and fences, and depriving the neophytes (as they called the partly Christianized Indians) of the venerable oaks on which they depended for food. The worst part, however, was that the town, by supplying Indians with food and employment, was allowing them "to live in their old freedom," so that they ignored the gospel.[2]

Anza had led a group of 235 impoverished settlers in 1775 from the province of Sonora, now Arizona, to settle the bay at San Francisco. Each of these 35 or so families were rewarded for their arduous trek with gifts of clothing, agricultural implements and tools, cattle, horses, a yoke of oxen, a mule, two sheep, two goats, and the promise of generous land grants. By the king's order, primitive agricultural tools were also given to the city dwellers and to the Indians to use at the mission. Before long the fathers, with the aid of their soldiers, had instructed a few Indians in the planting of crops. The Indians were attracted by offers of free food and clothing, a promise the padres could not always fulfill. In the first year, wheat was planted and a dam was constructed to irrigate crops of beans, lentils, peas, and corn. That first winter the fathers had also planted fruit trees, using cuttings brought in from other missions. The fruit trees were irrigated with well water brought by a ditch. While the grains and vegetables were for the profit of the missions, the fruit trees were for the fathers and the use of the community.

The main "crops" of the mission system were hides and tallow, which could be sent by ship for sale in Europe; the profits went to the king. Mission Santa Clara began with a handful of heifers, bulls, calves, horses, and mares donated by other missions. It is estimated that by 1830 there were 65,000 head of cattle within its control, making it one of the wealthiest in the chain. These Spanish longhorn cattle had a wild look because they were allowed to roam free, competing for forage with elk, antelope, and deer. In order to feed the growing herds, the Spanish broadcast seeds. One version claims that Father Serra broadcast wild mustard seed along El Camino Real in order to create a trail for those coming later. Whatever the reason, wild oats and mustard overcame the native bunch grasses and changed the look of California for good. Wild mustard still grows in our orchard and wild oats all over California.

The first mission was flooded by the Guadalupe in 1784. It was then relocated upstream. Captain George Vancouver saw the second Mission Santa Clara gardens in 1792 and noted a fine small orchard of apple, peach, pear, apricot, and olive trees, as well as vines. All, he said, flourished except the grapes, but he felt the failure was due to lack of knowledge on the padres' part, not lack of good conditions. By 1800 enough fruits were being harvested to supply both the mission and the pueblo. By 1805 the orchard was producing a surplus— enough, even, for peach brandy.

Courtesy Bancroft Library

The Santa Clara Valley Indians

The early Europeans left mixed accounts of what the Costanoan people were like. "They were dark, dirty, squalid, and apathetic," wrote the anthropologist A. L. Kroeber in 1925, relying on statements of early-day travelers Father Palou, on the other hand, in his journal of 1774, commented that the Indians were "well formed and tall, many of them bearded like a Spaniard, with long hair hanging like a mantle from their shoulders to their waists." The artist Choris saw them in the late 1700s. Observing their circumstances under the mission system he wrote, "I have never seen one laugh. I have never seen one look one in the face."[3]

The truth is, we know very little about the Costanoan Indians. The experts cannot agree on how long they lived in the Bay Area. The earliest authentic claim is 4,500 years, the age of the "Sunnyvale Girl" skeleton that was found in the lowlands near the bay in 1972.[4] Her teeth are ground down, the results of eating acorn mush mixed with sand. The Indians, as we have seen, were not farmers themselves. Their main food came from the abundant oak forests and creek beds, and from the freshwater marshes along the bay. They fished and hunted, and dug clams and roots with their digging sticks (the term "digger Indians" was used as an insult by early white settlers). Reminders of the Indians emerged in orchard plowing, when a farmer would come upon a mortar, pestle, or *metate* (flat grinding rock) left by an Indian woman, perhaps centuries ago. The shells of thousands of horn snails (*cerithidea*) can still be seen in a Los Altos orchard where Indians dined on this delicacy. The plants the Indians gathered to eat still grow in our orchard: the stinging nettle, monkey flower, hog fennel, miner's lettuce, cow parsnip, wild buckwheat, dandelion, and fiddleneck, to name just a few. Under the padres these hunters and gatherers became the unpaid laborers in an agricultural economy. Eventually, twenty-one missions were strung along the 700 miles of El Camino Real from San Diego to Sonoma. Each one was a day's ride from the previous one and provided a haven of safety in an essentially hostile countryside of unconverted natives. No one dared travel at night. These feudal outposts were empires to themselves, run like military camps with a few guards to enforce order.

A picture of Indians practicing the agricultural methods taught them by the padres is given by John Bidwell, an American farmer in the Sacramento Valley during the 1840s. While the missions by then were already divided into smaller rancho holdings, the manner of work was the same as it always had been.

The harvest of weeks, sometimes of a month, was piled up in the form of a huge mound in the middle of a high, strong, round corral; then three or four hundred wild horses were turned in to thresh it, the Indians whooping to make them run faster. . . . Next came the winnowing, which would often take another month. It could only be done when the wind was blowing, by throwing high into the air shovelsful of grain, straw, and chaff, the lighter materials being wafted to one side, while the grain, comparatively clean, would descend and form a heap by itself. In this manner all of the grain in California was cleaned. At that day no such thing as a fanning wheel had been brought to this coast.[5]

Despite these methods, primitive even by ancient Roman standards, the missions produced rich yields. The sheer quantity of Indian labor, the extensive plantings, and the factory-like nature of mission management combined with the natural fertility of California to create wealth for the king.

Mexican Rule

The Law of the Indies established by Spain in the sixteenth century decreed that within ten years of the missions being established the neophytes were to be freed and the mission lands turned over to them to operate as individual landowners and farmers. The political realities of colonial life and the difficulty of converting the Indians prevented any such accommo-dation, and soon mission life itself was threatened by the revolution that ousted Spain as a power from Mexico. By 1821, California was freed of Spanish rule and claimed as a Mexican colony.

Immediately the mission system was open to attack as a remnant of the king's presence. Influential citizens petitioned the government to release the fertile mission holdings to private use. This was accomplished by the Secularization Act of 1833. Measured by the square league (about 4,500 acres) these grants were made to private individuals who were soldiers or wealthy landowners, and to a few Americans married to Mexican citizens. Americans or foreigners who became Mexican citizens and converted to Catholicism were also eligible.

Forty-one land grants were made by the Mexican government in Santa Clara County.[6] While there were corridors of open land between the grants, most of the best land on the valley floor had been settled by the time the Americans swooped down on the county after the discovery of gold in California. Of the one thousand or so Indians still living within the confines of Mission Santa Clara just before it was broken up, only seven received grants of land. The others became rancho workers, dispersed to join renegade Indians in the San Joaquin Valley, or settled in the short-lived Indian villages around the bay.

The Rancho

The same transfer of lands that was a final blow to the Indians brought the rancho into brief glory. From 1822 until 1846, the Californios, as the Spanish-Mexican landowners were known, led a life of pastoral simplicity.

The basis of the economy was still hides and tallow. Each ranchero planted crops for the needs of his rancho. There were no cash crops to speak of until the Gold Rush, when the rancheros began to plant wheat to feed the miners. Until that time there was little cash; most payment was in kind. John Bidwell recalls in his account of the 1840s that there were few fruits planted except for the prickly pear that had long served as hedges to keep cattle from the grainfields.

Lasting imprints from the Spanish-Mexican period have been the many place-names; the architectural style of the ranch house and patio and of colonial-style buildings like the old Sunnyvale City Hall; community of property in California's legal system; and the heritage of fruits, vegetables, livestock, and grain. Mission-style agriculture remains to this day: the huge landholdings that require many workers—the so-called factories in the fields—are characteristic of California agriculture.

While the heritage of the colonial period provided many positive additions to California culture over the long term, in the short term there was nothing but hostility between the Californios who owned large tracts of land and the Americans who wanted to wrest it from them. From 1846 until the 1880s conflict and chaos ruled.

My father, speaking as a small farmer, and keenly aware of history, said to me, "You know, there are many people who believe that California still belongs to the Mexicans." It was easy to see that he was annoyed to think that, after 130 years of statehood, anyone should still consider California a part of Mexico.

Manifest Destiny and the Yeoman Farm Tradition

American immigrants to California brought with them certain ideas that fueled their claim to territory. Among them was the belief that America, by the God-given right of its "manifest destiny," should expand its boundaries to embrace the whole North American continent. The Oregon Territory came under American control in 1846 by negotiated settlement with the British, but the Mexicans were not as agreeable. They refused

to sell California and they insisted, with some reason, that Texas was their property. Texas, California, and New Mexico were ceded to the United States by the Treaty of Guadalupe Hidalgo that ended the Mexican War of 1846–48. Nearly 1.2 million square miles of real estate, for which we paid Mexico a mere $15 million, were added to American control. Many felt this was money to salve our consciences, since the war was never fully justified. Somehow, when we were celebrating the acquisition of California in the Sunnyvale City Hall Auditorium in 1948, none of this was mentioned.

While Manifest Destiny provided the broad, ideological framework for expansionism, the ideal of the yeoman farmer was equally important to pioneer settlement. The sturdy settler family, according to Jefferson, Webster, Jackson, and many other Americans, embodied the health and promise of the nation. At a time when seven out of ten Americans were still farmers, the yeomen were considered a committed band of citizens who toiled in the earth and on whom the defense of the country rested. Daniel Webster, a successful farmer as well as lawyer and statesman, commented to the Boston Legislature in 1840 that America's small farmers and freeholders drew "not only their subsistence but also their spirit of independence and manly freedom, from the ground they plough."[7] America, with its fertile valleys, its rich natural resources, was seen as the "garden of the world," and the yeoman as the gardener. Underlying this metaphor was the assumption that the founding of America and democracy was the fulfillment of the biblical promise of Eden. Through the distribution of land to individual families, the potential wealth of the nation was divided among many. The long shadow of aristocratic Europe with its history of wars, of a privileged class and a poor one, was left behind. Homesteading and expansion went hand in hand toward the Pacific.

The idea of homestead land for settlers had such currency in America that the Republican party, under the leadership of Abraham Lincoln, made it a main plank in its platform of 1860. The agrarian ideal of the yeoman farmer was thereby pitted against the aristocratic ideal of the plantation system and slavery. Even as the Civil War raged, Lincoln signed the Homestead Act of 1862, thereby ensuring, at least on paper, that land would be divided among small landowners in areas where no slavery would be allowed. The act was the logical conclusion of the Preemption Act of 1841, which had guaranteed settlers land at $1.25 per acre. An act of Congress brought the Preemption Act to California in 1853. The United States had been selling public domain land at auctions for $1.25 per acre since 1820 as a way of adding needed money to the federal treasury. Under the Homestead Act, land was to be free on the condition of settlement.

The discovery of gold in California would bring to the state a different breed of person from the typical yeoman settler. Single, aggressive, confident, and greedy, he intended to go home after striking it rich. A. A. Holcomb, father-in-law of George Worswick (mayor of San Jose 1902–10) was just such an example. "Alone I started out," he wrote about his 1850 journey west, "full of hope, sanguine of success, and in the full bloom of health . . . fully determined, and foolish enough to believe that I should return to my friends and the girl I left behind within the promised time—two years—loaded down with wealth."[8] But only a few were successful at the mines. Those who did not return home saw the great farming future that lay ahead for the state and quickly used the same language in describing that future as had been applied to the new territories in previous decades. As early as 1851, the image of "the garden spot of the United States" was applied to California and Santa Clara County.[9]

The influx of Americans and foreigners into Santa Clara County began after gold was discovered in 1848. It was this contingent of easterners and midwesterners who brought with them the deeply embodied notion that land was for the common man. Many of them came with the closely allied notion that land was for the taking. In 1849 some two hundred Californio families owned 14 million acres, mostly the best valley lands, flat, fertile and virgin. Many frustrated gold diggers resented this lopsided distribution. Henry George, the nineteenth-century land reformer and economist, wrote that the history of the California grants was one "of greed, of perjury, of corruption, of spoilation and high-handed robbery."[10] While it was the Californios who were displaced by Americans and immigrants, many Americans, much to their surprise, suffered in the ordeal as well. The Indians lost their land, and then the Californios. Before the Americans could claim dominance, a period of chaos and confusion reigned.

Notes

[1] Mission San Jose, founded in 1797, is located in Alameda County.

[2] *Informes* [unpublished agricultural reports of Mission Santa Clara, 1777–1832], University of Santa Clara Archives, 47. Also listed as *Annual Reports of Mission Santa Clara de Asis* (originals in Mexican National Archives).

[3] A. L. Kroeber, *Handbook of the Indians of California* (Berkeley: California Book Co., 1953), 466.

[4] Bert A. Gerow, "Amino Acid Dating and Early Man in the New World: A Rebuttal," Society for California Archaeology Occasional Papers, Contributions to Western Archaeology, no. 3 (Fullerton: California State University, Fullerton, Society for Archaeology, 1981), 1.

[5] John Bidwell, *Echoes of the Past* (New York: Citadel Press, 1962), 82. Reprint of 19th-century work.

[6] Clyde Arbuckle and Ralph Rambo, *Santa Clara County Ranchos* (San Jose: Rosicrucian Press, 1968). Deals with all the grants in alphabetical order.

[7] Quoted in Wheeler McMillen, ed., *Harvest: An Anthology of Farm Writing*, (New York: Appleton-Century, 1964), 101.

[8] A. A. Holcomb, "Along the Emigrant Trail: An Authentic Account of Pioneer Days as Recorded by A. A. Holcomb in his Diary While Crossing the Plains to California in 1850 and Again in 1859" (Unpublished ms., photocopy, n.d., California History Center Library, DeAnza College, Cupertino, Calif.), 4. Original with his granddaughter Mildred Worswick, Palo Alto.

[9] A. M. Williams to his father, letter published in *Missouri Courier* and quoted in *St. Joseph Adventure* (Mo.), Feb. 21, 1851, reprinted in Walter D. Wyman, *California Emigrant Letters* (New York: Bookman Associates, 1952), 134.

[10] Henry George, *Progress and Poverty* (1879).

Other Sources for Chapter 2

For the local Indians, see Bert A. Gerow, *An Analysis of the University Village Complex* (Stanford: Stanford University Press, 1968); Richard Levy, "Costanoan," chap. 45 in *Handbook of North American Indians*, vol. 8, (Washington, D.C.: Smithsonian Institution, National Museum of Natural History, 1978). The Bay Area as it was when the Spanish first settled it is described in David W. Mayfield, "Ecology of the Pre-Spanish San Francisco Bay Area" (Ph.D. diss., San Francisco State University, 1978), which includes a list of native plants and animals.

A lively account of Anza is J. N. Bowman and R. F. Heizer, *Anza and the Northwest Frontier of New Spain*, Southwest Museum Paper no. 20 (Highland Park, Los Angeles: Southwest Museum, 1967).

The early days of Mission Santa Clara are recorded in Gerald McKevitt, S. J., *The University of Santa Clara: A History* (Stanford: Stanford University Press, 1979); and in George O'Connell, S. J., *Woodstock Letters, A Record: Of Current Events and Historical Notes Connected with the College and Mission of the Society of Jesus in North and South America*, vol. 19 (Woodstock, Md.: Woodstock College, 1890, privately circulated). See also Robert L. Hoover, "Notes and Documents: The Death of Yóscolo," *Pacific Historical Review* 51, no. 3 (Aug. 1982):312—14. Informative general studies are Ralph B. Wright, *California's Missions* (Los Angeles: Sterling Press, 1967); and Sherburne F. Cook, *The Conflict Between the California Indian and White Civilization* (Berkeley: University of California Press, 1976).

For Spanish-Mexican society see especially Leonard Pitt, *The Decline of the Californios* (Berkeley: University of California Press, 1970). Its agriculture is described in Frank Adams, "The Historical Background of California Agriculture," in *California Agriculture*, (University of California Press, 1946), 1—24; and in John S. Hittell, *Resources of California* (New York and San Francisco, 1863), which contains excellent descriptions of Spanish cattle, the Spanish horse, etc. A vivid short study of the rancho that became Sunnyvale and Mountain View is Mary J. Gates, *Contributions to Local History, Rancho Pastoria De Las Borregas, Mountain View* (San Jose: Cottle & Murgotten, 1895). More recently, a study of ranchos in the eastern foothills of Santa Clara County and farther south has been compiled in Marjorie Pierce, *East of the Gabilans* (Santa Cruz: Western Tanager Press, 1976). The entire question of land grants is reviewed in W. W. Robinson, *Land in California* (Berkeley: University of California Press, 1979). See also Frances L. Fox, *Land Grant to Landmark* (San Jose: Pied Piper Publishers, 1978), with sketches by Ralph Rambo.

The classic study on the question of the westward movement is still Bernard de Voto, *The Year of Decision, 1846* (Boston: Houghton Mifflin, 1943); so, too, on the impact of the yeoman farm tradition, is Henry Nash Smith, *Virgin Land: The American West as Symbol and Myth* (New York: Vintage Books, 1950). For an overall view, see Don E. Fehranbacher, *The Era of Expansion, 1800—1848* (New York: Wiley, 1969).

Home and barn of Leon Renaud and his wife, the former Elsie
Pellier, daughter of Louis Pellier's brother, Pierre. Married in
1883, they had built this home by 1885, on land inherited
from Elsie's father. Vineyards (shown in background) stayed in
family until 1940. *Courtesy Mirassou Vineyards*

Santa Clara College in 1851. This was the second building on present site of University of Santa Clara. Original mission had moved three times until high ground was located far enough away from flooding of Guadalupe River. Earthquake and fire also took a toll. Vineyard is behind gate on far left; orchard was on opposite side of El Camino Real, which ran between church and orchard. *Courtesy Archives University of Santa Clara*

Don Secundino Robles (1811–1890) built this adobe some time before 1840 at what is now El Camino Real and San Antonio Road, Los Altos, and was then part of his 8,418-acre rancho. Photo shows holiday-makers posing before abandoned house in 1892, after Robles had died indigent; it collapsed in 1906 earthquake. *Courtesy Palo Alto Historical Association*

El Camino Real southward from University Avenue in Palo
Alto, 1900. *Courtesy Palo Alto Historical Association*

Spanish heritage is visible in Sunnyvale's colonial-style city hall on Murphy Avenue, here seen in 1950. Besides city offices it included a library, a large auditorium, and a basement where recreational activities took place in summer. The building was torn down to make way for downtown renewal in the late 1970s. *Photo from Camera Mart, Sunnyvale*

The Evans Jenkins grain farm on what is now Moffett Field,
c. 1876. Note skid house (in fence corner, far right) that
squatter could move from one place to another by horse.
Jenkins successfully gained title to his 155 acres by squatting.
Steam boat in background is under way from Alviso to San
Francisco. *Thompson & West* Atlas, *1876.*

Alfred Doten aged 61, still playing music, with two of his
children, Bessie and Alfred Jr. at the home of his ex-wife in
Reno, 1890. *Courtesy Dorothy Barton Webster*

Chief Lupe Yñigo (1760–1864), was granted 1600 acres of
land, present day Moffett Field. Doten wrote in his diary (April
11, 1858) of being told by "Old Ynego" (sic) that "when he
was a little boy his tribe was numerous about here—but all
have died, and he is the only one left. . . ." *Courtesy Archives
University of Santa Clara*

Man in bowler is mowing wheat near Murphy's Station, now
Sunnyvale, in late 1860s. *Photo by S. P. Saunders, Courtesy* San
Jose Mercury News

Hay being brought to a central point by four teams c. 1890.
Note use of mechanical "buck rake" to build stack and fields
cultivated as far as mountains. Scars of quarry, still there,
identify viewpoint as Cottle Road and Monterey Highway,
south of San Jose. *Courtesy Sourisseau Academy*

Overfelt family of east San Jose threshing wheat with their
Enright Steam Engine near Hillsdale Avenue, 1887. Cut grain
was fed from pile to the thresher with help of derrick (center
left) and grain emerged to be sacked at side of thresher (right).
Threshing crew traveled county with four-horse movable
cookhouse staffed by Chinese cooks. *Courtesy San Jose Historical
Museum*

Byron Walters of San Felipe Road in east San Jose shocks cured oat hay on the Fred Hassler ranch in the Evergreen district, 1949, a scene little changed from the 19th century. County's three main grain crops have been wheat, barley, and oats, with wheat the most important. *Courtesy* San Jose Mercury News

Two-stone, water-powered grist mill, Los Gatos Creek, built
1854 by James Alexander Forbes and shown here during a wet
winter, 1880s. Forbes went bankrupt but the mill continued to
produce flour until 1887. It marked the beginning of Los
Gatos. *Courtesy Los Gatos Library*

Drilling for water in the artesian district, Agnews, May 26, 1892. This and next two photographs illustrate stages of well construction and use. Here, two derricks provide leverage for boom to bring dirt up from bottom of well. *Courtesy Anthony and Ila Bravo*

Bringing in the water, new artesian well, Milpitas, 1916. Well was on Standish family pear farm; river in foreground is Guadalupe. *Courtesy Mrs. H. A. Oswald, Jr.*

Capped artesian well near Alviso, 1911. Capping made possible controlled use of water for irrigation, as here. Well was on Light-house Farm, then owned by Henry Bonetti but developed by Andrea Malovas. *Courtesy Archives University of Santa Clara*

Farmsite on hillsides in eastern foothills. Fruit trees, vineyards, and grains grace the hills. Photo by J. O. Tucker, c. 1900. *Courtesy Sourisseau Academy*

Bare-root cherry and apricot trees wait to be planted on Olson farm in Sunnyvale, 1980, replacing trees that have died.

Fred Martinez and Heriberto Torres of the Olson farm prepare the hole for a new tree in the winter of 1980. This small orchard is cared for by my brother for the City of Sunnyvale.

CHAPTER 3
LAND OWNERSHIP AND EARLY
AMERICAN FARMING: 1848–1880

IF YOU HAD NO LAND granted to you by the Spanish or Mexicans, you could come to Santa Clara County after the Americans claimed it, and buy land from a Californio. Buying land from the Californios was not difficult: they had land but little cash. The trick was to prove your title in the courts of the new country. There were many transactions in gold. Martin Murphy, Jr., whose extensive Irish-immigrant family eventually owned more California land than any other, bought almost 4,900 acres of Rancho Pastoria de las Borregas (Ewe Lambs Pasture) from Mariano Castro for $12,000 in gold in 1849. This land is the present site of Sunnyvale. Given the confusion of the times, even Murphy had to wait until 1865 for the Americans to confirm his title. Land was available from the public domain under the laws of preemption, by which the federal government allowed settlers to claim no more than 160 acres of land, and later through homesteading. Another method was used by the majority who became settlers and homesteaders by squatting first.

"What does it mean to be a squatter?" I asked my father. "You went out and put down markers," he explained. "Say you wanted to squat on this piece. You'd put a marker at that corner, and at that corner, at that corner there and there." He indicated a large square with his hand. "Then you registered it with the county clerk."

"Wasn't that out-and-out stealing?" I asked.

"Not if no one else claimed that land . . ."

"You mean you didn't have to pay a cent?"

"Well, of course there were the lawyers' fees."[1]

My father was born in San Francisco in 1899, just four months before the turn of the century. His parents and younger sister Elsie moved to Sunnyvale in 1901. His sense of place was bound up with the stories he absorbed like nourishment, stories of the people who came to Santa Clara County, who struggled with the land, stories of those who survived and those who lost.

The land we were talking about in relation to squatting was "Chief Indigo's Ranch." While Dad spoke some Spanish, and bits and pieces of several other languages, he pronounced the name of the Indian just as the Americans did when they began to pour into Santa Clara County after the Gold Rush. The Spanish, Yñigo, is pronounced Ee-*nee'*-goh. Yñigo's 1844 grant was called Posolmi, an Indian name whose meaning is lost. Also called Pozitas de las Animas (Little Wells of the Souls), after a spring that flowed for many years at the southwest corner of the property, his grant was one of the seven given to Indians when the missions were disbanded. Except for Yñigo, Roberto, and Marcelo, the Indians sold their grants and disappeared from history.[2]

Since 1933 Yñigo's grant, which fronts the bay, has been the location of Moffett Field, the naval air base in Mountain View. The Holthouse family, among others, lived on that land in Dad's generation and their children went to school with him. The brand under which they sold their fresh peas was "Yñigo," with a picture of an Indian chief who was portrayed—uncharacteristically—wearing a bonnet of the Plains Indians. Marcelo's grant, called Ulistac, now hosts high-technology firms and Great America, a large amusement park, in Santa Clara. These lands were divided into numerous farms that grew a myriad of crops in the one hundred years between the Indians and now.

In the early 1850s several different people squatted on Yñigo's property in the hope that lawyers would prove their claim against him. We know that Yñigo's tribe had lived along the Guadalupe River near the bay, that he had led the Indians who planted the famous Alameda—the pathway between the pueblo of San Jose and the Santa Clara mission—with willow slips taken from a nearby pond. We know that he was a weaver and a farmer who planted vegetables on his land grant. These he sold to the Americans and with the proceeds built adobe houses and possibly a wooden frame house. We also know that he was a rival in love with Marcelo, that he fathered many children, and that he was over a hundred years old when he died in 1864. Yñigo sold five hundred of his sixteen hundred acres but kept the bulk of his land, and these were the acres in contention.

In 1851 an act of Congress established a three-member land commission located in San Francisco to settle the disputes between those who claimed Mexican title and those who squatted on the land. According to the Treaty of Guadalupe Hildago (1848), the Mexican titles were to be honored by the Americans, but settling the titles was anything but simple. The original maps, when they could be found, were so carelessly drawn that there was room for error. The problem for the Californios became one of proving where one claim existed in relationship to another. Loose descriptions like "oak tree," "pond," or "willow" were open to challenge. Moreover, the lands that fell between the grants belonged in the public domain and were legitimately open to settlers. Every available piece of property was settled on by squatters, in the hope that property title could not be proved, in which case the squatter suddenly became a settler.

The process of settlement, by which Indian communal land was divided into missions, then ranchos, and then farms, left many broken people. Indeed, it left broken cultures: first the Indian and then the Californio. While the American star was on the rise, there were still many people of all races and callings who fell victim to the uncertainty of the times. A dramatic example of an American settler whose dream was broken is that of Alfred Doten, who came to the county in 1856. His story is of exactly the type that my Dad absorbed about those who came and went on the land.

Alfred Doten: American Hopeful

Alfred Doten, from Plymouth, Massachussets, was a Yankee forty-niner and a descendant of the first pilgrims on the Mayflower. In 1849 when Doten was twenty he developed the compulsive habit of writing daily entries about himself in leather-bound journals, a habit that lasted until the day he died. The journal, one man's witness to history, details farming practices and technology, markets, prices, crops, fairs, and such social events as the "musical evenings" that lasted until five in the morning.

For me, Doten's journal has a sense of the immediate, for he traveled El Camino Real, passing the land our own family would settle, and observing "the many fine ranches hereabouts." He met families who gave their names to roads: the Murphys, the McClellans, the Whismans, the Hollenbecks. Indeed, my father and my aunt went to Mountain View High School with descendants of the Emersons, people with whom Doten became involved. Doten's daughter returned to Santa Clara County and married one of our neighbors. My Dad knew the Barton family in Cupertino and Dorothy Barton Webster, Doten's only grandchild, is a friend of mine.

Doten's terse entry of October 25, 1855, tells the story of his near fatal accident in the gold mines: "Six years in California today—'flat broke and back broke'."[3] Like many others before him he turned his attention from mining to farming and came to Santa Clara County, where friends from his home state were already settled. He lived here from 1856 to 1862, changing location only once. Doten was popular. Among his many talents, which ranged from skill with a pen to carpentry, farming, and mining, he was a musician. His talents on the fiddle, flute, and banjo had made him welcome in the chilly evenings when men gathered together, huddled in crude flea-ridden miners' cabins, and tried to forget their fears and frustrations. Although he had come from a conservative family background, he soon found that drink, native women, and rowdy comradery took the edge off his failure in the mines.

By the time he came to work for Silas B. Emerson (a relative of Ralph Waldo Emerson), Doten was a chastened man. Despite the pain and discomfort from his injured back, he hired on as a farmhand, in the hope that, like thousands of beginners before him, he would be able to climb the farm ladder. Abe

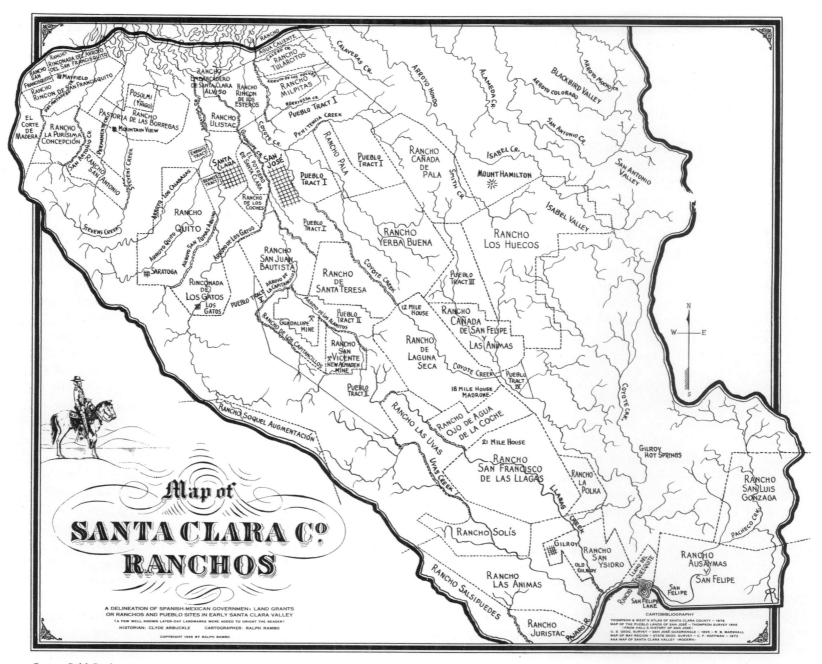

Map of

SANTA CLARA C⁰.
RANCHOS

A DELINEATION OF SPANISH-MEXICAN GOVERNMENT LAND GRANTS
OR RANCHOS AND PUEBLO SITES IN EARLY SANTA CLARA VALLEY
(A FEW WELL KNOWN LATER-DAY LANDMARKS WERE ADDED TO ORIENT THE READER)
HISTORIAN: CLYDE ARBUCKLE   CARTOGRAPHER: RALPH RAMBO

COPYRIGHT 1968 BY RALPH RAMBO

CARTOBIBLIOGRAPHY
THOMPSON & WEST'S ATLAS OF SANTA CLARA COUNTY — 1876
MAP OF THE PUEBLO LANDS OF SAN JOSÉ — THOMPSON SURVEY 1866
(FROM HALL'S HISTORY OF SAN JOSÉ)
U. S. GEOG. SURVEY — SAN JOSÉ QUADRANGLE — 1895 — R. B. MARSHALL
MAP OF BAY REGION — STATE GEOG. SURVEY — C. F. HOFFMAN — 1873
AAA MAP OF SANTA CLARA VALLEY (MODERN)

Courtesy, Ralph Rambo

Lincoln had described the farm ladder in 1859, before his election. It was part of the way in which property rights could be spread among the maximum number of owners. "The prudent, a penniless beginner in the world, labors for wages for a while, saves a surplus with which to buy tools or land for himself; then labors on his own account another while, and at length hires another new beginner to help him."[4]

Doten described Emerson's farm, where Emerson was squatting, along with many others, on Yñigo's property. In so doing he unwittingly described the rapid changes in agriculture since the coming of the Americans less than a decade before. The eccentric punctuation is Doten's.

Sunday, Aug. 13, 1854

. . . Emerson's ranch is situated about four miles to the westward of Alviso—It is well fenced and has a good substantial frame house, barns, [etc.]—There is but little timber on it; it is level and the soil is a rich loam—His greatest pest are the ground squirrels—they have destroyed much of his corn and a great many of his young trees; Many of his peach trees are girdled and nearly destroyed . . . Emerson is just finished harvesting his grain, hay [etc.], and will finish threshing out his wheat tomorrow he thinks—The wheat crop generally about here will turn out tolerably well this year—Emerson's place is rather lonely, as far as neighbors are concerned, but not more so than farms in the country generally are. . . [5]

From the hides and tallow of the early Spanish-Mexican agriculture, California turned to the export of wheat, wine, and wool. These were all goods that could be transported over long distances by ship. Early diaries indicate that little agriculture along American lines existed in Santa Clara County before 1846. A pioneer with the Bidwell-Bartleson party, Josiah Belden, suggested Americans did not plant wheat here until 1852 or 1853.[6] Emerson's farm, at any rate, produced grain, and it was grain, particularly wheat, that became king in the first period of American control. The immediate need was for flour to feed the miners. Emerson eventually would farm nine hundred acres in Santa Clara County and seven hundred of them would be in wheat. He gained title to lands in the Mountain View area south of El Camino Real, near Grant and Fremont roads. His squatter claim to the Yñigo property was denied.

Looking down at the valley from a point above Milpitas in 1861 Doten saw "farms, grain fields laid off in squares by fences [etc.]—belts & groves of timber, creeks, Penitencia, Coyote, Bay, Guadalupe [etc.] . . ."[7] The wheat grown in the valley was called "California club." Its origins are obscure but it was probably the same wheat that the padres had imported from Mexico. By 1853 "red Australia" and "Chile club," two hard and stout wheats, were introduced because they could take the long trip across the seas to the booming English, Russian, and Asian markets without damage.[8]

Farming Technology

Wheat farming on the American scale was considered a purely commercial investment and many individuals who took it up in these early days were more often concerned with profits than with establishing a way of life on the land. The early American subsistence farm, by which a family supported itself from the land, was yielding to cash farming—specialization in crops that a farmer sold for profit. Contributing to this commercial attitude toward agriculture was the introduction of farm machinery, which was developed to counter the lack of manpower. Labor-saving machinery was ideal for California's huge rancho farms. On some San Joaquin Valley spreads, plows were "ganged," or hooked up together, so that as many as thirty-five of them moved across a strip of land 400 feet wide, each pulled by a team of ten horses or mules. Some farms were as large as 36,000 acres.

C. H. McCormick, Virginia-born inventor and son of a farmer-blacksmith, developed a horse-drawn machine in 1831 that cut the harvest. Called a mechanical reaper, the machine doubled its function when it also stripped the grain from the plant. It is thought that the first combine harvester in California may have been tried in Santa Clara County in 1854.

53

The combine is only one of the many different types of new farm machinery which Doten described in his journal: "It is a large threshing machine drawn by twenty horses. . . it cuts a very even swath of twelve feet in width, taking off the heads of the grain, which pass directly into the threshing machine. The chaff blows out behind, and the clean grain runs out from a spout in the side, into the sacks which are hung on to receive it."[9]

This combine harvester saved human labor but required enormous animal power. Soon the steam engine was introduced for threshing and many other types of farm tasks: pumping water, sawing wood, and grinding grains. Doten commented on how the steam engine "never gets tired. . . . No horses to bother with & feed."[10] It did require three-quarters of a cord of wood and fifteen barrels of water per day. The big engines were moved by horses from farm to farm as needed; they were fitted with long driving belts to do the particular job required. The next step was to put wheels on this stationary equipment and so develop a steam engine designed to move itself. The first tractors were born. By 1868 a company in Pacheco, near Martinez, was manufacturing a steam tractor called the Standish Rotary Steam Plow. It was dubbed the *Mayflower*. Even though the steam tractors, called traction engines, were huge and expensive, they put power into the hands of the American farmer. In 1890 some three thousand steam tractors and almost as many steam threshers were built. They continued to be designed, built, and used until the 1920s—more than two decades after the compact gasoline engine was developed. Santa Clara County's most famous manufacturer of a steam engine was Joseph Enright, who began the Joseph Enright Foundry in San Jose in 1864 and patented his engine in 1875. Called the Patent Wood and Straw-Burning Portable Engine, Enright's model could burn stubble, a by-product of threshing. It was sent all over California and used in this valley into the twentieth century.

Doten detailed other labor-saving devices, such as the horse-drawn Willard's Patent Seed-sower and Harrow, which he said could sow twelve or fifteen acres of wheat a day with only one man driving.[11] Ten acres was the most a man could sow by hand in one day, so the machine increased efficiency by up to fifty percent. Of course, the increase in costs of the new machinery made it necessary to work more acres in order to pay off the higher capital investment. The San Jose Foundry, established in 1852, made such equipment, along with windmills, gangplows, and the Pelton Six-fold Horse-power Threshing Machine. From the beginning, the bigness of California farming was supported by an inventive local technology.

Artesian Wells

Another feature that distinguished Santa Clara County was an abundance of artesian wells. The best one in the valley, according to Doten, was the one on Emerson's ranch. "It is one hundred and ninety-four feet in depth, five inches in diameter, and the cool pure water flows from it at the rate of nearly fifty gallons a minute, in a steady unvarying stream, furnishing an abundant supply for the house, barns, cattle, irrigation purposes [etc.]."[12]

An artesian well is the result of geologic formations, usually inclines, that trap water beneath the soil under tremendous pressure. The first artesian well in the county was sunk in 1854; Emerson's probably followed in the same year. Beneath the valley surface, waiting to be tapped, were one million acre-feet of water. At first the Americans were so careless with this newfound resource that they let the wells gush out of control. How long it took for this great store of pure water to collect beneath the earth's surface cannot be determined, but we know that by the 1920s Santa Clara County farmers had drawn down the supply and were in need of more. Between 1915 and 1967 the land at Alviso sank 12.7 feet, indicating the depletion of the underground supply.[13] By the 1930s dams would be built in the foothills to help restore the water supply and prevent further subsidence. Almost 90 percent of water drawn from the underground source was for agricultural use up to the mid-1930s. Dams stabilized the water level until 1947. After World War II, urban use accounted for 65 percent and agriculture only 18 percent. From the early 1970s Santa Clara County has imported extra water to meet its needs.

There were two major artesian areas in the county. The larger of the two was the area immediately around the bay, ten to twelve miles in length and three to six miles in width. In 1864 the San Francisco and San Jose Railroad Company wisely put its tracks just above this line, for in times of heavy rains the area is subject to flooding. The other was in the area around Old Gilroy in south county called the Bolsa, or Exchange (perhaps because cattle were once sold there).[14] The presence of this abundant water induced the planting of strawberries as early as 1852; vegetables were also grown and lucerne for the cows in the dairies that were soon established there. By the 1870s Santa Clara County was the leading strawberry producer of California and Gilroy was known as the milk and cheese capital of the state.

Artesian wells supplied water under natural pressure, but by 1914 most of the 45,000 acres then irrigated relied on pumps. The number of pumping stations rose quickly once it became evident that irrigation created healthier trees and bigger fruit. Over the next twenty-five years, irrigated land more than doubled and was still on the rise ten years later.[15] At first, wind power was used to draw large quantities of water from the ground. Steam engines replaced wind power and were replaced in turn by gasoline engines and electric motors of ten, twenty-five, and even seventy-five horsepower. Many of these wells were located in deep pits in order to bring the source of power closer to the water, and more than one farmer lost his life or a limb trying to maintain his pumping plant.

The average well was capable of three-to-five hundred gallons of water per minute. In order to move water into redwood containers on the second or third floor of a tank house for storage of the family water supply, smaller engines of one, two, or three horsepower were used. The tank house was one of the most common features of the valley landscape. In my day windmills were already scarce. The hand pump was the most elementary device used by the early Americans. It was capable of pumping water thirty feet. My aunt told me of the one my grandfather installed on their property in Sunnyvale. His first chore at five in the morning was to draw the water for my grandmother to use in the kitchen and for the children to wash their faces.

Although Doten as farmhand undertook many duties related to the sowing and harvesting of grain, he also had to pick peas and beans. Another of his chores, since cattle still had the run of the land, was building fences to protect the crops. It would be twenty years before the farmers gained the upper hand over the cattlemen and forced them to construct costly wooden fences. Inexpensive barbed wire, developed in the 1880s, was a response to the problem.

Doten took over as manager of Emerson's land while the latter returned to Boston. During the harvesting, reapers broke often because the wheat was badly mixed with wild mustard. Doten took parts for repair to the two blacksmiths Morrison and Jenkins, who had a shop at Stevens Creek and El Camino Real. Jenkins, a Welshman, also was squatting on Yñigo's land; he eventually gained title to almost 160 acres. An early print of the farm shows the "skid house," used by squatters to fulfill residence requirements. Since it was on skids, it could be pulled by horse from place to place.

One more step up the ladder to farm ownership took place when Doten went into partnership with Emerson, sharecropping one hundred acres with a man named Miller. In Doten's case the arrangement was for the sharecroppers to receive half the profits while Emerson was responsible for seed, teams, plows, reapers, and land. Doten and his partner paid for their board and the harvesting. In the end the partners barely broke even and the work was strenuous and frustrating. As soon as ten acres were sowed the cutworms ate the seed and the land had to be sowed again.

The Squatter's Farm

By October of 1858 Doten managed to buy a 160-acre farm for $275—about $1.50 per acre. His quarter section was four miles north of San Jose and two-and-a-half miles from the little crossroad of Milpitas where the cornfields of the Spanish had been located. The sharecropping arrangement left Doten with only $160 in profit. Doten's greatest worry was money. His concern was justified: there was a dispute, requiring a third party to settle, over the money owed him for managing Emerson's farm; his cash was spent in paying for the farm; he gave a note for his wagon to Morrison, the blacksmith, from whom he borrowed money for supplies. Like most farmers he began in debt. Foremost in his mind was clear title of his land, for he was squatting on the property in the hope that the court battle, sure to follow, would be settled in his favor. Court battles also ate up meager cash reserves.

The Berryessa and Alviso Families

Doten was thrown into the middle of a celebrated dispute between two Californio families. The Rancho Milpitas was originally granted to Nicolas Berryessa (Spanish spelling "Berreyesa") in 1834 by the alcalde (mayor) of San Jose. In 1835 that claim was overturned by Governor José Castro in favor of José Maria Alviso, whose heirs were in possession of it when Doten arrived. To add to the confusion, American lawyers interested in their own welfare advised each family against its self-interest. Doten's land was in an area of one thousand acres south of Berryessa Creek, the original line, which was the southern boundary of the Alviso family's Mexican land grant. An American lawyer, a former butcher, convinced the Alvisos that they ought to claim the property on which the Berryessas had settled next door.

In the meantime the Berryessa family ran afoul of another lawyer, James Jakes, who convinced them to vacate their adobe and settle on their own land like squatters. He hired a

surveyor, parceled out the property in 160-acre allotments, and then claimed the vacated property himself; Don Nicolas Berryessa sued but lost and had to pay $500 in court costs besides.

Doten and other farmers had already built houses, barns, and fences, and planted crops. They immediately organized into a squatter's association and hired a San Francisco lawyer, Alfred A. Green, to pursue their case in court. The first decision, in March 1858, came down against the squatters. Some of them agreed to pay the Alviso heirs but others, like Doten, held on. The squatters were given a reprieve until the following July. While the case went on appeal, Doten proceeded to work his land. One of his first jobs was to repair his fences against cattle and sheep. He cleaned his well, repaired his windmill, and began to cut wood from his land for sale—one of his few sources of cash. Much of the business he conducted was actually trade. He also planted his kitchen garden, a feature of early American farms. Among his crops were potatoes, peas, beans, onions, turnips, carrots, beets, lettuce, radishes, squash, corn, watermelon, muskmelon, and peanuts, and several varieties of fruit trees, all purchased from local nurseries. At the same time he increased his chickens by breeding to supply enough eggs and meat for himself and to sell.

In March 1859 Doten was heartened by the decision of the U.S. Supreme Court to review the land title cases in California in relation to the grants. By July of the next year, however, the case had gone against the squatters and Doten agreed to settle his portion of the rent due at $112.95, agreeing to leave peacefully by September 1. Under the terms of the settlement the new owner, José Urridias, took Doten's improvements from his land, while trampling cattle and other natural hazards spoiled most of Doten's crops. No wonder the battles between squatters, settlers, and landowners were often so vicious.

Before Doten left Santa Clara County he recorded a murder; a suspicious fire had leveled a neighbor's house; and several hundred people marched on San Jose ready to battle over the disputed Yerba Buena Rancho.[16] In the case of the Rancho

Mortars carved in rock next to stream provided group of Indian women a place to grind acorns, C. A.D. 600. Photo taken on Isabel Valley Ranch, Santa Clara County, 1982.

Barbed wire and cattle footprints indicate modern man,
otherwise this 1982 Isabel Valley scene has changed little since
Indians roamed the land.

Sebastian the German shepherd snoozes after winter rain on Olson farm, 1980.

My mother, Rose Zamar Olson, holding, a box of prize Bing cherries ready for market, c. 1940. *Olson Family Collection*

Yemenite worker picks cherries on Olson farm, Sunnyvale,
1980.

Prunes are dropped down a chute from floor above into 100
pound sacks, guided by Heriberto Torres on the Olson farm,
1980.

San Jose Dried Fruit Company branched out into canning about 1882. Montezuma brand of Bonney and Boole probably represents an eastern firm that supplied labels to a San Jose cannery to fill an order under its own brand, a standard practice. Next three labels date from 1899 or later since they display griffin emblem of the California Fruit Canners Association, organized by fourteen canneries in that year. They warn consumer to empty can as soon as possible—a precaution due to inferior sterilization techniques of the time. Not until 1906, with Pure Food and Drug Act, did exact description of can's contents or net weight become a requirement.

The Woman's Fruit Preserving Association, a co-op, may have been associated with Mrs. J. M. Dawson (see Chapter IX) but there is no evidence to confirm this. Mount Hamilton brand was one label of San Jose Fruit Packing Company, Fifth and Julian streets, organized in 1875. It grew out of the first cannery in the county, established by J. M. Dawson in 1872. Canneries of California Fruit Canners Association merged with many others to form California Packing Corporation in 1916.
Courtesy Ralph Rambo

Dry yard of Dolly Stowell, used by my brother for Olson apricots, on farm established 1900 by her father-in-law, Charlie Lincoln Stowell (1980 photo).

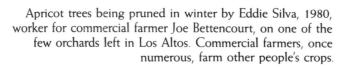

Apricot trees being pruned in winter by Eddie Silva, 1980, worker for commercial farmer Joe Bettencourt, on one of the few orchards left in Los Altos. Commercial farmers, once numerous, farm other people's crops.

Apricots just picked at Seven Springs Ranch, Cupertino,
being dumped into cannery box. Since 1981 my brother has
helped owner Dorothy Lyddon with orchard care and harvest
in exchange for share of crop.

Milpitas, the Berryessa family, rather than submit to ejection orders, armed themselves. The women wore knives and held boiling water on the stove "to scald any one who shall try to molest them. . . ."[17] Don Nicolas Berryessa came closer to madness with each family tragedy. Three of his sons became insane as a direct result of harassment by the squatters. His relative José Reyes Berryessa was lynched on what seemed to have been trumped-up charges and thereby lost claim to the rich Almaden quicksilver mine.

Doten's optimism was not destroyed by his notice to vacate. He undertook to buy one hundred acres of a rancho in Alameda County. But bad luck continued to dog him. That winter of 1861 his crop was inundated by one of the worst floods the Americans had yet experienced. Unprepared, they lost cattle and livestock as well as crops and property. The following summer was one of drought and the crops did not produce. The drought would continue for the next two years. With their herds destroyed, many Californios, too, were forced to put their land on the market for sale. Debt, the cost of defending their property, and the high interest rate on borrowed money combined to make it necessary to sell. Doten decided at this point to give up farming and return to mining, something he had promised himself he would never do again. But before he left the area he decided to take revenge on his enemy. In his diary for October 22, 1861, he recorded that "we came home by way of my old place—stopped at the old house [seven-line erasure] we drove to Milpitas—stopped awhile at the PO—drove on—big light where my old house was—stopped just below Weller's [one-line erasure] So 'old Jóse' won't get *that* house at all."[18] The irony is that before Doten left the valley to mine in the hills behind Milpitas, and then in Nevada, his case was reconsidered again and proven in *his* favor. But by then he was so deeply in debt that he transferred the Milpitas ranch to his hired hand to whom he owed wages. He left the county just as he came: broke.

The Californios fared no better, for the Berryessa's title was denied in 1869. In 1873 Don Nicolas died, a bitter and broken man. Many other Californio families had the land but lost it; squatters, dishonest lawyers, bad weather, hard times, and high interest rates were partly to blame. Human character played no small part. Recalling the fate of the Californios my Dad shook his head and said, "There are many stories of vast tracts of land lost in card games."

The Heyday of Wheat

Despite the losses common to Americans and Californios, the American presence was taking hold. Wheat, the major crop, would continue so until the 1880s, enabling many settlers to succeed. By 1875 there were five grist mills serving the valley; eventually there would be ten. Most of the local wheat was sent from the port of Alviso by scow, schooner, and steamboat to San Francisco for export. "All the roads in the county led to Alviso," my father commented. It was quickly seen that, despite the dry summer, California farmers could grow at least two crops of wheat by planting to catch the early rains and again before the soil dried out in summer.

Grain farming was dry farming. Yields were anywhere from 16 bushels per acre, typical of other parts of the United States, to an incredible 80 bushels per acre in some cases. Thirty and 40 bushels were the norm. The grain grew unusually tall under the oaks where the Spanish cattle had stood, protecting themselves from the hot sun—and dropping manure. This same manure was partly responsible for the huge vegetables the Americans grew in the early decades of their tenure.

By 1860 the California wheat harvest reached 6 million bushels. By 1870 it rose to 16 million bushels and income from it was twice that from mining. In 1870 Santa Clara County ranked fifth in wheat production, behind San Joaquin, Yolo, Solano, and Stanislaus counties.[19] In that year over a million bushels of wheat were produced in Santa Clara County. The peak was reached during the mid-1870s, with 1.7 million bushels. At that time, almost 185,000 acres of the valley floor were planted in wheat, barley, oats, rye, corn, and hay. In the

1880s, however, the midwestern fields began to produce, and California's days of supremacy in wheat were numbered.

The Beginnings of Fruit Culture

By 1868, as John Muir's description makes clear, orchards and vineyards were making a noticeable appearance among the Santa Clara Valley's waving fields of grain. As he traveled from Oakland to San Jose, he was impressed by the valley's fertility. "Its rich bottoms," he noted, "are filled with wheatfields, and orchards, and vineyards, and alfalfa meadows."[20]

The history of valley agriculture falls into four periods. First, as we have seen, came the early pastoral ranchos of cattle, hides, and tallow. After 1848, farmers created one vast field of grain. But even as grain continued, horticulturists were laying the foundations for the third period. Some, like the historian H. S. Foote, date the era of fruit culture from the coming of the transcontinental railroad of 1869, because it opened up needed markets. This was the prelude to the family farm era. A fourth period includes the present era, when the family farms have adapted to urban conditions.

El Camino Real and the missions had made California a colony for Spain. The colonizing weapon of the Americans was the railroad, which would link California to the rest of the country and Americanize it. Streams and creeks, running at will before, were harnessed by ditches to divert the winter floodwaters directly into the bay. The San Francisco-San Jose Railroad, laid down in 1864, was not as significant as farmers had hoped, since fares were high and the delivery points out of the way. Also, the railroad did not schedule trains at times convenient for reaching the San Francisco market early in the morning. The transcontinental railroad of 1869, on the other hand, linked Santa Clara County with national markets, and in the long run proved to be the vital connection that made fruit farming the leading factor in the county's economy.

Many of the land-grant squabbles were being settled in the 1870s and 1880s, and land whose title was no longer in doubt

became available for sale. Large ranchos where grain had been grown for up to thirty years experienced soil depletion. Unpredictable rain also made grain farming less attractive. And then there was the introduction of taxes. In 1873 when Santa Clara County had a population of 26,000, San Jose newspaperman J. J. Owens wrote that the large estates of one to twenty thousand acres would break up because "a system of assessing them at their actual value, just introduced, will soon induce the subdivision and sale . . . as the owners will find it too unprofitable to permit their lands longer to remain idle."[21]

The railroad itself created a change in the value of land. Before the locomotive, land in the San Joaquin, San Gabriel, and other valleys "was worth from ten to twenty-five dollars per acre. After the railroads were built, land went up to $200, $500 and $1,000 per acre."[22] The presence of the railroad was vital to the economics of fruit and vineyard culture. Goods that previously were in oversupply now had markets. Doten had noted in his journal that peaches lay on the ground for want of someone to use them. Before long, luscious fruits from Santa Clara County would enhance the diets and tables of people in New York and Boston, Philadelphia and Minneapolis. More and more partook of the feast, making fruit orchards economic and allowing a unique pattern of small family farms to emerge in Santa Clara County.[23]

Notes

[1] I taped this conversation with my father on Oct. 3, 1980.

[2] Arbuckle and Rambo, *Santa Clara County Ranchos,* 25, 36.

[3] Walter Van Tilburg Clark, ed., *The Journals of Alfred Doten, 1849-1903,* vol. 1 (Reno, Nev.: University of Nevada Press, 1973), 245. Hereafter cited as Doten (all references are to vol.1).

[4] "Address Before the Wisconsin State Agricultural Society, in McMillen, ed., *Harvest,* 146.

[5] Doten, 186.

[6] Doyce B. Nunis, Jr., *Josiah Belden, 1841 California Overland Pioneer: His Memoir and Early Letters* (Georgetown, Calif.: Talisman Press, 1962), 83.

[7] Doten, 597.

[8] Since California wheat hit these markets at a time when the usual supplies were limited, there was a booming demand for it despite the extra cost of transportation.

[9] Doten, 616.

[10] Ibid., 559.

[11] Ibid., 454.

[12] Ibid., 305.

[13] J. F. Poland and R. L. Ireland, "Land Subsidence and Aquifer-System Compaction, Santa Clara Valley, California, U.S.A.," ([Washington D.C.]: U.S. Department of the Interior, Geologic Survey, 1971.) Misc. Field Studies, map MF-336.

[14] William O. Clark, *Ground Water in Santa Clara Valley, California*, Water-Supply Paper 519 ([Washington, D.C.]: U.S. Department of the Interior, Geologic Survey, 1924), 79. See plates 14,15.

[15] *Soil Survey*, 174.

[16] The settlers claimed ownership over the grantee Chaboya, to whom it had been deeded in 1833. In that case, the sheriff backed down in face of their guns and battle was avoided. Eventually, Chaboya's claim was validated.

[17] Doten, 581.

[18] Ibid., 630.

[19] Thomas Thompson and Albert West, *New Historical Atlas of Santa Clara Co.*, (San Francisco: Thompson & West, 1876), 17. The figures are from a table headed "California Selected Statistics of Agriculture, 1870."

[20] William Frederic Badè, *The Life and Letters of John Muir*, vol. 1 (Boston and New York: Houghton Mifflin Company, 1923), 178.

[21] J. J. Owens, *Santa Clara Valley* (San Jose, 1873), 4.

[22] *Progressive Santa Clara* (n.p., 1904). Both this and the work cited in Note 21 are promotional pamphlets.

[23] Fruits as an integral part of our diet are now taken for granted. This was not so in 1871, when *Pacific Rural Press* declared (Dec. 2, 1871): "In every community there is a growing interest in fruits. They are beginning to be regarded, as they justly should be, as one of the essentials of a proper diet. They ought to hold an equal rank with bread and vegetables."

Other Sources for Chapter 3

Certain standard works on Santa Clara County were used in this chapter and throughout the book: H. S. Foote, ed., *Pen Pictures from the Garden of the World* (Chicago: Lewis Publishing Co., 1888); *San Jose Mercury, Sunshine, Fruit and Flowers*, [Souvenir of Santa Clara County] (San Jose, 1896); J. P. Munro-Fraser, *History of Santa Clara County, California* (San Francisco: Alley, Bowen & Co., 1881); Frederic Hall, *The History of San Jose*, (San Francisco: A. L. Bancroft & Co., 1871); Mary Bowden Carroll, *Ten Years in Paradise* (San Jose: Press of Popp & Hogan, 1903); Eugene T. Sawyer, *History of Santa Clara County, California* (Los Angeles: Historic Record Co., 1922); William F. James, *A History of San Jose* (San Jose: A. H. Cawston, 1933); *The Santa Clara Valley: Horticultural and Viticultural Newspaper* (San Jose, 1884-86). Thomas Thompson and Albert West, *Historical Atlas of Santa Clara County* (San Francisco, 1876):

Other works consulted include: J. N. Bowman and G. W. Hendry, "Posolmi, Middle 1830s to late 1840s," in "Nine San Francisco Bay Counties: 1776 to About 1850," vol. 7, 842-989; Paul W. Gates, *California Ranchos and Farms: 1846-1862* (Madison, Wis.: State Historical Society of Wisconsin, 1967); E. W. Hilgard, *Report on the Physical and Agricultural Features of the State of California* (San Francisco: Dewey & Co., 1884); *Biennial Report of the State Board of Horticulture of the State of California for 1885 and 1886* (Sacramento: State Printing Office, 1887), and for 1890-91 (ibid., 1892); [Sister] Gabrielle Sullivan, *Martin Murphy, Jr., California Pioneer: 1844-1884* (Stockton: University of the Pacific, Pacific Center for Western Historical Studies, 1974); George S. Wells, *Garden in the West: A Dramatic Account of Science in Agriculture* (New York: Dodd, Mead & Co., 1969) which includes an article on California's early wheat growing.

CHAPTER 4
THE HORTICULTURISTS AND
THE FAMILY FARM

CONSIDER THE FRUIT TREE and how it grows from winter wood, lifeless and bare. By an inner clock miraculous blossoms appear and transform themselves into fruit. I have often thought that an orchard is like a troop of dancers standing in place and moving in slow motion. This slow and quiet miracle is a metaphor of life itself, for the first command of the Bible is "Be fruitful and multiply."

The command came after Adam ate the apple (some say it was an apricot), but how could he refuse? Fruit is a plant's fleshy, ripened ovary enveloping its seed. Eve said to Adam, "Eat." She really meant "enjoy," for that is the root meaning of the word "fruit." Its surface, shape, scent, color, and taste are consumed directly along with its beauty, delicious flavor, and healthful nutrients. Fruit farmers recognize that what they do is something special. Perhaps that is why my father, along with many Santa Clara Valley farmers, referred to himself as an "orchardist." He might have said, like our friend Eiichi Sakauye, that he was a "pomologist"—a specialist in the growing of fruit—or even a "horticulturist," except that finding long Latin words somewhat amusing, he would have twisted the word into "yokamokalist," the name he gave to the new scientists and engineers whose culture slowly took over the landscape. If you asked him what these people produced, he would answer, with a broad mischievous grin, "Hootenannies."

Not that my father turned his back on science and technology—far from it! He was a scientific farmer, making use of new ideas from many sources. Horticulture (Latin for cultivation of a garden), a major branch of agriculture, is the science *and* art of growing fruits, vegetables, and flowers or ornamental plants. Medieval systems of agriculture, whose example the Spanish followed in California, included wild areas for timber and game; extensive fields for grains, forages, and pastures; and intensive kitchen gardens, often within closed walls like the mission gardens, where vegetables and fruits were protected from trampling and ruin by farm and wild animals. Santa Clara County had already seen these different phases of land use. Now, from the 1850s onwards, came the

turn of the horticulturists, the gardeners who, in a figurative sense, knocked down the mission garden walls and pushed the orchards, vineyards, and vegetable farms right across the plains and onto the hillsides, to the rim of the valley, even to the mountains, until the valley was one continuous garden.

The connection between science, the university, and agriculture was made a permanent part of American farming practices by the passage of the Morrill Act of 1862, which endowed colleges with public land for the study and promotion of agriculture and the mechanical arts. The University of California at Berkeley was founded for this purpose in 1868. The rational, square orchards, the vineyards that ran in symmetrical lines up the sides of hills, the orderliness of the valley, reflect book farming—science applied to the land. For the Santa Clara Valley, such farming was a development of the 1880s.

In our family, the scientific method of the universities was balanced by the intuitive method of the Middle East, for my mother, Rose Zamar Olson, is Lebanese. Her instinct to grow plants is part of her cultural heritage; the earliest agricultural communities are found in the region of her birth. By the time she was ten she was growing corn, peas, cucumber, squash, tomatoes, beans, and grapes in a plot that she tended in her village of Maschagara, thirty miles southeast of Beirut. She hoed, watered, and harvested crops that she sold by the roadside. Her methods reigned in the vegetable garden around our home. Orderly rows were not in evidence. Rather, the garden had a random, natural look, with everything planted in it growing in healthy abandon. Her skills worked just as well as my father's, and she continues to plant and grow her favorite vegetable crops and flowers as she approaches her eightieth year.

A student anthropologist had been referred to my mother because someone he asked said, "Mrs. Olson can grow anything." He gave my mother corn from an early Indian burial site, trusting her hand with these precious and ancient kernels. She did nothing special to prepare the seeds, but did prepare the soil, enriching it with manure. Then she pushed the seeds into the ground and watered. They grew! A hungry rabbit, loose from a suburban cage, ate the healthy plants before they reached maturity.

Pioneer Horticulturalists and Nurserymen

In allotting credit for the vast garden that was Santa Clara County it is impossible to single out any one nationality. Many nationalities would come here in the era of the family farm, bringing with them a variety of skills and experience. Horticultural expertise was only one reason these small-sized farms emerged as an unexpected pattern in the valley. There were other reasons as well. California, a new and virgin land, released creative energies. Far from being afraid of change and new ideas, newcomers were willing to try anything, to experiment with the land to see what it could best produce. The land, climate, and motivation were present in the right mix. Fresh fruit brought high prices in the years just after the Gold Rush, and this prompted many to begin fruit growing. Two men, Joshua Redman and Charles Clayton, took over the mission orchard in 1850, "reaping the benefit of the orchard, which at that time was very great, as fruit was scarce and consequently high in price."[1] The fruit sold at retail for fifty cents a pound. An apple in San Francisco sold for a dollar.[2] Santa Clara County's proximity to San Francisco made it a natural source of fresh fruits and vegetables.

The mission orchards were also used by the early Americans and immigrants who took cuttings with which to begin their own orchards and vineyards. Captain Elisha Stephens, guide of the Stephens-Murphy-Townsend party, came to the valley in 1849 and planted four acres of mission grapes where Stevens Creek Boulevard today crosses Stevens Creek, both named after him and both misspelled. Many others did the same. While newcomers made use of some native rootstocks, like the wild blackberry, plum, and California grape, better-quality produce could be had from varieties brought from the eastern United States, Europe, and Asia. The early nurserymen must be credited for giving Santa Clara County its firm start as a community whose economic base was orchards and vineyards. The first Americans to introduce grafted trees from the states to the West Coast came from Iowa. Henderson Lewelling crossed into Oregon in 1847 with wagons filled with trees set in boxes of soil. Three hundred trees survived. The same year he went into partnership in Milwaukie, Oregon, with William Meek, founder of the first nursery of grafted fruit trees on the Pacific Coast. The partners were joined in 1850 by Henderson's brother Seth, who brought a large quantity of fruit seed with him. In March of 1851 Seth took a shipment of grafted trees to Sacramento and sold them all immediately; they included apple, pear, peach, plum, and cherry trees.

Seth Lewelling holds a place of special importance in the history of Santa Clara County and our own family, for it was he who developed the Bing cherry in 1875. He named it after his Chinese cook, some say in lieu of the back wages he owed him. His political sympathies are reflected in the names he gave to other cherries: Republican and Lincoln. Henderson Lewelling is remembered for the Lambert, named after the owner of the orchard in which he developed it.[3] The Bing, the Republican, and the Lambert are only three of ten varieties that grow in our orchard, but the Bing and Lambert are two of the four most widely planted cherry trees in the world. Some of the finest examples of the Bing grow in Santa Clara Valley. While I never heard my Dad refer to himself as "Cherry King" of the valley, I have heard others do so. It was because his hand-packed boxes of cherries, few in number, sustained the highest quality, drawing the best prices on the New York market year after year. The cherries went by rail.

G. G. Briggs, in 1851, introduced peach, apple, and pear trees from New York to Yuba City and saw wonderful results. As was often the case with pioneers, he brought them "with no idea that they would succeed, but as a reminder of home." These three fruits, because of their widespread success in the East, were among the first to be planted in Santa Clara

County.[4] Locally, several Easterners and Europeans became involved in nursery operations. As far as the orchards are concerned, the most important was Louis Pellier, a Frenchman who settled in Santa Clara County in 1850. He came to the goldfields, but returned to his former profession as nurseryman, attracted to San Jose by its settlement of French people. He bought a piece of land and began to plant vegetables and pear trees. He collected seeds by paying the neighborhood children a penny for each one they brought him. The Peralta family adobe, with its pear trees, stood next door. Pellier Park in San Jose commemorates the spot today.

Pellier's brother Pierre came to work with him, bringing from France several varieties of grape cuttings. When, in 1854, Pierre returned to France to marry, Louis gave him a list of varieties he thought would do well in California. Pierre returned with his bride in 1856 and brought the cuttings—a whole trunkful. Among them was the *petite d'Agen*, a French prune named after Villeneuve, a village near Agen in southwest France, and cuttings of vines, pears, apples, and plums, as well as other varieties of prunes.[5] Louis Pellier immediately grafted the newly arrived prune cuttings to plum roots—the beginning of Santa Clara County's largest agricultural crop. He died in 1872, however, a decade before his tree emerged as the leading one.[6] All the prunes in the United States still come from California and over ninety percent of them are Pellier's.

Experiments with other kinds of fruit increased the range of possibilities for Santa Clara County. Commodore Robert F. Stockton, retired from his military and political career, purchased Rancho El Potrero de Santa Clara in 1847. In 1852 he had apple, peach, pear, nectarine, and apricot root stock sent from Hovey's Nursery in Massachusetts for the purpose of establishing a nursery of his own. With this shipment the first strawberries came to the county. Bernard S. Fox, a professional nurseryman from Ireland, accompanied the shipment. The following year he, too, opened a nursery in the area of the San Jose—Milpitas Road, adjacent to and crossing Coyote Creek,

just south of the present Schallenberger Road, it was called Santa Clara Valley Nurseries and Botanical Gardens. Fox went on to develop several pear varieties that were used in early plantings. His nursery was of special importance, for other nurserymen and fruit farmers settled next to it, each contributing something to the development of the prune. The French prune is small, and while it could be sold "green" or fresh there was not a widespread market for its use at first. The thought of drying it was still a long way off.

John Q. A. Ballou, a forty-niner from Vermont, bought his own homestead property just south of Fox's nursery and planted two thousand pear and apple trees there during the 1850s. In 1861 he obtained prune grafts from Louis Pellier that bore fruit in 1867. The next year, just before the railroad was completed, he sent eleven tons of dried fruit around Cape Horn. A fellow nurseryman and neighbor, George W. Tarleton, is credited with early graftings of the prune tree onto a damson plum stock. But it was John Rock (Johann Fels), a German-born nurseryman with property between Fox and Ballou, who saw the commercial possibilities of the prune and popularized it from 1868 on. Another German, B. Kamp, took grafts from Pellier and set out his trees in orchard rows.

Captain Joseph Aram, another retired military man who turned to horticulture, recounts how, in 1853, he met a man with a shipment of trees from the East. "They seemed about all spoiled and the man was discouraged. . . ." He bought the shipment and "was much pleased to find that I saved a great many of them and was able to get scions from them to graft and bud my seedlings. . . . For the little trees I started and grafted there was a great demand . . . and I sold $8,000 worth one year from that stock. We were astonished when we heard how soon the grafted trees came into bearing."[7]

It was not long before the horticulturists met together to establish a society to further their common interests. In 1853, under a spreading live oak on the property of Louis Prevost west of the Guadalupe River, the Pioneer Horticultural Society

B. S. Fox's nursery astride the Coyote River (right), between
Schallenberger and Berryessa roads in San Jose. Nursery was
one of several in district that helped make San Jose after the
Gold Rush the nursery capital of California. *Thompson & West
Atlas, 1876*

Pellier's home and place of business, City Gardens Nursery, at
N. San Pedro and Chaboya in downtown San Jose. This was
San Jose's first frame house, built with lumber from Oregon
and from around the Horn. *Photo by Alice Hare, 1902, Courtesy
San Jose Historical Museum*

California Nursery Co. at Niles, near Mission San Jose was
established when R. D. Fox, nephew of B. S. Fox, joined forces
with John Rock in 1884. It was a main source for orchard
stock for fruit growers all over California (photo before 1890).
Courtesy San Jose Historical Museum

Pierre Mirassou (center), with his two brothers-in-law, Philippe
Prudhomme (left) and Alfred Renaud (right), c. 1888. *Courtesy
Mirassou Vineyards*

Fruit orchards in Santa Clara Valley, c. 1900. Water tank on each farm indicates presence of well for family's needs. To judge from the small barns, these farmers did not process their fruit themselves, but sold it to a processor. Large dryyard appears upper left. *Photo by J. O. Tucker, Courtesy Sourisseau Academy*

"Vineyard in the sky" planted by Paul Masson during the 1890s in the Chaine d'Or (Golden Chain) area of the Santa Cruz mountains, so called because of its ideal conditions for producing fine grapes and wine. *Photo by Ansel Adams, 1959, Courtesy Paul Masson Vineyards*

Cattle being judged at Santa Clara Valley Agricultural Society
Fair, 1874, on present site of Hanchett residential district.
Seventy-five-acre fairgrounds had been purchased for that
purpose by 1859, six years after first countywide meeting of
nurserymen and horticulturists. *Courtesy Sourisseau Academy*

Indoor display at Santa Clara Valley Agricultural Society Fair, 1874. Note pears, grapes, wine, canned goods, flour, and indoor plants. *Photo S. P. Saunders, Courtesy Sourisseau Academy*

Field of onion seed at Pieters-Wheeler seed farm, Gilroy,
c. 1910. Santa Clara County was long considered the largest
center for the growing of flower and vegetable seed in the
United States. *Photo by J. O. Tucker, Courtesy Sourisseau Academy*

Knapp Plow Works, San Jose, some time after 1907 when Robert Knapp moved his business there to be near a main railroad branch. The plow, reversible at end of row and so suited to hillsides, was shipped all over the West, Hawaii, and the Orient. *Photo by J. O. Tucker, Courtesy San Jose Historical Museum*

San Jose, 1866: view northeast from courthouse along First
Street. Note box factory (left), an early supplier to fruit
industry. *Photo by J. T. Pollock, Robert T. Butcher and Eugene Butcher*
Collection, Courtesy Robert T. Butcher

San Jose, 1890: twenty-four years later the same photographer,
J. T. Pollock, climbed to the same spot and took this
photograph of the view northeast along First Street, recording
better than words the process of urbanization. St. James's Park
in foreground. *Courtesy Robert T. Butcher*

Congregational Church, Oak Street, Saratoga, 1890s. The charter membership included nine women and one man, who organized the first permanent church in Saratoga. *Courtesy Saratoga Historical Foundation*

Women packing apples at Butcher family farm, Santa Clara, in the early 1900s; Mrs. Arthur Butcher at far right. Outing was clearly as much recreational as vocational. *Courtesy Robert T. Butcher*

Long Bridge near Saratoga, here seen in the 1890s, was a favorite spot for picnics. *Photo by J. T. Pollock, Courtesy Robert T. Butcher*

Members of the Stelling family, farmers in Cupertino, enjoy a day at Aptos, on Monterey Bay, then as now a favorite spot for summer outings and vacations (photo c. 1900). *Courtesy Charles Stelling*

Springtime visitors, 1912, to farm of Frank Jenkins, Saratoga, descend from water tower after admiring view of orchard blossoms. *Photo by J. O. Tucker, Courtesy Margaret Jenkins*

was born.[8] The society met once a month, bringing flowers and fruits together for comparison and discussion. Santa Clara Valley's fruit-growing potential was put on display when the State Horticultural Society held a fair in San Jose in 1856. A wide variety of fruits was shown and people came from miles around to view their extraordinary quality. The Santa Clara Agricultural Society, representing the other branches of agriculture, joined with the local society, which was absorbed by it. By 1859, after an act of the state legislature, the Santa Clara Agricultural Society bought fairgrounds for regular displays.

Santa Clara County experienced its first setback in fruit growing in the late 1860s, just before the completion of the transcontinental railroad. Many new orchards grafted on improved stock came into bearing at the same time; the San Francisco market was flooded, so that growers were left with rotting fruit. While it was a temporary setback, it illustrated that a viable orchard economy needed wider markets.

The Orchards Spread Out

The first prune orchard to achieve a commercial success was that of E. L. Bradley, on Stevens Creek Road at Bascom Avenue, which was planted as an experiment in 1875. Ten acres of it yielded from $2,500 to $4,000 each season after the trees came into bearing, in 1881.[9] The combined yield for the following four years was $15,000. This success proved that prunes could grow without irrigation and that ten acres could provide a handsome income for a family.

Large-scale plantings of orchards can be dated from this point at the beginning of the 1880s. Suddenly grain lands became more valuable as subdivisions for fruit farms. A land boom followed. Spurred on by other stories of success, growers made haste with new plantings of prunes, grapes, and other fruits. The rush caught nurserymen unprepared: prices for nursery trees rose from 15 cents each to 35 and 40 cents. Trees were imported from the East to meet the demand.

The California Nursery Company, located in Niles just inside Alameda County, is of major importance in the story of fruit development. In 1884, John Rock and R. D. Fox, a nephew of Bernard Fox who had inherited his uncle's business, joined together and bought nearly five hundred acres of land just outside the county for the exclusive development of fruit trees. Under John Rock's direction the nursery became the best and largest on the Pacific Coast. A grower could choose from four hundred varieties of apples alone. Rock also specialized in prunes (he introduced the Imperial), peaches, apricots, plums, and cherries—a total of 1600 varieties of fruit trees by 1884. It was here that, in 1901, my grandfather bought his fruit stock. Sometime before his death in 1904 Rock sold the nursery to six businessmen. It has been in the hands of the Roeding family since 1917, when George C. Roeding took it over after his father Frederick C. Roeding, a well-known Fresno nurseryman, had bought it. George C. Roeding, Jr., and his son Bruce continue to operate California Nursery Company, though primarily as a mail-order business specializing in ornamentals rather than commercial fruit trees. Its original grounds have been developed except for twenty acres acquired by the state for Vallejo Mission Adobe State Park, named after an original adobe still on the site.

By 1892, the State Board of Horticulture could claim that Santa Clara County was "preeminently the horticultural county of the State," and that prunes—over 22 million pounds of them in 1891—were its principal crop.[10] The success of the prune, with that of the peach, pear, and apricot, was partly due to the rediscovery of the drying process. Since dried fruit could be shipped anywhere, it opened a wider range of markets, making small farms economical. The Egyptians, Middle Easterners, Romans, and Europeans had known about drying fruit and the use of sulphur to preserve it. Most eastern Americans had experience with drying apples in evaporators but few had any experience with prunes. Ballou and Tarleton began to dip the prunes in a solution of lye and boiling water, thus causing the skin to "check", or crack, and hastening the drying process. This process prevented "frogs," bloated prunes that ferment rather than dry.[11]

Another barrier to small-farm ownership was removed when the discovery was made, by accident, that drying prunes in the open air was more efficient than using evaporators. In 1887 the prune crop was so large that the growers, for lack of evaporators, had to resort to sun-drying. Before the discovery of sun-drying, the most favored dried prunes had been produced by the French method, which consisted of placing the prunes in ovens. During the four to six hours of drying, the prunes were turned by hand—a costly and time-consuming process. With the discovery of sun-drying, a hindrance to entering the prune market was removed, since the sun was available to anyone while evaporator ovens were expensive.

While sun-drying worked well on prunes, it made other fruit such as pears, apricots, and peaches turn black. In the 1870s a local pioneer, Henry Coe, began to correct this with sulphur. The cut fruit, before being left out in the sun to dry, was placed on trays, and housed overnight in a wooden shed in which sulphur had been ignited. Experiments by farmers in Visalia turned up the same results as Coe's: sulphur fumes preserved the color of apricots, peaches, and pears, and kept out insects as well. Soon dried fruit, packed in wooden boxes, was sent not only to the eastern United States but to Europe. By widening the market, the growers had passed another milestone.

From the 1850s onward (later in other areas), orchards were established in and around San Jose and Santa Clara. Pears were concentrated in the lowland areas north of San Jose and Santa Clara, where the annual flooding of the creeks did not damage their roots as much as it did those of other fruits. Early maps indicate numerous strawberry plantings in this region by the 1870s; the pears and other fruits were planted by the 1880s. Some families that began as farmers in the 1880s remained here through several generations, farming the land until the 1960s, when a disease known as pear decline hastened what the pressures of urbanization had already begun. These included the Westons, Brachers, Browns, Chinchens, Gallaghers, Frenches, Wilcoxes, Standishes, and many more. The Sakauye family had settled there in 1906. Some of these families, like the Gallaghers and Frenches, could trace their origin to families descended from the Alvisos and Berryessas. A few old families, like the McCarthys and Cilkers, retain a foothold in the area even today. Throughout Santa Clara County, farm families are remembered in place names such as Tantau Avenue, King Road, White Road, Hellyer Avenue, Cottle Avenue, Stelling Road, and McClellan Road.

Another early fruit-growing area when it first opened up was known as "The Willows." Later it was called "The Cherries" and finally, after the turn of the century, "Willow Glen." The name commemorated a dense thicket of willows that once grew throughout the region, southwest of San Jose along Los Gatos Creek—so dense that only the Spanish cattle had been able to thread pathways through it. Vineyards were planted by Antonio Sunol before 1850. The land was divided into ten-acre lots and cleared in the 1860s. At that time hops were planted, as well as strawberries; the latter did well until the lowlands emerged as a significant berry-growing region. Willow Glen had been The Cherries because the first commercial cherry orchards in California began there in 1868, when W. C. Geiger cleared and planted the fourteen acres he had bought for $100 per acre adjacent to Los Gatos Creek. In 1888 he sold his crop on the trees for $6,000—not a bad income from less than fourteen acres. By the turn of the century these remarkable virgin cherry trees, planted in deep loam, were still bearing, some as much as one to two thousand pounds of fruit, and the area became known statewide as premium orchard land.

Few had suspected in the 1860s that much of the valley could be planted in orchards. An admitted exception was the "thermal belt" which extended east to Almadén Valley and west to Mountain View. Vineyards and orchards in this area were more protected from early frosts. Los Gatos and Saratoga, two towns in the belt, are nestled in the foothills of the Santa Cruz Mountains. Both were primarily lumber towns, but an early orchard was planted in Los Gatos in 1860 when a nurseryman, J. F. Kennedy, moved there. He had come to the county with Bernard Fox and the shipment of fruit stock for Commodore Stockton. Kennedy's neighbors planted orchards when they saw that his succeeded. Gilbert Fancher, from New York, pioneered 40 acres of almonds almost next door sometime after 1862.

Orchards and vineyards were planted in Saratoga in the 1870s. One of the first prune orchards was established by the Reverend William D. Pollard (remembered in Pollard Road) who came from Indiana in 1876 and bought 40 acres of land. He planted pears, peaches, apricots, and prunes, reporting after five years that he earned $550 an acre from the prunes and $300 an acre from the peaches.

In 1883 Dr. George Handy, an eye specialist from New York, decided to become a fruit farmer. He bought a former grain ranch halfway between Saratoga and Los Gatos and called the canyon on it Glen Una, after his daughter. On his 450 acres he planted 125 acres of prunes, probably the largest planting in the county up to that point. Eventually, for a time during the 1890s, the Glen Una, which was taken over by his son-in-law Frank H. Hume, became the largest prune orchard in the world; it had 350 acres in prunes alone, and an annual income ranging from $35,000 to $44,000. Prune growing on a large scale had become a reality in Santa Clara County. More typical was William Rice who, in 1876 along what is now the Sunnyvale-Saratoga Road, planted his 30 acres in 17 acres of prunes (10 silver, 7 French), 1 acre of apples, and 4 acres each of apricots, peaches, and pears. For him as for many, the secret of survival was a diversified crop.

At first these were looked upon as foolish investments, doomed to failure because of the thin soil and lack of water.

Dry farming, except along the creeks, came into being in these areas. Widespread irrigation would not be practiced until after the turn of the century, when electric power and turbine engines became available for bringing water to the surface. Even so, dry farming of orchards, much to the surprise of doubters, worked, and the orchards prospered. Misgivings were expressed about the ability of the soil to bear fruit in the Mountain View area. But when, in 1890, some of the small ranches planted in the 1880s began to produce fruit at the rate of $200 per acre, "the wise hay ranchers," according to a local historian, "said no more."[12]

The Berryessa area and to the south Evergreen, beneath the eastern foothills and near the concentration of nurseries on the San Jose–Milpitas Road, were also developed in the 1880s. Lands formerly in grain were ideal for orchards and vineyards. Certain other lands in these hills were fine for truck gardens, with such crops as early spring peas, while others were good only for grazing. In such areas a mixed pattern of agriculture emerged and has left remnants visible to this day. Meanwhile, prunes were beginning to appear around Gilroy. Before this time the only fruit trees there had been in kitchen gardens for the use of families handling cattle or growing grain. Dairies had prospered in this area since the 1850s (they continue to do so) and vegetables grew successfully because of the artesian water supply. Already the center of the county's cheese industry, Gilroy went on to become one of the primary prune growing areas. Apricots and vineyards were widely planted.

One of the last areas converted to orchard lands was the one known today as Los Altos Hills. Although a farmer named John Snyder had vineyards and orchards in the area in the 1870s, these lands were long considered good mostly for cattle grazing and grain crops. After the turn of the century, venturesome farmers began planting orchard trees and found that they thrived without irrigation. The Blenheim and Royal apricots were heavily concentrated here, but a varied pattern of agriculture emerged with dairies, chicken farms, wineries, orchards,

1977

Unfiltered **Mirassou**

Santa Clara

Cabernet Sauvignon

Produced and Bottled by Mirassou Vineyards
San Jose, California · Est. 1854 · Alc. 12% by Vol.

VINTAGE 1979

Charles Lefranc

A Founder's Wine

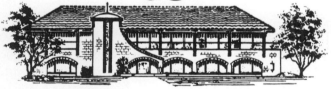

MONTEREY COUNTY
Fumé Blanc

Here is one of the most remarkable full-bodied dry wines of
its kind. Fumé Blanc means white smoke and is made predominantly
from the SAUVIGNON BLANC grape. Sauvignon Blanc prospers
and reaches perfection in Monterey County, producing a wine
of extraordinary fragrance and breed.

PRODUCED AND BOTTLED BY
ALMADÉN VINEYARDS, SAN JOSE, CA   BW 145
ALCOHOL 12.5% BY VOLUME

stock farms, and truck gardening side by side. In the upper regions, a ranch like the O & O, belonging to Louis Oneal, raised horses until the 1940s. Others ran cattle.

Vineyards and the Wine Industry

Santa Clara County became an early center for growing table and wine grapes. During Prohibition grapes were used for juice but grapes for raisins have never prospered here. The Mission grape did not suit the county's early French and German settlers. It was, however, the dominant grape until the 1880s, when more attention was paid to stock from the eastern United States and Europe. In 1884 there were just over 1,500 acres of vineyards planted in the county. The annual *Report of the State Board of Horticulture* reported an increase to 11,000 acres in 1892. Grapes were planted not only on the valley floor but also on the undulating, gently rounded hills that link the valley to the mountains on east and west. Professor E. W. Hilgard of the University of California at Berkeley attested in 1884 to the fine composition of the soil: "The higher lands of the valley are a lighter sandy loam, gravelly on the east and west, while those of the hills on either side are a cinnamon-colored loam, with a reddish-brown subsoil, well adapted to grape and fruit culture."[13] These lands did indeed prove to be excellent for vineyards; some even claimed that the wines of West Side—now Cupertino—were the best produced in California.

Vineyards as well as orchards began to appear in the mountain regions during the 1880s. To make possible the planting of vineyards on hillsides, a special horse-drawn plow, reversible at the end of a row, was developed by Robert Knapp. This invention is still in use in steep areas. There was enough produce in the area of the Santa Cruz Mountains for one depot, Wright's Station, to ship a carload of fruit a day during harvest. The best table grapes came from this area.

Charles Lefranc, considered the father of winemaking in Santa Clara County, bought a wagonload of grape cuttings from the Santa Clara mission and began his wine operation by the early 1850s. Lefranc located his vineyard south of San Jose at the mouth of the Almadén Valley. Later he imported French vines and grafted these to native California grapes that he found growing along the banks of the Guadalupe. He excelled in making white wines, clarets, brandy and even sherry. Lefranc married the daughter of an earlier French settler and vintner Etienne Thée. Lefranc's daughter married Paul Masson who worked at New Almadén vineyards, owned by her father. He became a partner with his brother-in-law, Henry Lefranc. Paul Masson, from Burgundy, decided he would create a sparkling wine in Santa Clara County to rival that of Champagne in his native France. Going into business on his own, he bought property on Pierce Road above Saratoga and, in customary style, created a French-type winery complete with the facade of a European church. After an illustrious career, during which he garnered praise for his premium wines and champagnes, he sold his vineyard in 1936 to Martin Ray, a businessman turned vintner. A fire destroyed the winery in 1941, but Ray recouped and sold the business to Joseph E. Seagram in 1943. Seagram still retains a major share. As for Almadén Vineyards, it belongs today to National Distillers. The Lefranc family is remembered, along with Thée, in the eighteen-acre vineyard that surrounds corporate offices in Almadén Valley.

Mirassou Vineyards, based in Evergreen, traces its history back five generations to Pierre Pellier, who settled on the land purchased by his brother Louis, the nurseryman, in 1862. While there were earlier vineyards in the area, Pellier's would outlast the others and survive grape phylloxera, Prohibition, family disputes, and resettlement of the vineyards themselves in Monterey County in the late 1960s. Pierre Pellier's daughter Henriette was taught winemaking by her father. She married Pierre H. Mirassou in 1880 and together they ran a successful operation. Mirassou Vineyards is now the oldest family wine business in the United States.

The early grape plantings were nearly wiped out in the late 1890s by the dreaded phylloxera, a small wingless insect that attacks the roots of vines. The flat lands of Mountain View and Cupertino, where large vineyards had been the most characteristic feature of the landscape, were then subdivided and converted into smaller-sized family farms. As resistant stocks were developed, the new plantings took place in the hills. All the dead vines had to be pulled out. A special device, based on a system of pulleys and powered by animal strength, was developed for this purpose by a one-armed inventor named Edmund Boden, originally from England.

The vineyard I remember most was Heney's in Cupertino, which produced a fine cabernet under its own label of Chateau Ricardo. One hundred acres had been planted in 1882 by William Heney, a San Franciscan who joined in the vineyard boom of the 1880s on the West Side. When "the louse," as farmers called it, struck in 1898, Heney sent to France for resistant stock and replanted the entire vineyard, probably by 1902. By the time I saw the vineyard in the early 1940s it had passed from the Heney family to another owner. I remember it as it was then because my mother and I went there once, climbing under barbed wire, down through a creek infested with poison oak, and up to the vineyard to gather a few of the tender young grape leaves. Such leaves are used in cooking throughout the Middle East and stuffed grape leaves was one of our favorite dishes. It was a particularly beautiful vineyard, stretching up the gently rolling foothills. The red brick winery had a simple, rectangular authority as it stood on a plateau against the rugged hills of Montebello Ridge that surround the Stevens Creek area. Today, homes fill the former vineyard where Highway 280 passes at the intersection with Grant Road.

Clearing the Land

Some lamented the destruction of the oaks as the land was cleared for orchards. Describing the "grand old oaks," E. S. Harrison wrote in 1887: "Your days are numbered. The axe of

Utility is already at your base. . . . The spirit of your twinkling leaves shall re-appear in the rosy wine . . . your souls will rise again in the fruits that will make this section famous. You die that others may live, and thus you are compensated."[14] But then some oak trees would remain to shade tractors, to provide shelter for people cutting apricots, or just because a farmer hated to see an oak go. And a few would remain to grace shopping centers.

Before the orchards took over, agricultural lands were divided into three categories: wheat, cattle, and chaparral. Wheat land was usually good for most crops, while the cattle grazed on land not good enough for wheat. At first, chaparral was considered worthless, but this opinion was changed by the work of men like Hilgard who saw that it could be used for vineyards and orchards. Also, the railroad, whose owners were trying to promote the West, found a use for chaparral roots as domestic fuel, paying six dollars a load for them in the early 1870s. Gradually, according to one eyewitness report, "there came a demand for the roots as fireplace fuel that paid and often more than paid for the clearing," which was usually done by Chinese contractors. Only after it had been cleared did the chaparral's value as grape land become apparent. The same witness estimated that the major clearings were in the 1880s and 1890s, when the first large-scale plantings took place.[15] The roots of chaparral are extremely hard and make good charcoal.

Swampland took longer to reclaim than chaparral but promised equally rich rewards. In the Gilroy area a swamp had resulted from the Llagas River. Slowly that land was drained by ditches, making it suitable for the alfalfa and rye grass that brought in the dairies. Swampland continued to be a problem in north county until the 1920s, when a mosquito abatement district was formed to drain the freshwater marshes in the Palo Alto and Mountain View areas. Small berry and vegetable farms were set up here as well as dairy, rabbit, and chicken operations. The soil was, in some areas, too tough for tree

94

culture; blue adobe required a blast of dynamite in order to prepare a hole big enough for the roots. Nonetheless the soil was rich and yielded good berry and vegetable crops.

The removal of so much cover left ground animals without food supplies. Soon rabbits, squirrels, gophers, and mice proved to be a nuisance to farmers. The walnut orchards are plagued by squirrels to this day, while gophers continue to survive in healthy numbers. One elderly man told me that he, like other children of the time, was employed to catch gophers at ten cents a tail. Ingenious devices were used in orchards to frighten birds, who enjoy fresh fruit as much as people do.

The Poor Man's Paradise

The presence of the horticulturists and their nurseries was only one reason Santa Clara County would emerge as a fruit-growing region characterized by small farmers. Soil, weather, and water were preconditions for success. Free solar power, which bypassed expensive evaporators (also called dehydrators), helped the quality of dried prunes to surpass the French product. An international market developed for "Santa Clara Valley Dried Prunes." The market for fresh California produce was enhanced by the development of refrigerated rail cars that used blocks of ice to keep produce cold; the ice, replaced every three hundred miles, left a telltale water drip on the railroad ties.[16] Cold-storage houses were built for keeping the produce until shipment. Fresh cherries, grapes, plums, and pears shipped best to the eastern markets. By the turn of the century, Santa Clara County produce was being sold in Kansas City, Omaha, Chicago, St. Paul, Minneapolis, Boston, Denver, and New York. San Francisco and Los Angeles offered local markets, as did the canneries (see Chapter 9).

The widened markets increased the economic advantages of fruit growing. The word was broadcast by boosters, the real estate developers and capitalists. The San Jose Board of Trade, forerunner to the Chamber of Commerce, took shape in 1886

(replacing an earlier board of 1874) with the purpose of bringing more people to the county. The population of Santa Clara County in 1885 was only 35,000, but it was considered one of the most populous counties in the state. *Santa Clara Valley, Its Resources, Advantages and Prospects, HOMES FOR A MILLION* boasted the title of one brochure, in 1888. This was an era of expansion when the West, eager to make the American dream a reality, approved of the Pacific Rural Press's comment that "California is so good a state, that the 'truth, the whole truth, and nothing but the truth,' should be set forth for the benefit and information of all people."[17]

What the truth was came into question as the rosy picture of how easily one could succeed at farming was challenged. "Men who come to California and Oregon" wrote John S. Hittell in 1882, "often complain that they have been deceived; that they have been led to believe that they could get rich with little exertion, and that life would be much easier for them than it had been in the Eastern states whereas they find that they are, in fact, subjected to keener competition than they ever witnessed before, and that instead of getting rich with little work, they remain poor even with hard work."[18] To counter such complaints, an article on Santa Clara County stressed how one man, in one year, could earn enough to buy his own farm. "The farm-laborer can not always command, as was the case last harvest, from $2 to $4 per day and board; but the statement can not be too often reiterated, that, even in so thickly settled a county as Santa Clara, one year's wages will enable him to become a farmer."[19] The unidentified writer goes on to say that the laborer can buy a team of horses with his earnings of one year and sharecrop with owners of large farms, thus hastening the time when he can gather enough money to purchase his own farm.

The booster activities succeeded: by 1900 there were over sixty thousand people in the county. Statistics illustrate that there was truth in Santa Clara County's particular claims, for farm size began to decrease. By the middle of the 1880s more than half the farms in the county were still in tracts of 400 to 640 acres or larger.[20] By 1900, within fifteen years, more than half were in parcels of 50 acres or less. The average size of an improved farm was 50 acres by 1910. By 1920 that same average would drop to 41 acres. Only four counties in the state, two of them urban areas, could boast lower averages for improved acreage: Santa Cruz, Trinity, Los Angeles and San Francisco counties. The trend continued: in 1950 the average was 32 acres.[21]

Prophetically, a 1911 publication had stated that "the great and wonderfully productive Santa Clara Valley is fitly termed the 'Poor Man's Paradise.'"[22] Even Jefferson could not have foreseen the yeoman tradition working out its destiny on this unexpectedly small scale.

Notes

[1] J. P. Munro-Fraser, *History of Santa Clara County* (San Francisco: Alley, Bowen & Co., 1881), 542.

[2] H. S. Foote, ed., *Pen Pictures from the Garden of the World* (Chicago: Lewis Publishing Co., 1888), 171.

[3] U. P. Hedrick, *The Cherries of New York: Report of the New York Agricultural Experiment Station for the Year 1914*, 22nd Annual Report, vol. 2, pt. 2 (New York: J. B. Lyon Co., 1915), 63, 103, 151.

[4] Though apples were planted in kitchen gardens and are still grown commercially, they never became a major fruit crop here. After the 1880s, the peach and pear became second only to the prune. By the 1920s, however, the peach had been displaced by the apricot. Eventually, Santa Clara County would be the state's foremost producer of prunes, apricots, pears, and cherries.

[5] The difference between prunes and plums has been well defined by Edward J. Wickson. "All prunes are plums, but all plums are not prunes. A prune is a plum which can be dried without the removal of the pit without fermenting—the result being a fleshy pulp with a high degree of sweetness. All plums which will not do this are not prunes even though the word may appear in their California common names." *The California Fruits and How To Grow Them*, 9th ed. (San Francisco: Pacific Rural Press, 1921), 272. In 1965 my father and another prune grower, Will Lester, travelled through Villeneuve. They found it to be a small

village in a hilly area not unlike the western foothills of Santa Clara County. The soil is alkaline and the French prune is still grown there. A medieval tower of the Knights Templar still stands as a reminder that the prune was brought to France by the Crusaders from Asia Minor.

[6] Louis Pellier [nephew], *A True Account of the Introduction of La Petite d'Agen into Santa Clara County by Louis Pellier in December 1856* (San Jose: N.p., 1931); "History of the Prune," in *Report of State Board of Horticulture, 1891* (Sacramento: State Printing Office, 1891), 95; Robert Couchman, *The Sunsweet Story* (San Jose: Sunsweet Growers, 1967) 11.

[7] [Capt.] Joseph Aram, "Early Days in Santa Clara," *San Francisco Examiner*, April 20, 1889.

[8] When Prevost's property was subdivided in the 1870s it was called Live Oak Park. His well-stocked, highly diversified nursery was next door to that of Antoine Delmas, a noted French nurseryman responsible for introducing several varieties of new grapes to the county. The name survives in nearby Oak Street, and there are still numerous oaks in the area.

[9] Couchman, "Pellier Introduced the Prune," 18.

[10] "Santa Clara County, "*State Board of Horticulture*, (Sacramento: State Printing Office, 1892), 241.

[11] The use of lye in preparing corn was a practice of many American Indian tribes. William Archdeacon, Chicago author, published a recipe for using lye to remove the skin of peaches in 1876.

[12] Mary J. Gates, *Rancho Pastoria De Las Borregas* (San Jose: Cottle & Murgotten, 1895), 25.

[13] E. W. Hilgard, *Report on the Physical and Agricultural Features of the State of California* (San Francisco: Pacific Rural Press, 1884), 47, 52, 112. For a map showing the various types of soil in the valley, and what was grown on them in 1958, see *Soil Survey*, 44.

[14] E. S. Harrison and Charles Oberdeener, eds., *Santa Clara Valley, Homes for a Million* (San Jose: McNeil Bros., 1887), 119.

[15] William S. Cooper, "Vegetational Development upon Alluvial Fans in the Vicinity of Palo Alto, California," *Ecology*, 7, no. 1 (Jan. 1926), 18.

[16] John F. Stover, *American Railroads*, (Chicago: University of Chicago Press, 1961), 164.

[17] Publisher's preface to Hilgard, *Report on the Physical and Agricultural Feature. . . .*

[18] John S. Hittell, "Land for Settlers," in *The Commerce and Industries of the Pacific Coast of North America*, (San Francisco: A.C. Bancroft & Co., 1882), 84.

[19] "One of Our Farming Counties," *Overland Monthly*, Sept. 1873, 241.

[20] *Report of the State Board of Horticulture* (Sacramento: State Printing Office, 1892), 239.

[21] The official definition of "farm" has been changed nine times since 1850. Since 1975 it has meant a place from which $1,000 or more of agricultural products were sold during the year in question. By earlier standards a farm had not less than ten acres and $250 in (1959, 1964, and 1969), sales.

[22] *Sunnyvale, the Manufacturing Suburb of San Francisco* (Sunnyvale: Sunnyvale Chamber of Commerce, 1911), 49.

Other Sources for Chapter 4

The standard histories of Santa Clara County include information on horticulture and other kinds of farming, along with biographies of individuals who helped pay for publication. Among them are: J. P. Munro-Fraser, *History of Santa Clara County* (San Francisco: Alley, Bowen, & Co., 1881); H. S. Foote, ed., *Pen Pictures from the Garden of the World* (Chicago: Lewis Publishing Co., 1888). The latter is especially useful because of Foote's special feeling for the county as a center of farming. He also published a magazine on orchards and vineyards called *Santa Clara Valley: Horticultural and Viticultural Newspaper* (San Jose, 1884–86). In 1896 the *San Jose Mercury News* published *Sunshine, Fruit and Flowers*, a promotional book that portrays individual farms in detail. Eugene T. Sawyer, *History of Santa Clara County* (Los Angeles: Historic Record Company, 1922) also has much information on local farming history as well as biographical sketches. A good association history is E. J. Wickson, *California Nurserymen and the Plant Industry, 1850-1910* (Los Angeles: California Association of Nurserymen, 1921).

I made extensive use of promotional materials that were widely distributed throughout the United States to attract newcomers to Santa Clara County. They were often illustrated and included names of farmers and the location of their farms and vineyards. Typical are: Board of Trade of San Jose, *Santa Clara County*, vol. I, no. 1 (San Francisco: W. B. Bancroft & Co., 1887); E. S. Harrison, *Central California, Santa Clara Valley: Homes for a Million* (San Jose: McNeil Bros., 1888); California Development Board, *Santa Clara County, California*, ([San Jose], 1915); and various publications of the Sunnyvale and San Jose chambers of commerce.

Valuable historical information on fruit trees and their culture is to be found in E. J. Wickson, *The California Fruits and How to Grow Them* (San Francisco: Pacific Rural Press, 1912). This book was revised and renamed; the ninth edition (1921) is called *California Fruits*. Early information is in John S. Hittell, *Resources of California* (San Francisco: A. Roman & Co., 1863). The marshlands and their role in early agriculture are discussed in Arthur Coffman, *An Illustrated History of Palo Alto* (Palo Alto: Lewis Osborne, 1969). The most complete history of local wines and vineyards is Charles L. Sullivan, *Like Modern Edens* (Cupertino: California History Center, 1982); see also Ruth Teiser and Catherine Harroun, *Winemaking in California* (New York: McGraw-Hill, 1983).

A useful map of the county in 1889 shows the division of lands into small parcels and lists owners: *Official Map of the County of Santa Clara, Compiled from U.S. Surveys, County Records and Private Surveys and by the Tax Lists of 1889 by order of Board of Supervisors*, by Hermann Brothers, [San Jose], 1890 (original in Map Collection, Stanford University Archives). Statistics on agriculture in Santa Clara County are found in the U.S. *Census of Agriculture*. Material on early agriculture in Saratoga is from Florence R. Cunningham, Saratoga's *First Hundred Years*, ed. Frances L. Fox (Fresno: Valley Publishers, 1976).

CHAPTER 5
TOWN AND COMMUNITY

GOING TO BUY SCHOOL CLOTHES was an excursion that we looked forward to for days. My mother drove the three of us in the 1938 Plymouth to San Jose, to walk South First Street where shops abounded. In an earlier age the farm family might make an annual trip with horse and buggy for supplies. We knew where to find exactly what we were looking for, and we made the rounds. When my sister Jeanette and I were old enough, we traveled into San Jose by bus and shopped on our own, using money we had earned working in the summer's fruit harvest. Each shop had its own character and we knew them like old friends: Woolworth's, Hart's Department Store, Blum's, Roos Brothers, Hale's, Appleton's, Prussia's; shoe stores and the old-time Stern's leather shop, restaurants, and fine movie houses like the Victory, the Fox, the Padre, and the nearby Hester— everything a "big city" could supply.

This downtown was a far cry from the way San Jose, the first city of California, began. The city was also its first capital, in 1849, but this designation did not last long, for the legislators found no decent housing nor any decent meeting place. What they did find was enough liquor to counter the wet and mud. The new state government's brief tenure in San Jose earned it the title of the "Legislature of a Thousand Drinks." Even in the 1860s, San Jose's reputation as a town awash in liquor was supported by its ratio of saloons (forty-four) to churches (six).

Santa Clara County as the Garden Spot of the World

San Jose's frontier character changed as families moved in and established schools, churches, and a stake in the future. By the turn of the century it had developed into an elegant and prosperous place, and thought of itself as second only to San Francisco on the West Coast. It was the focal point of one of the finest agricultural districts anywhere in the world, a fact that was put forth in countless brochures on the virtues of coming to settle in the Santa Clara Valley.

The rhetoric of the yeoman tradition was employed to describe the county, even though the word "yeoman" was seldom used. Mary Bowden Carroll, a society writer for a San Jose newspaper, published a book in 1903 that carried the endorsement of the Chamber of Commerce. The book, *Ten Years in Paradise*, drew on every aspect of the notion that Santa Clara County embodied all the possible good that men had been seeking since the beginning of time. The virtues to be found in this paradise included a climate where people did not need to fight frigid cold or searing heat. The mild weather made possible a long growing season and a wide variety of abundant crops. Large harvests could be had with a minimum of work because of the exceptional fertility of the soil. Adam need not sweat too profusely here.

The natural goodness of the place added to health. Examples abounded of individuals who arrived ill, only to thrive working outdoors as farmers. Physical rejuvenation inspired mental happiness. Finally, the culture of the county, the education, and the transportation, were so modern that nothing was lacking but people to fill this paradise and make it a living Eden. Santa Clara County's egalitarian nature was stressed: "The king to which the people of this valley bow is the monarch of mind and manner, for great wealth does not denote the possession of superior qualities and does not carry with it the right of greater privileges."[1]

A few years before, an article by the Honorable David Belden (1832–1888), a respected judge of the Twelfth District, had emphasized the county's egalitarian nature; social events and other types of recreation enjoyed by few in eastern communities were, he claimed, "the practice of the many" in San Jose.[2]

You did not have to be a wealthy person to join in this paradise. Carroll comments:

There are many improved ranches of ten acres which are paying a big interest on the money invested, because the labor is so light that it can be done at all times, except during the harvest season, by one man with a team. Of course, it would be foolish to think that the majority of the people here are fast becoming rich by the culture of fruit and the vine. Still it is a self-evident fact that nearly all who do cultivate the soil are far removed from poverty. Many of the farmers here will testify that one hundred and sixty acres of farming land in many sections of the East could, with profit, be exchanged for ten acres of this fertile soil.[3]

Within the county we have place names that indicate the currency of the garden idea. Paradise Valley is in Morgan Hill. There is a hill in the Saratoga foothills called Mount Eden and a location along the railroad near Coyote called Edenvale. The name Sunnyvale echoes the theme, while the Valley of Heart's Delight is a nickname that conjures visions of an Edenic garden of goodness *and* pleasure, for here the contradictions that bothered our first parents have been resolved. Even if some of these names were chosen by promoters, name and reality in most cases were as close as one could hope. Santa Clara County was all that the slogans indicated.

Valley Towns

Each of the fifteen towns in Santa Clara County has its own story of how settlers came to that particular spot and why. The common thread that runs through these histories is the establishment of a business or function that served the agricultural interests of the area. Both Los Gatos (1850) and Saratoga (1851) began where mills were built to grind grain into flour for local use. An embarcadero or landing half a mile up the Guadalupe Slough served the Spanish and Mexicans for shipping their major products: hides, tallow, and later quicksilver from the New Almadén mines. In 1851 a more direct route to the bay was discovered and named Steamboat Slough after the new means of locomotion. The new town of Alviso grew up there, about half a mile from the abandoned embarcadero.

Well into the twentieth century, it functioned as the county's primary port for agricultural products; it was the advent of the truck that ended Alviso's usefulness in this role. Today, it is a marginal residential area.

Many towns developed because they were in a spot on the road to or from San Francisco. The name of Mayfield can be traced to a local farm so called in 1853. In 1855 a post office was established and the San Francisco—San Jose stage stopped there with a pouch of mail for the entire county from which the letters marked "Mayfield" were extracted. Mountain View had a similar beginning, in the early 1850s. Milpitas began in 1856 when Frederick Creighton built a store on the main road between San Jose and Oakland; a post office and hotel followed in the same year. But each of these communities served as an agricultural center. Even Campbell, founded with a quite different purpose in mind, followed the general trend: in 1885 Benjamin Campbell subdivided land to create a town free of alcoholic beverages (each deed included a clause prohibiting the sale of liquor), but it was fruit growing and processing that made the town prosperous. Another dry town was Palo Alto, first called University Park. It was the creation of Leland Stanford, who established it in 1887 as a place where Stanford students could avoid the twenty-five saloons of Mayfield, some two miles to the south.

The breakup of the vast estates belonging to the Murphy family, estimated to be over seventy thousand acres in 1860, accounts for three towns in Santa Clara County alone. Martin Murphy, Sr., had arrived with his wife and nine children in 1844 and settled on a rancho in southern Santa Clara County. His family spread out around him and throughout California. They lived like county gentry, running their estates on a sharecropping basis for the most part; their land was used for grain and cattle. My father remembered that the Sunnyvale branch of the family had its own railroad car to travel between home and San Francisco. The new taxes on property added to the Murphys' need for cash, but the main reason for the

Carl Johan Olson and Hannah Louise Merck: San Francisco, 1898.
Olson Family Collection

breakup of their estates was lack of motivation. The second and third generations were not farmers, and while they could have planted their own choice lands into orchards, they sold them instead to others who did. Morgan Hill (1892) and San Martin (1895) were carved out of subdivisions of Murphy family lands. Sunnyvale, at the other end of the valley, was also brought into being from Murphy lands by a developer, in 1898. By 1900 only San Jose, Santa Clara, Gilroy, Los Gatos, and Palo Alto were incorporated. Los Altos was the handiwork of a Southern Pacific railroad executive and others who put land on the market after 1907, when the Peninsular Railroad completed its interurban electric train service connecting Palo Alto and Mayfield with Cupertino, San Jose, and Los Gatos. Even before then, Los Altos and the hills behind were emerging as a first-rate area for growing apricots. The Crossroads, or West Side, changed its name to Cupertino in 1900 but retained its crossroads character until 1955, when it incorporated and succumbed to urban sprawl.

The small towns fed San Jose and brought it business and prosperity. San Jose returned the favor, providing them with banking and manufacturing services, as well as supplies and technology. This pattern, the outlying towns and cities like spokes connected to a central hub, was typical of farm communities across the United States. When urbanization came to the Santa Clara Valley after World War II, it shattered the symmetry of the long-established connections. The downtown shopping area of San Jose sank into a slump after the suburban shopping centers were established during the late 1950s.

The cities began at different times but they began in the same way. Mountain View, one of the oldest in the county after San Jose and Santa Clara, began in 1850 as a stage stop between San Jose and San Francisco; it was not incorporated until 1902. Its center, like Gilroy's, was moved when the railroad passed at a different location. Clustered around the stop was a general store, a post office, a blacksmith's, a livery stable, and a hotel. Later there was a butcher shop, a pharmacy, and a doctor's, all interacting to form a unit, and all doing business with the farmers in the surrounding countryside.

One Immigrant Family: The Olsons

The town of Sunnyvale was originally just a train stop called Murphy's Station. When my grandparents Carl and Hannah Olson responded to an advertisement, there was a post office and a school, both built in 1898. The advertisement, probably in a San Francisco newspaper in 1900, was placed by Walter Everett Crossman, a real estate developer from San Jose who had come to the county in 1887 from Wisconsin, just at the time land sales began to boom. The headquarters of his real estate business was in San Francisco. He became owner of two hundred acres of the Murphy Rancho in 1898 by paying $38,000 to its owner Patrick Murphy. According to a biographer, "when the owner [Martin Murphy Jr.] of that ranch died the family rapidly dissipated the fortune he had left, and Mr. Crossman was finally called to take charge of the estate."[4]

W. E. Crossman looked at the wooded oak grasslands of the Murphys' rancho and saw a town—not just an ordinary town, but a factory town. By 1908 his publicity reached the pages of *Sunset*, a magazine published by the Southern Pacific Railroad. "What do you think," he asked, "of a California town where machine shops and canneries and paint and roofing factories and iron works are set out among shading live oaks, and the cottages of employes [sic] are covered with roses or brushed by bearing fruit trees? That's Sunnyvale, down the peninsula from San Francisco just about where the fair Santa Clara valley opens out its loveliness like a big geographical fan."[5] The notice that attracted my grandparents promised a free train trip, a free barbecue, and generous terms of sale. Crossman also offered free land for factories if companies would move to Sunnyvale. In this way the Joshua Hendy Iron Works, a world-famous manufacturer of mining equipment, was induced to locate in Sunnyvale after the 1906 earthquake. When families

103

came to find work in the factories or to farm, Crossman sold them lots at $150 to $200 an acre.

My father remembered W. E. Crossman. "He wore spats, a diamond ring on his finger, a Stetson hat and a vest with a gold watch fob, and he smoked a cigar." Though he seemed the typical real estate promoter, he had the reputation of being an honest broker and even an idealist. But his dream was never quite realized, at least in his lifetime. The earthquake of 1906 shook up the real estate market, leaving the area's reputation badly damaged. Crossman transferred his interests to C. L. Stowell and C. C. Spalding, two Sunnyvale real estate brokers, in 1915. He then acquired income property in Los Angeles and retired in 1916.[6]

Hannah Louise and Carl Johan Olson were typical of the immigrant families who first settled in the new town of Sunnyvale. Shortly after the birth of their children, they began their search for the ideal place to settle a family. My grandfather had been in the United States since 1888 but still had not settled down. He worked on a railroad in the Midwest. He carried nitroglycerine in the blasting of the Eureka harbor and he worked for the Stauffer Chemical Company when it was located in North Beach in San Francisco. Because this job caused him respiratory problems, his doctor said he should live in the country. He and Hannah had met at a Swedish church in San Francisco and married in 1898. They relied on their faith to guide them in finding the right place to live. Their prayers were coupled with weekend trips that Grandfather took around the bay. At the time Murphy's Station was called Encinal, Spanish for "live oak" (its name was changed in 1901 because another town claimed the same title). Crossman, the promoter, dubbed it the City of Destiny, and is credited with the new name, Sunnyvale.

They didn't need to look twice. Grandmother, a woman six feet tall, large-boned, had worked as a cook for Senator William Andrews Clark from Montana (his house on The Alameda required a staff of four to run). She and Carl had saved their money and bought their five acres outright at $150

an acre. They had enough money left over to build their house. Byrnal Brynelson, a Danish carpenter, was hired to do the job at $2 a day. The three-room house cost them $300; a well dug to eighty feet cost them $150, and the family moved in with $25 left of their savings. One of the first tasks confronting my grandfather was to cut down one of the large oaks for firewood. All cooking was done on a wood-burning stove, which also provided heat for the house during the winter months.

They chose property on McKinley between Taaffe and Murphy streets because it was directly across from the Encina School, a large two-storied structure that served Sunnyvale's growing population of immigrants and footloose Americans. All grades were taught together in the same room. The town's population included Irish, English, Swedes, and Portuguese. There was a French family or two, as well as Canadian, Yugoslavian, and German settlers. Given the number of nationalities, it is surprising that there were no more than fifteen or twenty families in Sunnyvale when my family first settled there at the turn of the century. By 1910 there would be a population of two thousand.

Although my grandparents had been raised in rural communities in Sweden, they were not farmers by trade. When they planted their first cherry orchard they were doing so with the unbounded optimism that attended the American adventure. To that optimism, however, they added a large dose of careful planning; as little as possible was left to chance. A diligence and steadfastness, a dedication to the welfare of their family characterized not just their dream but most of the community's. Hard work attended every day.

Like so many other newcomers without experience in farming, my grandparents watched and listened, asked questions and forged ahead. Before Crossman's promotion of Sunnyvale, most fruit trees were located in the kitchen gardens of grain farmers. Murphy's orchard is said to have been the first one after 1850 in this area, but many, such as Emerson's, followed his. The Thompson and West *Historical Atlas* of 1876 indicates

Projection of Sunnyvale commissioned by real estate developer
W. E. Crossman in 1906. El Camino Real curves slightly
(center left), while Southern Pacific Railroad bisects the map.
The distribution of oak trees is probably fairly accurate.
Courtesy California History Center

W. E. Crossman (right), c. 1900; railroad track and Murphy's
woods beyond. Crossman's dream was to make Sunnyvale into
a manufacturing city set among fruit trees. *Photo from Camera
Mart, Sunnyvale*

Crossman (in bowler, far left) uses his bicycle to visit a customer in process of building a house on one of his lots, c. 1900. *Photo from Camera Mart, Sunnyvale*

Encina Grammar School, Sunnyvale, 1899: view northward
from McKinley Street. In 1901 my grandparents bought five
acres of open field on the south side of McKinley, just across
from this school, which my father and aunt attended. *Photo from
Camera Mart, Sunnyvale*

R. Trevey & Co.'s store at Alviso, a typical example of turn-of-
the-century one-stop shopping. Touring car (right) dates photo
as before 1910. *Courtesy San Jose Historical Museum*

Campbell Avenue, Campbell, c. 1900. Central Santa Clara
Fruit Company (left) was only one of town's several processing
companies, many of them co-ops. *Courtesy Campbell Historical
Museum*

An electric car of the Peninsular Interurban Railroad about to travel the Mayfield cutoff, completed 1908, from Mayfield (now California Avenue, in Palo Alto) to Saratoga, c. 1910. Land along route was opened to development and young people could commute, via connecting line, to college in Santa Clara or San Jose. *Courtesy Cal Street*

Schoolchildren and their mentors dressed to walk in the parade
at the Saratoga Blossom Festival, an annual event from 1900 to
1941. *Courtesy Saratoga Historical Foundation*

Parent-Teacher Association dispenses refreshments at Saratoga Blossom Festival, 1926. Many such organizations contributed to this general outpouring of community spirit. *Courtesy Garrod Family Collection*

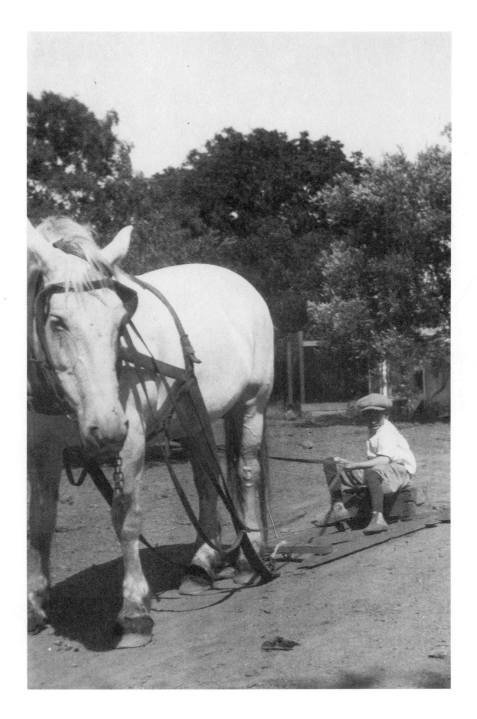

Robert T. Butcher with barn-door sled hitched to his horse "Dolly" at the Butcher family farm in Santa Clara, 1923. Horses in 1920s were still used for farm work but were fast becoming relics—or pets. *Courtesy Robert T. Butcher*

Patrick Lyons, Irish immigrant, pours a toast with family members in field on his property at El Camino Real and Saratoga-Sunnyvale Road that became Olson farm. *Courtesy Frank Lyons*

Will Weston, Jr., sits on the slab which smooths the pear orchard, 1936. "Pears have been good to us," Will senior wrote in 1966, "and the approach of urbanization, to our regret, threatens us." By 1971 most of the orchards were sold. *Photo by Burton Crandall, Courtesy Nancy P. Weston*

June spraying of pear trees at Will Weston's ranch, 1936. *Photo by Burton Crandall, Courtesy Nancy P. Weston*

Dick Garrod poses with big pear at Garrod family farm,
Saratoga foothills, 1923. *Courtesy Garrod Family Collection*

Birthday party for Cuyler North (second from top of fruit
ladder) and his sister Frances (bottom) at Northurst, the family
farm in Cupertino, in 1898. *Courtesy Frances North Martin*

Anton Andrade, Portuguese foreman of Will
Weston ranch in Santa Clara lowlands, picking
pears, 1936. *Photo by Burton Crandall, Courtesy
Nancy P. Weston*

Women "facing" 25-pound boxes of prunes by hand at Los Gatos Cured Fruit Company, c. 1910. The rate was 10 cents per box, but bread was 5 cents a loaf. *Courtesy Sun-Diamond Growers*

the kitchen orchards that surrounded isolated farm houses. The first commercial orchards may have been planted by W. S. Hollenbeck, followed by G. H. Briggs, in the same area south of El Camino Real in the 1880s, during the orchard rush. Both had been grain farmers from the 1850s. By 1893, Charles O. Bocks had planted fifty-five acres of cherries on Hollenbeck Avenue. People thought he was crazy. The largest cherry orchard in the world at that time, it earned him the title of Cherry King, and proved how well suited the soil was to fruit production in this area.[7]

Charles and Cora Bocks, who inherited half this land from C. O. Bocks, and Charles's brother Lester, who inherited the other half, were our neighbors when I was growing up. Bobbie Bocks, Lester's daughter, was my closest friend. We used to ride our bicycles on the dirt roads through the fruit orchards, traveling for a couple of miles at a time without emerging from them. In 1917 when Charles Bocks settled on the land, the cherry trees were dead, nothing but stumps, perhaps from the same type of disease that is destroying our cherry orchard. One possible explanation is that this orchard, according to Charles Bocks, was irrigated by water from the D. M. Delmas Dam, which had been built across Stevens Creek in the late 1880s to water Delmas's five hundred acres of grapes. Delmas, a famous trial lawyer and son of French nurseryman Antoine Delmas, shared the water without knowing that it carried along with it a deadly disease. According to Otis Forge, all the orchards watered from that dam died of oak root fungus. Charles Bocks replaced most of the trees with prunes, which bore too heavily, and apricots and pears. His brother also planted other fruit, but it was eventually discovered that pears grew there the best. As Cora Bocks said, "We were poor for years, not that we are so wealthy now, but there just was no cash."

My grandfather did not worry about such difficulties. Basing himself on the proven experience of those who had come before, he dug the holes for the cherry orchard. The new trees were put in place by 1902, and with them the family's hope for the future. Trees from the California Nursery in Niles were about fifteen cents each. Since it takes seven years for a cherry orchard to come into bearing, my grandfather took other jobs at the new factories. Grandfather, six feet two inches tall, angular with a dry wit, worked for a time at the Goldie Machine Works, and then at the Joshua Hendy Iron Works, which was the largest manufacturing company in the county (it became today's Westinghouse plant). He took any job offered, including odd jobs for the Murphy family, he frequently read his Swedish Bible, he enjoyed singing hymns—and of course, he was called "Ole."

The Summer of Baling Hay. In order to earn needed cash, the Olson family, like many others, hired on to work with a hay-baling crew, probably in the summer of 1905. Up until the time of the horseless carriage, Santa Clara County supplied San Francisco with the hay to feed its horses. The area north of Sunnyvale that reached to Mayfield (today California Avenue, south of Palo Alto) was widely planted in hay as well as grains and plants for seeds. Since equipment to bale the hay was expensive, crews, led usually by the equipment owner, went from farm to farm to do the job. The crew members earned up to $3.20 each a day.

Ethnic identity was still an important factor in these early communities. My Swedish grandparents worked for a Swede, John Pierson; he had settled in Mountain View along with his brother, who ran a grocery store.[8] Pierson had a Monarch Junior haypress that was made in Hayward. His team of twelve horses were used two at a time, circling four times to press one bale of hay. After pressing eight bales, the two horses were replaced by fresh ones. All the while the entire team fed on the farmer's hay. There were Portuguese crews as well, and spirited encounters resulted on weekends when these crews came together at a watering hole like The Outside Inn in Mountain

View. Their competitive spirit erupted in slurs and name-calling, one crew accusing the other of adding dirt to the weight of each bale. After a few drinks there were fist fights. My nondrinking grandparents were not involved.

My grandmother was cook, while my grandfather worked with the men. Dad, aged six at the time, was big enough for small errands like running to get the day's supply of milk. Being cook meant working from dawn to dusk. First was breakfast for as many as six men, my grandmother's two children, and herself. By the time that was finished, it was time to start lunch and prepare a morning snack of coffee and rolls. There was an afternoon break as well, and then the big meal at dinner time. Sleeping quarters were under the sky; the men snuggled under blankets while my grandmother and the children slept in the cookhouse. The job lasted for six to eight weeks after school was out in June. When the season was finished, my grandmother vowed never to do that work again.

Even before the cherry trees came into bearing, pressure was put on the family to sell four of their five acres. The price kept going up and finally Grandfather yielded. It meant moving the house to the corner of McKinley and Taaffe. It was on rollers when the great earthquake hit on April 18, 1906. Grandfather ran into the basement hoping to hold the house in place! My father was thrown to the floor and my aunt hid under the bedcovers fearing for her life. By some miracle the only local damage was to the chimneys in town. But then, there wasn't much in town to damage.

The Olson Dairy. With the four acres sold my grandparents had the money for other farmland. In 1906 they purchased a five-acre piece on the Old San Francisco Highway from another longtime Sunnyvale family, the MacDonalds. Hay was raised there to feed the horses and Ruth, a Jersey cow. My grandparents had decided on a dairy to help their cash flow. Ruth gave a pure rich milk, but she allowed no one else to draw it from her except my grandmother who, on the rare occasions

when she was sick, had to get out of sickbed to do the job. The children helped deliver the milk, hopping off the wooden wagon with their pitchers in hand. The lady of the house would come with her pint or quart measure and the milk was transferred. The cost was a dollar a month for a pint a day and two dollars for a quart, delivered to the door. My grandmother kept the accounts and carefully watched what was spent.

This cash helped them to buy the necessities and a few amenities—hair mattresses to replace the mattresses of cornhusk, curtains for the windows, and cloth for new clothes. Within ten years the Olsons were doing well enough to go to San Jose and buy their own "surrey with the fringe on top" from Hatman & Normandin, the carriage makers. My Aunt Elsie recalled that on Sundays the surrey was taken out of its shed and hooked up to the horses; soon the family was off to visit friends. She also remembered that it was kept immaculately clean—a symbol of the family's growing security, emotional no less than material. August nights, when the moon shone brightly, my grandmother would ask her husband to get out the surrey and take her for a ride. The Olsons were taking hold in the New World.

From Frontier to Community

While drinking had been one of the favorite pastimes of miners and squatters, it was frowned upon by the wives and mothers who were making their influence felt in the settling of new communities. Alfred Doten had noted temperance preachers in Santa Clara County in the early 1860s and himself attended several meetings where temperance sympathizers and churchgoing people gathered to promote abstinence. By the 1880s the temperance battle was a national one. In Santa Clara County it was fought on a small scale by such protagonists as Leland Stanford, with his efforts (after 1887) to dry up Mayfield. The only way he could impose a "no saloon" rule was to buy the entire town piece by piece (in 1925 it was finally annexed to Palo Alto and disappeared as a legal entity). In a promotional booklet of 1911 the claim was made that "Palo Alto has no saloons, no vicious resorts, no bums." One of the longest battles over the status of alcohol was fought in Los Gatos, where the issue was put before voters several times before alcohol was prohibited in 1906.

When Prohibition did pass in 1919, there were several reasons why it was difficult to enforce in Santa Clara County. The communities were isolated; two hundred gallons of wine were allowed for family use anyway; and what went on in the hilly regions was difficult to control. The ethnic makeup of the county also contributed to its title as "the wettest dry county in the United States." Local French, Italians, and Yugoslavs had made their own wine for years; some even distilled spirits. A local Yugoslav farmer brewed a clear drink from prunes so strong it was called "white lightning" or "jackass." It was really slivovitz, a time-honored liquor made in Yugoslavia where prunes also thrive along the Dalmatian coast. The farmer gave it to his friends at Christmas time.[9]

Social Structure and Social Events. The few families of the town and the scattered farming families of the outlying districts made for a close community in which everyone knew everyone else. Few, if any, remained anonymous. All problems, successes, failures, and quirks were noted and stored in the memory of the community. Until the end of her life, my aunt (1901-1983) could do fine imitations of the various people who had stopped in to visit at their little house opposite the school, in the early part of the century. Each immigrant group went through the baptism of ridicule. My aunt never forgot being jeered at because her parents could not speak perfect English.

Social life in the valley centered on church activities, which in turn were organized along both religious and ethnic lines. Catholics and Protestants, while friendly as neighbors, maintained their distance in matters of worship. Social clubs often reflected religious and ethnic differences, and exclusion was not unusual. White Anglo-Saxons were at the top of the social hierarchy, but other groups could and did counter by organizing their clubs for the benefit of their members. There were social organizations for Italian Americans in San Jose. The Sociedad Cervantes Española was formed in 1929 to aid the Spanish and Mexican residents of Sunnyvale and Mountain View. The Chinese in San Jose had their tongs and joss houses. There were Buddhist and Shinto churches. Paul Mariani, Sr., denied membership in the Masons because he was Catholic, founded the Napredak Club for Yugoslavs in the late 1930s. Other organizations like the Odd Fellows, the Grange, the Lions, and the Elks created community activities that did much to set the pattern of town life.

Entertaining in the home was the major social event. Having friends for lunch or dinner on weekends was for some families a weekly event. Because the weather was so often agreeable, weekend outings were also the rule. Families traveled in their buggies, or by interurban rail—later, by car—to one of several outstanding country retreats. Alum Rock Park, established in 1872, was a favorite place to take a picnic lunch and stay for the day. Pacific Congress Springs, a resort since the 1860s in the Saratoga foothills, was the valley's answer to Saratoga Springs in New York State. It was a fashionable place for wealthy San Franciscans until it burned down in 1903. Santa Cruz and Capitola were places for weekend trips or family holidays. Camping out in the backwoods of Mount Hamilton was for the hardy; the steep and twisty road was said to have 365 turns. A hotel was established on the western side of Mount Hamilton at Smith's Creek. Hunters went into the hills for deer and other game.

Year after year the county fair featured agricultural products from across the valley. Women took the competitions seriously and spent both time and effort to can the best preserves and make the finest quilts. The fair, first organized in the 1850s, was an annual event to which the whole family came. Fruit farmers competed with one another for top ribbons and awards, while stock and poultry, grain and cheese—everything the valley produced—was on display.

The Blossom Festival. One of the most celebrated events in this annual routine was the Saratoga Blossom Festival. Begun in 1899, it was held off and on until the beginning of World War II—a true springtime celebration. It was attended by people from around the world, for nowhere else could the human eye see 125 square miles of orchard bursting into bloom at the same time. The festival featured a great variety of attractions: sports, hymns and prayers, songs and parades representing the valley's past, plays and recitations. Special trains were scheduled to bring visitors from around the bay. Many families arrived in their buggies to see the sight of Santa Clara Valley in full blossom. It was the collective expression of a people whose goals and purposes were integrated with the internal rhythms of nature.

It is easy to understand why Senator James D. Phelan, a successful San Francisco businessman who built the Villa Montalvo in the Saratoga foothills, was reluctant to broadcast the wonders of Santa Clara County. For he understood very well that sharing this special bounty meant destroying it. He remarked about 1918 that he feared the day when the valley would have been discovered, for the incoming flood of humanity would be "devastating." Nevertheless, he continued, "if settlers come to make their permanent homes and to become assimilated in an orderly way in our communities, we shall give them welcome."[10]

And give them welcome Santa Clara Valley did.

Notes

[1] Mary Bowden Carroll, *Ten Years in Paradise* (San Jose: Popp & Hogan, 1903), 152.

[2] [Hon.] David Belden, "The Garden of the World: As It Is Now," in *Pen Pictures from the Garden of the World*, ed. H. S. Foote (Chicago: Lewis Publishing Co., 1888), 26.

[3] Carroll, *Ten Years in Paradise*, 132.

[4] B. D. Hunt, *California and Californians* (San Francisco: Lewis Publishers, 1935), 101.

[5] Sunnyvale Land Co., *What Do You Say to This?* (Sunnyvale, n.d.). Reprinted as a brochure from *Sunset*, Feb. 8, 1908.

[6] "W. E. Crossman Sells Sunnyvale Interests," *Sunnyvale Standard*, Sept. 3, 1915, 1.

[7] Taped interview with Charles and Cora Bocks, Saratoga, Calif., May 1980.

[8] My father heard John Pierson tell the following story about his trip to the United States from Sweden as a sailor on a Swedish bark. The crew rose up against an oppressive captain and threw him overboard. They then agreed to tell the same story when they reached port, namely, that the captain was swept overboard by heavy seas.

[9] This same Yugoslav, who shall remain nameless, sold his land for a shopping center. In the heavy rains of 1981 and 1982, two separate cave-ins took place on that land. Revealed beneath the tarmac of the parking lot were two identical wood-lined compartments, dry and sound, which extended down over fifteen feet. Those who remembered that this had been a neighborhood of bootleggers during Prohibition were not inclined to take the compartments for septic tanks or wells.

[10] *Santa Clara County, California: The Valley of Heart's Delight* (San Jose: V. S. Hillis [early 1920s?]), 3. This pamphlet was found in the Higgins Collection, Shields Library, University of California at Davis. It is a revision of an earlier version published just before the Panama-Pacific International Exposition of 1915.

Other Sources for Chapter 5

The material on my family was based on taped interviews with my aunt Elsie Olson Rothermel Kay (1901—1983) and my father, Ruel Charles Olson (1899—1980), and on family papers.

Ralph Rambo, born in 1894, stands out as one of the finest authors to capture the quality of life in Santa Clara County during the heyday of orchards and before. His drawings and stories are to be found in several booklets published by Rosicrucian Press in San Jose between 1959 and 1970. They include: *Looking Backward, 1900* (1959); *Almost Forgotten* (1964); *Remember When* (1965); *Me and Cy* (1966); and *Adventure Valley* (1970).

In addition to the standard bibliographical material on Santa Clara County, listed in Chapter 4, I have relied on several local histories. The California History Center at De Anza College, Cupertino, has published booklets on several communities, including Seonaid L. Khorsand and Jane Lawes, eds., *Sunnyvale, City of Destiny* (1974); Seonaid L. McArthur and David Fuller, eds., *Cupertino Chronicle* (1975); and Ann Connor, Alice Marshall, and Seonaid L. McArthur, eds., *Los Altos Reminiscences*, 1976. See also Kay Peterson, ed., *Sunnyvale Collage* (Sunnyvale School District, 1981), a useful compilation by a retired teacher.

Interviews with old-timers were put together by Students of the Community Experimental Based Alternative School at Fremont High School and distributed by them in 1978 as *Prune Pits: The Collective Stories of Early Sunnyvale-Cupertino Residents* (in collection of California History Center).

W. E. Crossman's real estate company, the Sunnyvale Land Company, published several publicity pieces. One of the first is *Our Lands: A District Comprising the Richest Land in the Santa Clara Valley, Where Fruits and Vegetables Find a Ready Market at Home* (Sunnyvale: Black Cat Press, 1907). This article was enlarged and reprinted in *Sunset Magazine* in February, 1908, and subsequently became the brochure cited in the text. A more complete promotional brochure was published about 1911; called *Sunnyvale: The Manufacturing Suburb of San Francisco*, it listed most of the industries, with photographs, and described the agriculture of the city.

An excellent study of transportation systems within the county is Charles S. McCaleb, *Tracks, Tires & Wires* (Glendale: Interurban Press, 1981).

Frank Norris was at Casa Delmas, the 500-acre vineyard of D. M. Delmas, and wrote a vivid description of the large-scale wine making there for *The Wave*, Oct. 1895.

CHAPTER 6
ONE FARM AND THE
CYCLES OF WORK

THE CYCLES OF WORK on our farm were typical of the many family operations throughout the valley. There were farms where managers and hired help did all the labor required, but they were in the minority. In order for a family farm to succeed, it was necessary for each member to help in the daily tasks and the annual harvests. It was a way of life in which the smallest child participated. One of my earliest memories is of being with my mother in the apricot orchard that surrounded our home. Perhaps I was five years old, which would place the year about 1943. It was bitterly cold and I was wrapped in a woolen hat, jacket, and scarf against the dampness and ground-level fog. My mother had on her faded three-quarter-length jeans, which we called pedal pushers. She wore the same pair when she had a chance to go fishing. That day, in the dead stillness of winter, her head was wrapped in a bandana, and she was wielding a pitchfork with an intense concentration that characterized everything she did. Petite, only four feet eleven inches, she weighed a mere ninety-eight pounds as a young woman.

What my mother was doing was collecting the "brush"— the clippings from pruned orchard trees—and burning it. Certain fruit trees, including the apricot, peach, and plum, require pruning; last year's growth is cut back to produce a stronger growth the next year. Pruning is both art and science and a skilled group of people was hired every winter to do it at an hourly wage. My mother saved precious cash by burning brush herself. She gathered up the trimmed branches into a pile where they were set alight. The thin twigs and branches burned in a special way. A tunnel would develop, creating the effect of a volcano. The smoke would rise in wisps, filling the air with the pleasing scent of burning wood that would taint our clothes and hair.

My presence there was voluntary. To keep warm, I picked up the twigs that fell from the pitchfork as my mother carried it loaded to the fire. I would add my lot to the fire, warm myself for a few minutes, and then find myself a low-lying tree with welcoming branches to climb in. The apricot tree has a

tough, crusty exterior like the prune tree. Both are fragile. The walnut tree and the cherry tree, in contrast, are smooth-barked and sturdy—perfect for scrambling into and building all manner of suspended houses. (It was a rare farm that didn't have a tree house. The arms of aged oaks found yet another use. If there was no regular tree house, the children found their own favorite tree and, as in my case, built a rough tree house with a few planks and a lot of imagination.) My mother's work did not stop with burning brush. She also ran the fruit stand. But some explanation is required to fill in the gap between my grandparents' and my parents' tenure on the land.

From 1910 to 1918 the dairy business grew, but just barely, with only three cows to milk. In the meantime my grandparents had bought land north of the railroad tracks, in the artesian belt, where they grew tomatoes and other vegetables for the San Francisco market. My father recalled taking the fresh vegetables by horse and buggy to Alviso, where they were put on board a schooner for the early-morning produce market. Levy Zentner handled the sale on a commission basis in San Francisco.

The Cherry Orchard—and Next Door

My grandparents bought a cherry orchard from a Sunnyvale minister, John Thomas McCart. The Reverend McCart had bought six acres from the Lyons family (of whom more later) and planted the trees in 1906. Some of those old trees still survive.[1] His one-and-a-half story house burned down when his daughter took a kerosene lamp upstairs shortly after the room had been doused with gasoline to kill the bedbugs. He sold the property to my grandparents about 1913 and left town. The cherries were coming in fine and my grandparents operated a redwood-shed fruit stand on El Camino Real, selling to the passing traffic. In 1913 El Camino Real was paved to accommodate the new horseless carriages. Dad recalled that he and other children rode their bicycles on the new macadam before the two-lane road was opened officially. A sign was posted warning that the speed limit was 15 miles an hour.

It was during World War I that my grandparents decided that Sunnyvale had become too crowded, and that the new health requirements and the attendant inspectors for dairy production were more than they wanted to deal with. Their answer was to move out of town into the country. Initially, the land south of El Camino Real was cattle and wheat land belonging to the Lyonses, an early Sunnyvale family. Daniel Lyons was a soldier of fortune from County Cork, Ireland, who hired himself out to the Mexican government. In return for service, sometime before the end of Mexican authority in 1846, he was granted 640 acres just south of the Rancho Pastoria de las Borregas, from Hollenbeck Road east along El Camino Real. His deed was not confirmed by the American authorities, but this property was in a corridor of land between Santa Clara and Los Altos that, since it did not fall into a Spanish or Mexican grant, was open to homesteading. The name Homestead Road in Cupertino reflects this fact.

Lyons, a bachelor, hired a lawyer, W. T. Wallace, to defend his claim in the American courts. Wallace was successful in securing an American patent for Lyons and for payment received 250 acres of prime agricultural land. This piece would eventually be the fertile Spaulding-Caulkins ranch. When, after 1913, it was planted in cherries, apricots, and prunes, the oaks were cut down. What could not be sold as firewood was gathered into an acre of oakwood six feet high and burned.

Because Daniel Lyons had no family he sent for his brother Patrick, who came to California from County Cork in the 1860s (he sent for his wife and four children later). Eventually there would be ten Lyons children, seven of whom survived to inherit what was left of the Lyons estate.

Pat Lyons had a varied farm operation on his land, situated on the southwest corner of El Camino Real and the Sunnyvale-Saratoga Road. A watering trough for the cattle stood at the corner.[2] Cattle grazed and grain was raised within picket fences. There was a dairy adjacent to the large rambling redwood farmhouse, which also had an outside cooking area that could easily accommodate the entire threshing crew.

The main problem facing the Lyons family was the same that confronted many of the old landowners: a lack of cash. During the economic slump of the 1890s, Pat Lyons gave parcels of land in lieu of cash to pay his bills. He was, by all accounts, a convivial man who loved his family, enjoyed his friends, and enjoyed living. On his deathbed, he was prayed over but also toasted by the family priest: "This will be the last one you'll have on this side, Patty." By the time he died, in the early 1900s, there were only forty-nine acres of land left to divide among his seven living children. It was one of these parcels of flat, rich soil, laced with gravel and perfect for cherries, that the Reverend McCart had bought and planted.

After my grandparents bought the piece from the Reverend McCart, they went on to buy the seven-acre parcel next door developed by Martin Herstich, a Yugoslavian immigrant from Dalmatia, who had married one of the Lyons daughters. Martin was a good farmer who knew what he was doing; he had been foreman for Pat Lyons. On the seven acres he planted the apricot trees where my mother and I were gathering brush about three decades later. He built the redwood frame house in which we lived. He sank the well outside our door and fitted it with a hand pump. He erected the barns for the horses. He even dug a wine cellar, under a toolshed, and made claret there; it was a musty, earthen hole that fascinated us because of its spider webs, old barrels, and heavy scent of wine and earth. Everything was going very well until his wife died, in 1917. Shortly after, he sold the property to a Scandinavian seafaring man named Victorson, who tried farming for two years before he decided he couldn't make a living at it. It was Victorson who sold those seven acres to my grandparents.

The Family Moves to El Camino Real. So in 1919 the Olson family moved from downtown Sunnyvale to the Lyons property and took up residence in the house that Martin Herstich had built.

Herstich had planted a row of walnut trees enclosing the apricots. The walnuts fronted the highway and extended in a lane back from the road to the house.[3]

By the time I was a child the highway had been widened, and the only walnut tree left was the one I liked to hide in on hot summer days. Before I was born the hand pump had been replaced by a water tank that stood atop a tall platform supported by redwood studs and cross bracings. My uncle John Sayig had planted a baby rose that covered the structure with a profusion of small pink blossoms. When my grandmother moved to the farm she planted china lilies and "naked ladies" (belladonna lilies) along the drive.

My father had made the decision early in life that he wanted to be a farmer and only a farmer. He reasoned with his parents that since he was fourteen and able to work a plow, he should quit school and start farming. He was a good student at Mountain View High School, where he had been a freshman in 1914. My immigrant grandparents believed that education was a necessity and resisted the young boy's suggestion. He countered that it didn't matter how much school he attended, he would never, but never, wear a white collar and sit behind a desk. He would be a farmer. To that kind of resolve my grandparents couldn't say no, so my father took up the life he loved.

The Types of Jobs

My father's day began at 5:00 A.M.; in harvest time, it extended to 9:00 P.M. As a young man my father worked for other farmers, plowing with a team of horses to earn extra cash. Horses were important in the early days of Santa Clara Valley agriculture. Many daily tasks revolved on their requirements: early feeding, late feeding, cleaning the barns, carrying the manure to the orchards, mending the horse equipment, the "tack" (harness and other trappings), and the many implements and vehicles they pulled. The horses required hay and grain, so property was set aside to grow these expensive items. This involved planting, tending and harvesting, "shocking" (piling up the sheaves), threshing, baling, hauling, and stacking in the barn.

The fruit trees, too, had their cycle of work. Once the holes were dug and the trees planted, they required constant care. Many different diseases and pests can attack a tree: San Jose scale, an insect that can destroy prune trees and other fruits; the codling moth, which settles in pears, walnuts, and apples; worm borers, which attack the trunk and require each tree to be examined and each worm to be cut out. Spraying to counter the pests was a job that was done more frequently as more remedies were found.

My father's sister, my Aunt Elsie, recalled tasks the family did together. "We would sit in the kitchen around that round oak table with the kerosene lamp in the middle, cutting the potatoes for planting. Each piece had to have one or two or three eyes. We would do that the night before the planting. My father believed that the best time to plant potatoes was when the moon was full."

While the immigrants brought with them some of the folk heritage of the old country, the next generation would quickly learn the American way of farming. My father's attitude was progressive. He attended meetings to hear about the latest in fruit culture. He believed in the new idea that the trees did better if they were irrigated. In order to control water as it flowed from the ground, ridges were made in what is called a checks-and-squares pattern. A new job was created and a new piece of equipment required, pulled first by horses and later tractors. Water from the wells was diverted into the ditches and as more and more people irrigated their orchards, often sharing wells, water was scheduled for night use. The farmer or a hired hand patrolled the flowing water, to make sure it didn't break and run away, and to divert the water to the next area when the ditches had been filled. That running water in the brown earthen ditches was one of the most pleasurable sights. It bubbled up from the ground with a never-forgotten gurgle.

130

It was a joy for children to wade in the irrigation ditch and not too unusual to be thrown into the muddy brown water, as happened to my cousin Louise Sayig (now Mrs. Peter Orlando). My brother and his friends were the culprits.

How much water should be given to the trees and how often the trees ought to be irrigated through the year were subjects of hot debate in our family, my mother claiming my father used too much water, my father defending his practice with the high quality of the product. From late spring through the beginning of fall, the trees were irrigated as many as five or six times. After each irrigation, when the ground was dry enough, the land was disked to turn the soil and make it flat again. Many farm children enjoyed running under the trees with the smooth, freshly turned soil under their bare feet. Blackbirds followed the disk looking for worms.

Women as Farmers: My Mother.   Hard physical labor was often done by women. Widows or women who had inherited property from their fathers or women determined to be farmers on their own did the work themselves if there was no alternative. One widow in San Jose put four children through college on the proceeds from her forty acres of prunes. She worked the horses and plow herself. While the census of 1920 listed only 363 women farmers in Santa Clara County, less than ten percent of the total, most farm wives were an integral part of the system and could be considered farmers too.[4] There were also a few cases when husbands abandoned their families, leaving the wife to fend for herself, and even a few where the husband did not take to hard work, forcing the wife to become the breadwinner.

Inheritance laws favored an equal distribution of property between male and female offspring. Thus it was that by the time my grandparents died the land was divided between my father and his sister, Aunt Elsie. My aunt never ploughed or pruned, but she did sell her peaches from the edge of the Sunnyvale-Saratoga Road. I remember being with her as she sorted the peaches by size and quality; the Crawford peach was her favorite. When she subdivided her remaining acres, she named the street Crawford Drive. My father did the work on her piece for a share. Eventually he bought ten of her twenty acres.

My immigrant mother left Lebanon in 1921 because she had heard that in the United States the streets were paved with gold. She set out at the age of seventeen on a cattle boat that took her to France. She was diagnosed, incorrectly, as having the eye disease glaucoma. Denied entry papers to the United States for that reason, she went to her brother in Mexico and stayed with him seven years, helping to raise his family of seven children. When she contracted a severe case of malaria, she became desperate to leave Mexico. In 1929, with the help of family and friends, she arranged a visa under another woman's name and entered the United States as a tourist. It was while living with her sister in Sunnyvale that she went to work for Charlie Olson at his fruit stand, just three blocks away.

This was in the early 1930s, a time of strong anti-immigrant feelings in California. Her marriage to my father was not looked upon favorably by his parents. After all, my mother was Catholic and from an exotic country, not even European, while they were Protestant and from northern European stock. But when the first child—my sister Jeanette—was born, in 1934, they made a peace offering. My grandmother came to visit, took a good look at the sparkling white clothes hanging on the line, and decided that this woman who could speak Arabic and Spanish but little English, couldn't be all bad.

My father was to say in one of my interviews with him that the neighbors ostracized them because of their mixed marriage. But when I asked my mother if she felt this, she said, "I was too busy working to notice if they did."

The work she did complemented my father's. She ran not only the house but the fruit stand. She had the blood of a mercantile race in her, and she knew with a sure instinct how

Rose Zamar and Ruel Charles Olson San Jose, 1933. *Olson Family Collection*

to wheel and deal. Rosie, as she was known, held her own with the men she dealt with. In the cherry season she would rise at four in the morning, wash or iron, and prepare meals ahead. By six she was in San Jose at the Grower's Market on Tenth Street to buy produce for the stand, and at eight she was ready for business on El Camino Real. Her day stretched until past dark.

After the cherry crop came the apricots. She closed down the stand and ran the apricot-cutting shed, supervising as many as one hundred young people who came from the town and surrounding area to earn money for school clothes or, in many cases, to add to the family income. Very often whole families came together to work through the entire season.

Children's Work. Children were an important factor in the seasonal work. They were paid the same as adults for piece-work, by the bucket of prunes picked or tray of apricots cut, and they worked alongside the adults. Our long summer vacation in the United States harks back to the time when school was let out so that the children could help their families with the all-important harvest.

The cycle of harvest work on our farm began with the cherry crop, which comes into bearing in the middle of May. We three children helped out with the fruit stand, packing cherries with the Italian and Mexican women. More often, though, we packed cherry baskets for sale and waited on customers. I also remember sweeping the floor at the end of the day or early morning.

When the cherries were finished the apricots began, about the Fourth of July. I can remember beginning the apricot-cutting season full of anticipation because I was going to earn money with all the other children. In order to dry apricots, they first must be cut open carefully, the pits removed, the two apricot halves laid on an eight-foot redwood tray, sulphurated, and then put in the sun to dry. The job of cutting 'cots fell to children and families. The tedium slowed us down, and it wasn't difficult to begin trouble by throwing a mushy apricot at someone across the open shed. But we worked, and we managed to turn some of it into play as well. That lasted from July to August. My mother was floor lady [supervisor], helping us to finish our trays and seeing that the tally card or tickets were correctly punched for the number of trays cut.

Just as the apricot season finished, the prune season began. Mom went into the orchards to supervise the picking. Hordes of young children, often whole families, came to work. It is important to note that most of our crew were local people, although my father did occasionally hire migrant workers. Most were in our school and belonged to families who were a settled part of the community. Mom organized the work to make sure the ground beneath the prune trees was picked systematically, and that all the prunes were taken off the ground where they had dropped, heavy and purple, full of natural sugar. Branches of prune trees were so laden that they were held up with long pine props. Occasionally the props were used to shake the prunes down from the trees, but the secret of Santa Clara County prunes was that they were allowed to ripen in their own sweet time. There were as many as four pickings of the same orchard. Today the fruit is tested for sugar content. Then a mechanical shaker takes hold of the tree, under which a canvas skirt, like an inverted umbrella, has been placed. The fruit drops into the skirt. There is usually only one picking as opposed to our four.

A bit of local humor had it that Louis Pellier, the man who, it will be remembered, introduced the French prune, was the best educator in the Santa Clara Valley. The reason: children picking prunes on their hands and knees had such a good taste of physical labor that they determined to go to college and avoid doing such menial work for life. This story illustrates the shifting attitude toward manual labor. At one time it was an honest way to earn money; Americans and immigrants alike were happy to take it. Today, however, it is looked down upon. It offers less money and fewer benefits than other kinds of work. As a result, we have come to rely more on laborers from Mexico and mechanical devices.

All the time my mother was working in the fields she hired a woman to do the housework. She enjoyed the out-of-doors and the type of work she did there. After the prunes were picked, washed, and dried in the dehydrator she helped in scraping them off the trays. Only then would she go back into the house to continue her chores there. There was produce to can, bread to bake, clothes to wash and iron, and school to think about.

My Father's Work. My father, too, was carrying on his routine of work: the organization of the men in the orchards, the women in the packing shed. For many years he relied on Italian immigrants who drove to Sunnyvale from San Jose's Goosetown, everyday during harvest to pick the cherries.[5] Salvadore Ricaboni was foreman through the 1930s and 1940s. His wife, Sarah, was the number one cherry packer, as my father called her. Several wives of pickers joined her in helping to hand-pack the Bings for the eastern markets.[6]

Dad hauled the fruit to the farm buildings. It was one of my joys to break away from work and ride with him to the orchards. Here the men were high in the cherry trees, on "snake ladders" of forty feet in some instances. Musical Italian voices emerged from hidden sources. Yes, and they sang too. Dad would confer with Salvadore about the number of buckets each tree yielded and how long it would take for the picking to cover a certain area. The two of them would load the Model T truck, formerly a milk wagon, with the buckets of luscious red cherries, and we were off again to the packing shed.

This, in the early stages of farm labor, was hand work done one bucket and one box at a time. Over 92,000 tons of dried prunes were produced in Santa Clara County in 1937. Before the age of motorized forklifts, such a crop represented thousands of man-hours in back-breaking labor, as the fresh fruit was moved from the orchards to the processing plants. Then they were sorted by size and then into sacks, which were hand-filled one shovelful at a time. The sacks, each weighing one hundred pounds, were finally loaded on the truck beds, hauled to their destination, and unloaded one more time.

While there were men hired to do this work, much of it was done by the farmer himself. There was hardly a farmer who worked the long hours, the punishing routine from day to day, from month to month, from year to year, who did not grow old looking something like the crooked branches of the trees. As my brother grew in strength he took on more of the hard physical labor that my father had done: lifting buckets of fruit from the orchard to the packing house, from the packing house to the shipping station or the cold-storage plant; carrying ladders to the field and back; bringing down boxes to be washed and putting them back; spreading out trays to be cleaned, then lifting them heavy with fruit to the carts for the sulphur house or the dehydrator. Today, my brother walks with back pain.

The Diary of Charles Forge. Otis Forge of Cupertino, now in his eighties, has had a long life as farmer as well as engineer. He and my father used to sit together and talk about their common interests, their indomitable spirits as well matched as their rugged faces and bent bodies. Otis's father, Charles R. Forge, a ship's engineer by training, having nearly lost his life at sea more than once, had decided to keep his feet on the ground and be a farmer. He said, "It's less money, but you live longer." He settled in Santa Clara County around the turn of the century, buying property first near Fremont Road and the Sunnyvale-Saratoga Road, and then on Homestead Road. With meticulous care he kept a daily journal of his life from about 1906 to 1940.[7] It is a testament to the endless round of chores, the things to be fixed, the nurturing of the vegetable garden, the livestock, the trees, the house, the well, the windmill, then the pump, the equipment. And what made it all worthwhile, the children.

Three days out of a period of fifteen years have been chosen to represent the cycle of work.

Monday, Feb. 19, 1906. Cloudy early then fine. Got up [at] 6. I worked washing machine and Niels [Niels Buck, a hired hand who later farmed for himself] churned & made butter. Cut out irons & wood for side draft for my plow. Pruned in P.M. Rain guage [sic] showed .25" last night. Drilled irons for plow. . . . Filled up oat box at noon. Cloudy sunset. Set traps [for gophers] under oak trees. Apricots & Almonds in bloom & peaches will soon be out. Weeds growing very rapidly.

Aug. Friday 14, 1914. Fog early. . . . Got up [at] 6. Fed chicks & milked. Picked peaches N. of house. After breakfast we all picked near east line. Fred hauled in full boxes & got away for the Canners about 9:30 with 150 boxes. Otis & I picked till noon. Fred scattered boxes around from wagon when he got back. I ran housepump and washing machine. . . . War rages in Europe near Brussells [sic] & other places. Fred & Otis & I picked peaches in P.M. Have 10 tons of my own out & 4 tons of Niels ['s].

Feb. Sat. 12, 1921. Fog A.M. Fine P.M. Ther[mometer] 45–60. Calm. Got up [at] 7. Made fire. Fed chicks & Mat fed stock & milked. Read papers. Otis went to Santa Clara as usual [to school] and did not come home till supper time. I worked on spray rig. Found strainer broken so drove to San Jose to Bean Spray Pump Co & got new wire mesh. After lunch we filled up tank & ran 3 tanks in P.M. Rig ran very well. . . . Apricot bloom coming out fast. Almond in full bloom.

What Charles Forge documents is a way of life, with the work punctuated by family gatherings and by friends coming and going, the children being bathed on Saturday night, the Sunday dinner after church, the community meetings, the occasional picnics, the coming of the gasoline motor and the automobile, the trips to San Jose for supplies, the crops coming in and being sold, the money being put aside for the future, the births and christenings, deaths and funerals—the cycle of work so intertwined with the cycle of life that they mesh like two vines planted when young and grown to old age.

I asked Otis Forge specifically about the Great Depression and his comment was, "What do you mean? It was all depression!" For those who loved the life it was work well invested in clean living, honesty in relationships, and, ultimately a sense of well-being. Otis and my father, like other men and women of that generation, saw it as both a good way of life and a way to earn a decent wage. My father was asked by a student historian how, if he had the chance to do it over again, he would live his life. "Exactly the same way", he replied. "I loved every minute of it. It was a good way to make a living and be your own boss."[8]

Notes

[1] The one my father considered his favorite is pictured on page 16.

[2] Information on the Lyons family from taped interviews with Eileen Brynelson Milan, granddaughter of Patrick Lyons, and with Frank Lyons, Jr. Eileen Brynelson's grandfather had built my grandparents' house in 1901–02. The Lyons house at the southwest corner of El Camino Real and the Sunnyvale–Saratoga Road, built before 1875, was torn down in the 1950s to make way for yet another shopping center.

[3] Our driveway was short, but many of the farms had long approach roads, lined with trees, that created a break in the flat earth and heightened the horizon above the orchards. Eucalyptus and poplar were favorites for this purpose, but willows, palms, pepper trees, sycamores, ash, and even some conifers were used.

[4] U.S. Department of Commerce, *Census of Agriculture 1920* (Washington, D.C.: Government Printing Office, 1922), 348.

[5] Goosetown straddles the Guadalupe River in an area bounded by San Carlos and Willow streets, in one direction, and, in the other, Bird and Orchard avenues. Before 1900 it was occupied by Irish; the Italians who succeeded them were in turn succeeded by Mexicans.

[6] The Black Tartarian cherry was the first to be shipped from Santa Clara Valley to eastern cities, but by the turn of the century the Bing began to replace it as the foremost shipping cherry. See A. C. Butcher, "Cherry Culture," *Monthly Bulletin of the State Commission of Horticulture* 3, no. 8 (August 1914): 319–327.

[7] These journals are still in the possession of Otis Forge, who intends to donate them to the Bancroft Library, University of California at Berkeley.

[8] Pam Sherwood, "R. C. Olson's Story: There's Nothing Like the Soil or Ground Itself," in *Prune Pits: The Collective Stories of Early Sunnyvale-Cupertino Residents*, compiled and distributed by the Community Experimental Based Alternative School at Fremont High School (Typescript in collection of California History Center, Cupertino, 1978), 66.

Other Sources for Chapter 6

Since this chapter deals with family history, it is largely based on my own experiences. Other source materials are cited in the notes.

On the question of child labor in the orchards, one of the best accounts is Thomas A. Bailey, "The Fruits of Child Labor," in his *The American Pageant Revisited* (Stanford: Hoover Institution Press, 1982), 20–24. Bailey, a well-known historian who was born near the Bradley prune orchard on Bascom Avenue in San Jose, found the work tolerable and a positive influence. For a contrary view, see Rudy Calles, "Prune Heaven," *Pacific Historian* 23 (Spring 1979): 58–65. His family's experiences were those of migrant laborers. Closest to the experience of children working on our own family farm is told in Janet Lewis, "Apricot Harvest," in *Good-bye, Son and Other Stories* (New York: Doubleday & Co., 1946), a short story set in Los Altos. A taped interview on June 3, 1979, with the late farmer Alton Burkhart of Los Altos Hills revealed that his experience with children and adults working during the summer was very positive, similar to that described in Lewis's story and experienced by us. The point to be underscored is that for most young people of migrant families, the reality of picking prunes at low pay was neither fun nor a step to future betterment.

Family cutting apricots under oak tree in Cupertino,
mid-1920s. *Courtesy Burrel Leonard and California History Center*

Frances and Cuyler North, with friend Althea Porter (right), photographed in 1894 by their father, ex-New Yorker Gabriel North, at his fruit farm on Homestead Road, Cupertino, which he had bought in 1887 after seeing a railroad advertisement. *Courtesy Frances North Martin*

Wilma M. Peters, aged five, imitates her father Jack Peters's work in tree irrigation at his ranch on Hollenbeck Avenue, Sunnyvale, c. 1917. It was great fun to slosh about in the mud on a hot day. *Courtesy Roger Bibb*

Caramie, my mother's sister, at soda fountain of the first store she ran with her husband, John Sayig on Taaffe Street, Sunnyvale, 1928. Like my mother, she was an immigrant from Lebanon. *Courtesy Louise Sayig Orlando*

Yuba Model 12 tractor, Detroit-made but California-designed,
with track mounted on two-inch ball bearings; if track broke,
bearings were scattered, to be mistaken later by archaeology
buffs as Spanish cannon shot. Here, woman and her dog disk
and slab orchard, c. 1915. *Courtesy Sun-Diamond Growers*

Young Harold Butcher sweeping off hay wagon at family farm, Santa Clara, 1913; hay (behind wagon) will soon be hoisted into loft. *Courtesy Robert T. Butcher*

Prunes being sacked for shipment in John Leonard's packing house, Cupertino, c. 1930. Packing has ceased but building still stands, at center of Vallco industrial and commercial park. *Courtesy Burrel Leonard and California History Center*

Chinese workers operating prune dipper of Charles Oscar Bocks, son of a German immigrant, at Saratoga-Sunnyvale and Homestead roads, c. 1895. Bocks employed over one hundred Chinese, housing them in a barn on Hollenbeck Road not far from our property. *Courtesy Charles and Cora Bocks*

Thomas Foon Chew (in straw hat) c. 1925, with other Chinese in town that may be Alviso, since boardwalk indicates floods were usual. Chew was a cannery owner, inventor, successful farmer, and much-admired citizen. *Courtesy Gloria S. Hom*

Children of Thomas Foon Chew's cannery workers at school he started for them, Alviso, c. 1924. School was racially integrated, unlike most schools which forbade Chinese attendance. *Courtesy Gloria S. Hom*

The Aihara family, c. 1935; they lived and worked on our farm during the 1930s and 1940s, and were "relocated" to a prison camp in 1942. Left to right: Chitose (Dorothy), Torano with Ben on her lap, Hatsune (Helen), Teikichi, known as George, and son George. *Courtesy of George Aihara*

Vincenso Picchetti, (center) foreman of Villa Maria from
1872-1877 was encouraged by the fathers to purchase 160
acres of land on Montebello Ridge. *Courtesy California History
Center*

Tsunegusu Yonemoto and family in Yonemoto carnation nursery, Murphy Avenue, Sunnyvale, c. 1945; note sons in uniform. Land was purchased in son Fred's name in 1915 to evade ban on Japanese land ownership. *Courtesy California History Center*

Mexican farm laborer in vineyard, 1976. Even today, without Mexican labor, the crops of Santa Clara County would not be picked. *Courtesy* San Jose Mercury News

"Mexican Grandmother," by Dorothea Lange, 1936. Lange lived in Oakland and came through Santa Clara Valley many times. This woman is somewhere in the lowlands, near a creek, picking tomatoes. *Courtesy Library of Congress*

Dust Bowl Americans in search of work in Santa Clara Valley,
c. 1935. *Photo by Dorothea Lange, Courtesy Oakland Museum*

Cannery workers on strike in Santa Clara County, 1930s.
Their sign, written on a cannery apron, reads "This is our
motto Stick together If You want to Win." Eventually they did,
and today all cannery workers belong to a union. *Courtesy
Sourisseau Academy*

Apricot load of nonstriking grower is dumped by growers protesting low price at Schuckl & Co., Sunnyvale, 1939. At issue was canneries' offer of $30 a ton versus growers' demand of $42.50. *Courtesy Sourisseau Academy*

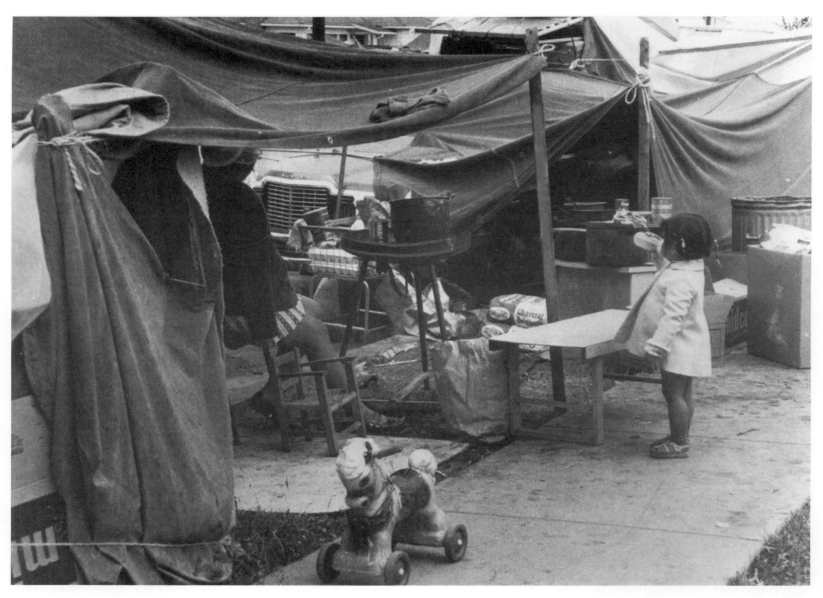

Among the legitimate complaints of migratory farm labor is poor housing, as shown here somewhere in Santa Clara County, 1972. *Courtesy* San Jose Mercury News

CHAPTER 7
IMMIGRATION, LABOR, AND
THE AMERICAN DREAM

THE DAY HAD BEEN LONG *and tiring, and his body ached with it. It seemed to him that from the time he had been strong enough to lift a bucket or carry a box, his life had been a repetition of moving from one crop to another. . . . But what seemed so futile was the fact that the rewards for such labor were so small—even with an entire family working. They barely made enough to subsist.*[1]

For many the American dream has been the chance of a better life for one's family. For some it has been wealth alone. But there is more to the dream than material success or personal gratification. Justice, fairness, dignity, freedom from fear and from poverty, and freedom to worship are all part of the vision that has drawn so many to our shores. Some say the dream is just that, but people from around the world still come, risking life and limb to get here.

In the Santa Clara Valley many ethnic and cultural groups came together to form a microcosm of American life. While the dream was realized for many, others experienced failure. There are the stories of exceptional success like that of Henry Miller, a German immigrant who landed in San Francisco in 1850 with six dollars in his pocket. He went to work as a butcher and began to buy cattle. In partnership with Charles W. Lux he amassed over one million acres of grazing land in three western states. Miller, who was known as the Cattle King, had his headquarters at the Bloomfield ranch in Gilroy. His enormous financial success did not protect him from tragedy, for his happiness was shattered by the early deaths of many members of his family.

Then there is the story of a Spanish immigrant who came to America via the Hawaiian pineapple fields. His ambition gave him the local title of King of Spain. During World War II he left his wife in order to manage a farm for a woman whose husband was serving in Europe. When the war was over he was fired, and his own loyal wife took him back.

Eventually, he saved enough to buy a farm. But the land itself was not very good and the trees did not bear well enough to cover his debts. He couldn't face losing all he had worked for, and one morning he was found hanging from a branch of one of his trees. His wife's words at his graveside will always be remembered by those who knew this family. As she threw in the traditional handful of earth she said, "You wanted dirt, here's your dirt."

Somewhere between these two extremes of success and failure is the story of an Italian family. Sal Noto, an engineer by profession and a book collector and student of Jack London by avocation, fictionalized his family experience in the short story quoted at the beginning of this chapter.[2] His parents Joseph and Frances were children of Italian immigrants. They made their living working in the fruit orchards. The elder Noto also worked as a middleman, buying, picking, and selling crops. One year, income was so short that Joseph Noto picked mustard greens, plentiful in most orchards before plowing, bundled them, and sent them to the eastern markets to earn cash.

Joseph Noto's dream was to own his own land. After success with a grocery store, he and his wife bought seventeen acres of prune trees in San Martin, south of San Jose, in 1956. But the orchard, well past its prime, could not support the family, and they opened a fruit stand nearby. Their margin of success, like that of many other families, was minimal—just enough to support them. Some money was made when they sold their $17,000 investment four years later for $29,000. With that money they bought ten acres of former vineyard land in Morgan Hill, just north of San Martin, for $10,000, later selling eight acres at a profit in small lots. This experience, typical for many, underscores the fact that farmland became more valuable as urban or suburban real estate.

These stories represent the spectrum of success and failure.[3] But if the ideal could be attained via the farm ladder, it was not easily attained by all, for there were whole groups against whom an intense hatred developed in California. Their story deserves special attention because they were excluded by law not only from land ownership but even from working, whether on farm, or in factories, ports, and mines.

The Chinese

An anti-Chinese movement that later affected Santa Clara County's farm industry began on San Francisco's waterfront in the 1870s. It was in this context that one cannery in the county advertised its product as packed by "white labor only."[4]

The Chinese had come to California just after the Gold Rush to fill the need for huge numbers of workers who would work for low pay and under adverse conditions. While they had hoped to strike it rich in the Golden Mountain, as they called America, most remained to do other types of hard physical labor. It was the Chinese who broke the rock and laid the track over the High Sierra for the railroad that connected California and the West with the rest of the country in 1869.

When that job was done the Chinese turned to other occupations. In Santa Clara County they built wineries, laid roads, and cleared land of underbrush for planting. Not only did they work for wages below what a white man would accept ($1.00 a day compared with $2.50 to $4.00), but they lived under conditions that a white man would not abide. Without wives and families, they slept in barns, barracks style. Housing of this type was considered part of their pay. There was a redwood barn on the Bocks family property on Hollenbeck Road, just around the corner from our farm. It could sleep the one hundred Chinese who harvested and processed the fruit. When not on contract the Chinese gathered together in Chinatowns up and down the valley. Mountain View had a small Chinese population from the time of the railroad. Even though it was illegal, the Chinese ran gaming parlors (there was one in Sunnyvale) that were frequented by whites as well as Chinese. Gilroy had a well-defined Chinese sector of town, while Los Gatos and Saratoga had smaller pockets of Chinese who worked as domestic laborers and laundrymen.

The anti-Chinese movement began in San Francisco, during the depressed 1870s, when white workers turned their resentment against Chinese working on the docks for lower wages than they. It was there that Denis Kearney, a rabble-rousing grassroots agitator, introduced the slogan, "The Chinese must go." The second largest population of Chinese after San Francisco was in San Jose. The city itself was ahead of Santa Clara County (itself the first county in the state to do so) in voting to keep the Chinese out of California. In 1882 the Chinese Exclusion Act was passed by Congress prohibiting Chinese immigration through 1892. In 1892 the prohibition was extended for another ten years, and in 1902 Theodore Roosevelt signed a bill denying further Chinese immigration with very few exceptions. In addition, only Chinese who were American citizens by birth were allowed to own land (of course, some Chinese immigrants got around this provision with forged papers).

Nonetheless the Chinese had already made a major contribution to the agriculture of Santa Clara County. Even after Kearney's anti-Chinese legislation was passed, the Chinese controlled the county's strawberry business through the sharecropping system that had been established after the Gold Rush. The fact was that only Asians would "stoop to labor" in the fields to grow the exacting strawberry. To protect themselves, the Chinese had organized into "tongs," brotherhood groups not unlike unions. Each tong was controlled by one man who negotiated on behalf of the group. Without the cooperation of the tongs, the strawberries were neither planted nor picked. The white owners would have paid less than the one dollar per day that was the going rate for Chinese labor, but the power of the tongs maintained that rate. If the farmer did not agree to it, he had no help.

Despite all the obstacles there were Chinese who prospered within the system. Thomas Foon Chew, known as Tom Foon, built an empire in the canning industry. His father, before the turn of the century, had a small cannery in Alviso where he packed tomatoes. Tom joined the cannery in 1906 and expanded into many new areas. His mechanical ability was responsible for several new ideas in canning. It was he who developed machinery to automate the packing of green asparagus. Before 1920 only white asparagus, picked before it emerged from the soil, was canned, and only by hand. Foon went on to rent two thousand acres in Isleton, near Sacramento, to grow asparagus for his cannery. His canning and farming empire, the product of an agile intelligence, fell as a result of his untimely death in 1931.[5]

The Japanese

As the numbers of Chinese decreased because of the restrictive legislation, another group began to enter California with a different purpose in mind. Most of the early immigrant Chinese never intended to stay in California. Their intention was to make money to give them a good life once they returned wealthy to their homes in China. Not many accomplished this goal.

The Japanese intent, no doubt formed as a result of their crowded island condition, was to own a piece of American soil, farm it, and settle their families here. In 1887 there were only four hundred Japanese in California. Even then there was antagonism toward them. With the exclusion of the Chinese, the Japanese began to fill the demand for cheap labor, and by 1910 there were over forty-one thousand in the state. While the Chinese could not buy land, the Japanese could, at first. By 1919 the number of Japanese had risen to over eighty-seven thousand. More than half were either farm owners or farm workers. The whites' fear was that the Japanese were not only depriving Americans of jobs but farming land at a rate that would turn California into a Japanese settlement.

The contributions of Japanese to California agriculture were in fact significant. They are credited with beginning successful rice growing in the Sacramento Valley on lands previously unsuited to any agriculture. Between 1909 and 1919 they were leaders in such crops as beets, celery, berries, and grapes. The total value of crops produced by Japanese increased from $6 million in 1910 to $67 million in 1919. Nevertheless, the Alien Land Law of 1913 prevented Japanese from acquiring land, and from leasing it for more than three years.[6] The Japanese

got around the law by acquiring property in the name of their American-born children. Despite this, by 1919 only 843 acres were owned by Japanese in Santa Clara County and another 4,284 were leased under sharecropping arrangements.[7] The anti-Asian feeling of California culminated in the Exclusion Act of 1924, which prohibited any further immigration of Japanese, Chinese, and even Hindus (although these last numbered only about twenty-six hundred in 1920).

To put the anti-Japanese movement in perspective, there are numerous stories indicating that on a personal level, the relationship between Japanese and Americans could be not only cordial but exactly the opposite of the discriminatory official attitude. One example involved the Sakauye family north of San Jose, pear growers who in 1942, under Executive Order 9066, were forced to leave land they had owned since 1906. It was left in the care of their neighbors, the Edward M. Seely family, who took good care of it and returned it to them when they came home. The Sakauye family had cared for the neighbors' dying grandmother when Edward Seely had gone to Ireland with the navy in World War I.

Then there was the Aihara family, who had lived on our farm from the early 1930s. George Aihara arrived in California from Washington in the first decade of the new century. In 1913 he married Torano Ishiwara, a woman of unusual character and strength, who would not marry in Japan because her mind was set on coming to America. Through the picture-bride arrangement, by which Japanese women, chosen by their photographs, were admitted to the United States as prospective brides, she joined her husband-to-be in Seattle. Her Japanese name means "tiger in the field," and she did in fact come from a village in Japan where women enjoyed high status as owners and inheritors. Four children were born, all native Americans, and raised under the careful eye of their mother.[8] Alas, she succumbed to cancer in 1937. Perhaps it was a blessing that she did not live to see her American dream shattered when, during World War II, her family, along with the other four thousand Japanese in the Santa Clara Valley, were forced to leave everything within twenty-four hours and go to camps in Wyoming, Idaho, Colorado, Nevada, Utah, and Arizona. The Aihara family was sent to Arizona; I remember as a young child during the war visiting their empty house and garage. I had no knowledge then, at five or six, of the terrible ordeal they were enduring, but I knew and obeyed my parents' order not to touch anything as the people who lived there would return. Both the Aihara boys served in the United States armed forces after initially being turned down because they were Japanese. My father had provided them with character references to the effect that "there are no people I would trust more than these young men."

Throughout the time of the relocation camps, loyal Americans in Santa Clara County held property for their Japanese friends, returning it after the war. There are also a few stories of those who would not return it. But the valley's friendly reputation was communicated to the returning refugees, and more Japanese settled here after the war than were here before.[9] Finally, the McCarran-Walter Immigration Act was passed in 1952. It struck anti-Asian legislation from the books, enabling land ownership, citizenship, and civil rights so long denied.

Farm Labor

Historically, farm labor was barely separated from the farm family in terms of community status. Along with the members of the family the self-sufficient farm employed a "hired hand" who lived with them until he was ready to strike out and farm on his own. Or it might be that the hired hand remained so all his life, living and dying within the circle of a particular family.

The change to commercial farming had a profound effect on the relationship between farm owners and their labor force. With the advent of the modern farmer-businessman, a foreman hired large numbers of strangers to work, thus making the relationship purely economic. The employer's feeling of responsibility toward his workers and the worker's loyalty to the employer were lost.

In California the effects of this change were striking. In order to keep the price of labor down and to disrupt the organizing efforts of domestic laborers, growers recruited workers from China, Japan, the Philippines, Mexico, and other areas. To quote a California legislative committee of the 1870s, "To develop [the state's] latent resources and vitalize all her powers, we need sound, liberal, farseeing Legislators; men who can mould and harness *all* inferior races to work out and realize her grand and glorious destiny."[10] Wages were often low, working conditions harsh, and living facilities inadequate. In response, farm workers began to organize at the turn of the century. Confrontation between growers and workers was often violent and bitter.

The Industrial Workers of the World—the IWW or "Wobblies"—decided at a series of meetings in 1905 that they would organize the unrepresented mass of American workers, including migrant laborers. Their target was the western United States. In 1909 they attempted to organize the labor pool congregated in Fresno that supplied workers for San Joaquin Valley farmers. The organizers were jailed. Later attempts at various locations resulted not only in jailings but in riots and even deaths. While no gains can be said to have been made for the farm workers in the early years of the new century, the issue was at least clearly before the state, and Governor Hiram Johnson ordered a study of migrant labor problems in 1913. The irony was that the "inferior races" to which large growers looked for a labor pool would later include fellow Americans.

Unionization: Costs and Benefits. In the Santa Clara Valley the conflict between capital and labor was mitigated by the region's unique pattern of family farming. Even so, such conflict was and is by no means unknown. It was at its height from 1929 through the 1930s. Pickers, organized by the Cannery and Agricultural Workers Industrial Union (CAWIU), struck the pea, pear, cherry, and dairy industries. This particular

157

union was Communist led. In some cases—the pear strike of 1933, for instance, which involved the pear growers north of Santa Clara—the strikers achieved their goal of increasing their hourly wage there, from $0.175 an hour to $0.20 and $0.25.[11] In other cases no gains were made; wages were even lowered in one. Some strikers were jailed, others blacklisted. While improvements were made for some agricultural workers, there was no permanent union to represent field workers, who had no successful labor union of their own until the United Farm Workers of California under the direction of César Chavez, emerged in the late 1960s. By then, Santa Clara County was no longer a prime agricultural area.

There can be no doubt that most local growers looked on the unions with distrust. For the small farmer, the margin of profit is too small to absorb union pay scales. And then there is the process, sometimes difficult, of dealing with unions through collective bargaining and the relevant state agency, the Agricultural Labor Relations Board. Labor conflict in 1983 in Gilroy prompted one large garlic grower, a third-generation farmer, to quit farming and turn his attention to land development. The union had demanded the right to say which crop one farmer should plant.

Unionization in the canneries followed a different course. Even though some canneries used only white labor, there were few labor problems until the early twentieth century. One of the first cannery strikes in California is recorded in San Jose in 1917. The issues were low wages, the number of working hours, and union recognition. The union in question was the Toilers of the World, made up of elements of the International Workers of the World and the American Federation of Labor (AFL). It had the support of San Jose church leaders such as the Reverend W. L. Stidger, pastor of the First Methodist Church, and Father William Culligan of St. Joseph's Catholic Church.[12] Although the union was successful in this instance, it disappeared from the scene when America entered World War I and unionism became unpatriotic.

Many of the workers in the canneries in this early period were of European stock—Spanish, Italian, Portuguese, or Yugoslavian. High-school teenagers and college students followed the immigrants into the canneries, but their motive was to earn money through the summer so that they could continue their education. For the immigrant, and often the immigrant children, cannery work was a profession in itself.

During the 1930s union organization gained acceptance within the canneries, but not without violence and disruption of lives and property. The first major strike of the period was launched against five of the largest canneries: California Packing Corporation (CPC), Richmond-Chase, California Canning Cooperative, and the F. M. Drew Cannery. Two CPC canneries were involved; the issue was a 20 percent reduction in wages. It was the CAWIU that did the organizing, and on August 1, 1931, twelve hundred workers struck all five canneries. During this strike there were mass meetings in San Jose, police confrontations, and arrests; finally, it failed, but it had shown that the canneries could be unionized. By 1938, after the AFL replaced the CAWIU, they were.

Right up to the 1960s there were as many as twenty thousand people in Santa Clara County who worked in the canneries on a seasonal basis. When we were growing up it was well known that working in the cannery was a well-paying job, although the work was hard and tedious. What we didn't know was that much agony and hardship had been borne to ensure the workers a decent wage scale and acceptable working conditions.

Farmhands on the Olson Farm. Our farm is a microcosm of the farm labor experience. Numerous nationalities came to Santa Clara County and took the jobs available on local farms. There were two classes of worker on our farm: those who lived there year round and those who came for the harvest. As was typical in small family enterprises, those who stayed year round developed a close relationship with us. Those who came for the harvest usually returned year after year because they trusted my father and his dealings with them. Buck Wentworth drove

Buck Wentworth, one of the farm workers who lived on our ranch. He drove tractor, dipped the prunes, fixed any number of broken things, and in his spare time sat for hundreds of hours watching the traffic rush by on El Camino Real. *Olson Family Collection*

our tractor for us from the early 1950s until he died in his trailer on the ranch in 1963. Nick Moholous, a Greek immigrant, worked for us on and off for years. When he became ill, we placed him in a nursing home. He so disliked being confined that he escaped, and no doubt died somewhere as a John Doe. Tilio Tope, an Italian, fled to California from his home in Boston after knifing his wife's lover. When he died, my father contacted his family who, never interested in him before, suddenly wanted his possessions. My father boxed up his pair of shoes, a pair of pants, and his hat, and sent them to Boston.

There was something sad in these lives. These men had given up on the American dream and did not even participate in the struggle to achieve it. Cheap wine, cigarettes, their work, and later TV, were the sum of their lives. Yet they were part of the extended circle of people who mattered in our lives. We remember each for what he was, a human being with specific characteristics, specific foibles and quirks. The stories about their lives are part of our lives. Like many farmhands, Buck drank too much. On one occasion, while under the influence, he lost the motor of his fishing boat in the river; on another, he drove the tractor into an apricot tree and knocked it over. But his conflict with John Rose, a local builder who died in 1984, summarized the proud and stubborn character of these men. The conflict arose because each considered himself to be an expert in many areas. It didn't end until 1963. John was remodeling our apricot cutting shed, and Buck had nothing but criticism for the way he went about it. One morning Buck failed to emerge from his trailer as usual and my brother went to check on him, only to find that he showed no life. My brother called John to come and verify that Buck was no longer breathing. "Yes, he's dead" he said, hammer in hand— and quickly returned to his work. In the meantime the Mexican workers had gathered at the door with their hats in their hands, reciting the Rosary.

Buck's own reminiscences still rattle in our brains. We were never sure if his family came from Iowa or Ohio (probably they had been in both), but he told of how his grandfather lay dying during the fall of his last year at home, and how the grave was dug before the freeze of winter in anticipation of his burial. When the old man finally died and his body was placed in the coffin for the funeral, suddenly it was remembered that he was well over six feet tall and the grave was too short. There was nothing to be done but to put the body and coffin in the barn, where the cold kept it frozen—until spring, when the ground and grandpa thawed out.

The Great Depression created yet another class of unwanted migrants: a floating, landless class of Dust Bowl Americans who came to California thinking they could find work and land on which to squat. Instead they found communities that turned them away in fear and anger. Between 1935 and 1939 more than 350,000 such migrants entered California by car, looking for work. Many of them were farmers forced off their land by the long drought in Oklahoma and Texas.[13]

Such a family (their name is lost to us since my father died) came every year from Porterville in southern California to pick prunes. I remember their pitched tent in the orchard, the mattresses they carried on the roof of their Ford, and their angular thinness. Dad took to saving the man's paycheck until the family was ready to leave, otherwise he would have spent the money on drink as the season progressed. They were called Okies, since they spoke with the distinctive twang of Oklahoma.[14] But there was another so-called Okie who came to the ranch as a farmhand with his family. Eldon "Hank" Lindstrom, his wife Sally, and their two children came to work for my father in the late 1940s. They stayed for several years, carefully saving their money until they had enough to buy their own twenty-acre farm near Turlock, California. This was yet another example of success via the farm ladder.

During the Great Depression, Mexicans began to move north in search of work. In 1942 the federal government began the bracero program to replace the men who had gone to war. Mexicans were brought up by train to the Santa Clara depot, where farmers would meet them. Housing and food were supplied. Since the end of this progam in 1964, illegal Mexican aliens have entered the country to fill the need for farm labor. Without them, there would be no crops harvested in Santa Clara County or across much of the state.

One family came to Santa Clara County in 1945 and settled near us on a neighbor's farm. Louisa Martinez was the mother of seven children, five sons and two daughters. Her family left Guanajuato about 1913, at a time of unrest and revolution in Mexico. Her father worked in the mines of Kansas and then, in 1919, the family came to California. Frank, one of the sons, has worked for us since 1950. Two of Frank's sons, Ernest and his brother Junior, who now has a young family of his own, were both born on the ranch and still live there.

Another Mexican family makes its home on the ranch. Heriberto and Consuela Torres and their three children have lived there since the 1970s. But the Mexicans are not the farm's only residents. Yemenite workers were brought to the United States under an agreement with King Saud of Saudi Arabia who negotiated for other Arab countries with President Truman just after World War II. The Yemenite men are excellent workers; most of them send their earnings home, in the same way as their Mexican counterparts. They come to our ranch in the early spring to pick cherries and stay through apricot harvest. Most travel on to the San Joaquin Valley where they cut asparagus and then pick grapes. A few of these men have made our farm their home away from home, and have adopted my mother as their own. When my father was still alive, Synon, their boss, would come and discuss world politics. His English was not the best but these two old men enjoyed each other's company, and could sit for an hour communicating in a way the rest of us barely understood. Now, Synon's friend "Shorty," a tower of strength no more than five feet tall, brings my mother gifts of fresh lamb, often slaughtered on the ranch for his own needs. Frank Martinez, too, regards my mother as if she were his own. He worked so long beside my father and my brother that he became truly part of the family. He was one of those who kept vigil at the hospital just before my father died.

160

While the farm ladder no longer works in Santa Clara County, pockets of the old value system still exist. But land has become too expensive. The American dream has been pared down from farm ownership to home ownership, and from that to ownership of a condominium. In this era of lowered expectations, it is important to remember that the dream has never worked for all. The miracle is that it has worked for so many. We are still a ray of hope for many people around the world.

Notes

1 Sal Noto, "Valley of Heart's Delight," *Pacific Historian* 24 (Spring 1980): 39.

2 Information on Sal Noto's family experiences is from a telephone conversation of Dec. 8, 1983.

3 Of course, the farm ladder in Santa Clara County worked well only as long as there was land enough to farm and the family farm remained a viable economic unit. The heyday of family farms was in the mid-1920s, when the county had nearly seven thousand of them. By 1959 there were just under half that. See James, *History of San Jose*, 158; and Soil Survey, 41. Although there is no generally accepted definition of "family farm," as a minimum it connoted a farm where most of the labor, except at harvest time, was performed by family members, who expected ownership to remain in the family. Today's family farm might be a family corporation, a modern agribusiness, or other highly mechanized farm still under family ownership.

4 San Jose Mercury, *Sunshine, Fruit and Flowers*, 200. The Flickinger Cannery in Berryessa claimed that its fruit was "all packed by white men and women, who are required to exercise care that neatness and cleanliness shall characterize all their work." The canning label emphasized, "Packed by White Labor."

5 James Wright, "Thomas Foon Chew," in *Chinese Argonauts*, ed. Gloria Hom (Los Altos Hills: Foothill Community College, 1971), 20–44.

6 State Board of Control of California, *California and the Oriental* (Sacramento: State Printing Office, 1922), 228.

7 Ibid., 48.

8 Taped interview with Mr. and Mrs. George Aihara, Jr., and Helen Aihara Kitaji on July 20, 1980.

9 Phone conversation with Eiichi Sakauye, Dec. 6, 1982.

10 Quoted in Maisie Conrat and Richard Conrat, *The American Farm* (San Francisco and Boston: California Historical Society and Houghton Mifflin Co., 1977), 196.

11 Christina Fernandez, "Research Notes: San Jose Cannery Strike, 1931, and Santa Clara County Pear Pickers Strike, 1933" (Unpublished paper for Dr. Albert Camarillo, Department of History, Stanford University, 1975).

12 Stuart Jamieson, *Labor Unionism in American Agriculture*, U.S. bulletin 836 (Washington, D.C.: Bureau of Labor Statistics, 1945), 65–66.

13 State-Wide Committee on the Migrant Problem, *Migrants, a National Problem—and Its Impact on California*, introductory statement by Chairman Harrison S. Robinson (Sacramento: California State Chamber of Commerce, 1940).

14 My brother John became friendly with a young boy, Richard Kemper, who had settled in Sunnyvale from Oklahoma, and picked up his Oklahoma accent from him. For years after my brother was nicknamed "Okie."

Other Sources for Chapter 7

For Henry Miller the Cattle King, see Patricia Snar Simon, *Henry Miller, His Life & Times* (Gilroy: Gilroy Historical Society, 1980).

Useful information on the anti-Chinese movement in San Francisco labor unions is to be found in William Martin Camp, *San Francisco: Port of Gold* (New York: Doubleday, 1947). Early canneries and unionism are covered in Ann Krooth and Jaclyn Greenberg [interviewers], *Harvest Quarterly* Nos. 3 and 4 (double issue), 1978. For later developments, see William Braznell, *California's Finest: The History of Del Monte Corporation and the Del Monte Brand* (San Francisco: Del Monte Corp., 1982).

An excellent fictional account of the pear strikes of the 1930s is to be found in Jose Antonio Villarreal, *Pocho* (New York: Doubleday Anchor Books, 1970). See also ibid., "The Valley Was Kind to Us," *San Jose Mercury-News*, Oct. 17, 1979, 9B. Another Chicano novel that deals with prune pickers and Santa Clara County is Raymond Barrio, *The Plum Plum Pickers*, (Sunnyvale: Ventura Press, 1975). Like John Steinbeck in *Of Mice and Men*, Barrio describes large farms, managers, and the migrants—in this case, Chicano families—who try to retain their dignity while earning a meager living.

An interesting pamphlet on the Japanese in California is California Joint Immigration Committee, *California's Answer to Japan: Japan's Honor Not Hurt by the Immigration Act* (Sacramento: State Printing Office, 1924). It emphasizes that the exclusion of the Japanese from American citizenship is based on economic factors, not personal ones. For a different view, see M. Browning Carrott, "Prejudice Goes To Court: The Japanese & the Supreme Court in the 1920s," *California History* 62, no. 2 (Summer 1983): 122; and Roger Daniels, *The Politics of Prejudice: The Anti-Japanese Movement in California and the Struggle for Japanese Exclusion*, (Berkeley and Los Angeles: University of California Press, 1962).

CHAPTER 8
MARKETS, GOVERNMENTS, AND COOPERATIVES

I N MARCH, ROSES WERE IN BLOOM, *and the orchards of the Santa Clara Valley had begun the slow procession of fragrance and blossom which was to last another full month; first the almonds, then Imperial prunes, then apricots and French prunes, and peaches, cherries, apples, pears—the almond trees breaking into green as the apricots turned snowy, apricots in green leaf as the prunes came into blossom, apples and quinces mixing leaf and blossom on the single twig.*[1]

In the early spring the farmer took his last breath of calm from the slow winter months, for ahead of him and his family lay sixteen-hour days. It was our custom to get into our car and drive beneath the orchard trees, savoring the scent and feel of blossoms drifting downward on the soft breezes. From a point on the edge of the valley we could see the panorama that lay at our feet, blossoming trees in every direction.

Each variety bore a crop that needed to be picked, sorted, packed, shipped, or delivered to a cannery, a dry yard, or a packing house. For these were the market choices in handling fruit. The local markets, including fruit stands like ours, were one outlet. The name of San Jose's Market Street recalls the time it was a market for local farmers to sell their produce. Through the San Francisco market, more than fifty percent of the valley's produce reached the eight other counties surrounding San Francisco Bay. Los Angeles was another not quite so local market for fresh fruit. There were eastern markets and worldwide markets, from Europe to Asia. Santa Clara Valley's fruit, fresh, canned, or dried was a welcome treat to the people of northern Europe. Over the years we, like many farmers, made use of most of these markets.

Even as a small child I felt the excitement and tension surrounding the question of what to do with the crop. Whether to sell the apricots directly to the cannery or to dry the crop was a gamble that could result in a measurable difference in profit. When the cannery price was too low, many farmers, Dad included, decided to go through the expensive process of

cutting and drying. Then the dried crop was sold directly to a distributor.

Markets: Drying and Canning Fruit

The number of canneries and dried fruit processing plants grew in proportion as the orchards spread. By the end of the 1890s, Santa Clara County was the world's largest center for canning fresh fruit and processing dried fruit. By 1920 it held forty canneries and thirty packing houses. The county's dominance in this field was maintained until the 1960s, when the orchards declined and the canneries and packing houses began to disappear.

The cannery and dried fruit prices were communicated from farm to farm by the buyers who represented the individual firms. These men knew the farmers well. We children knew them by their firms if not their names. One was a CPC buyer, one was from Schuckl, one from Richmond-Chase, and one from Pratt-Low. The buyers and the farmers would huddle as we small children hung around the edges of the group, listening to the important discussions of price. Who was offering how much? It was in this way that one generation learned from another about a business that everyone thought would go on forever.

The farmer who wants to survive must not only succeed in producing a crop, but in selling it; he is a businessman in a high-risk business controlled by the laws of supply and demand and by forces beyond his control such as railroad freight costs. The tremendous increase in the planting of prunes in the 1880s resulted in huge surpluses in the 1890s. World War I and World War II stimulated new plantings to meet the needs of the time. Dismal prices followed, leaving the farmer with barely enough to support his family. Prunes at one and a half cents a pound brought little bread to the table. The pre–World War I price had been three to four cents a pound. It was always clear to the farmer that, from the markets to the weather, he had a minimum of control. The areas of risk were reduced if, like my father and many others, a farmer spread his effort over more than one crop. It was for this reason that we grew cherries, apricots, and prunes; if one crop or one market failed, as it often did, something could still be salvaged.

The close relationships that might develop between buyers and farmers meant little when company profits were involved. Firms that might have done business with a family for years would suddenly turn their backs on it when they could no longer profit from that business. In many cases the canneries themselves suffered financial stress, if not bankruptcy. There was often tension, bordering on hostility, between the farmers, the canneries, and those who handled dried fruit. During the Great Depression, hostility broke into violence. It wasn't only the workers who organized into unions. Their efforts were paralleled by the efforts of small farmers to organize into co-operatives against the big business interests so that David could have at least a toehold against Goliath.

Fresh Produce Markets

By far the most significant market for fresh fruit was in the East, since that was where the majority of the American people lived. Getting fruit there was and is expensive: it has to be packed in boxes (formerly made of fine, clear pinewood, though many boxes are now of cardboard), stored in a cold-storage plant, carted by expensive refrigerated railroad cars, and finally handled by an agent who charges a fee at the auction when the produce is sold. Add to this the price of picking the fruit and the cost of fertilizers, sprays, and orchard equipment. It is the hope of the grower that by the time the final tally is made, he will have some profit to meet his debts, which include taxes and a bank loan taken out to finance his crop. When farmers organized, the businessmen to whom they owed money, the railroads who charged them a high

freight, and the canners and processors who paid little for their crops were often the targets of their wrath.

L. A. Gould, a Santa Clara orchardist, shipped the state's first carload of fresh fruit east in 1869, shortly after the railroad was completed. "The first season's shipments amounted to thirty-three tons of pears, apples, and grapes, and plums; in 1870 seventy carloads, or about seven hundred tons were sent." [2] Gould continued to ship to the eastern states, Australia, China, and Hawaii. [3] Later the packing plant of Abram Block stood amid Gould's orchards. It was a fixture for years, at Scott Lane and El Camino Real. [4]

John Z. Anderson, an early pear grower from Santa Clara (and later from San Juan Bautista), shipped the first carload of pears packed in ice to the eastern market in 1875. John Z. Anderson's namesake and grandson, John Z. "Jack" Anderson, was one of the few farmer-legislators from Santa Clara County. He was a popular Republican who served in Congress from 1938 to 1950. The family's pear orchards in San Juan Bautista were recently sold.

The auction system, begun in 1886 for California fresh fruit, aided growers by setting up a mechanism by which their fruit could be distributed. Patterned after the already existing Florida fruit auctions, it enabled distributors to buy produce as it came to Chicago. By 1900 individual auctions were being held in many cities; the largest one was (and still is) in New York. Colonel Harris Weinstock, a Sacramento merchant and an early advocate of California fruit interests, was instrumental in getting the system adopted.

A network of middlemen stepped in to accommodate the need for fruit handlers. Some, like Porter Brothers from Chicago, were national firms that set up local offices in Santa Clara County. [5] Similar distributors emerged to handle dried and canned fruit. Before long, specialized dealers were handling each specific fruit. We shipped cherries with Louis DeLucca, an independent fruit dealer, for many years. Then Day and Young combined with DeLucca. In its heyday the firm could

handle forty to sixty grower-packers. Today Bill Young, under the label of Sunshine Shippers, takes care of the seven remaining independent packers, the Olsons included. The cherries are rushed to eastern markets by air.

Government Lends a Hand

Not only has government intervened to aid the farmer in marketing his produce, it has become deeply involved in his welfare on many other levels. The Morrill Act of 1862, by establishing land-grant colleges, created a vehicle for educating the farmer. The Hatch Act of 1887 established experimental stations for research vital to farm development all over the United States. There are nine in California alone. Even before the Hatch Act, Santa Clara Valley had California's first experimental station, located by the state government at Cupertino on two acres of land donated in 1884 by John T. Doyle, prominent lawyer and vintner, for the purpose of studying vineyards and grapes.[6]

Early work in Santa Clara County by researchers from Berkeley included studies on rust-resistant asparagus stock that enabled the asparagus industry to establish itself in California after the turn of the century. The University Experiment Station at Berkeley also conducted studies, like the one on the importance of bees in French prune orchards (1918), that applied directly to Santa Clara County. Beehives in prune orchards became a part of the landscape as a result.

To better serve the fruit interests, the Deciduous Fruit Field Station in Mountain View was established in 1920 on three acres of land rented from A. W. Ehrhorn, a cherry and pear grower on Calderon Avenue, just off El Camino Real. Its first report concerned control of brown rot in apricots. (The second largest crop in the county was apricots.)[7] By 1925 the station was closed; another, smaller station opened in the Willow Glen area in 1926.[8] Finally, in 1928, the Deciduous Fruit Field Station on Winchester Road in San Jose began operations; it

has been turning out a steady stream of relevant agricultural information ever since.

However productive, these stations could effect little without a vehicle to communicate their findings to the farmers. And so, in 1914, the Smith-Lever Act created the Cooperative Extension Service. Due to the entrenched position of the county commissioner of agriculture, Santa Clara County did not participate in this program until 1944, when the War Emergency Food Production Program was established, and it was years before the Extension Service and the commissioner worked smoothly together.[9] Nevertheless, when Dad had a problem with his trees, he would call the Extension Service to advise him. He also made use of the university system by attending classes and lectures at the Davis campus. My brother still does both, as do most farmers who care about producing a viable crop.

State Agencies. Since agriculture became the number one industry in California, the state has also had a natural interest in its progress. From the 1850s commissions were established to foster agricultural ends. The most important agency, today's Department of Food and Agriculture, grew out of such early groups as the Board of State Viticultural Commissioners, created in 1880 to counter the deadly infestation of phylloxera. The underlying premise was simple: if the farmer had no crop to market, the state would lose income, farms would fail, and people would suffer. Even though the commission was abandoned in 1895, as a result of the economic depression of the 1890s, its proposed program led to the state's first quarantine law, in 1899; a law that served as a model to many other states.[10]

The State Board of Horticulture, created in 1883 to protect California's tree crops from infestations, was replaced by the Department of Agriculture in 1919, when the various areas of agriculture were drawn together into one state agency. To make closer contact with the farmer, the County Boards of

Horticultural Commissioners were established in 1881. Their name was changed to County Agricultural Commissioners in 1930. They report to the Department of Food and Agriculture, supplying statistical data on county agriculture, and function as the local inspectors of weights and measures, and as pest controllers.

Santa Clara County appointed Edward M. Ehrhorn its first horticultural commissioner in 1895. Ehrhorn, after growing up in Mountain View on the farm that was later the site of the Experimental Fruit Station, had trained in Europe and studied at Stanford University. He went on to become a deputy director of horticulture for the state. In his first report as county commissioner, he outlined the special pests that afflicted the county in 1895: the peach-root borer, the green vine hopper, black scale, and phylloxera. In one case, thirty pounds of the hoppers were gathered by hand in a day from an infected vineyard; there are about 43,500 hoppers to the pound! During his term at the state office, the quarantine law was passed.[11]

The present county commissioner is Greg Van Wassenhove. At one time the staff of the department was as high as thirty-two. Today it is fourteen. While Gordon Spencer, Van Wassenhove's predecessor, saw a continued need for the post, he conceded that, since there were few farmers left, the department's main job would be to monitor pests and diseases that appear on the urban scene, but threaten agriculture.[12] Just how devastating such pests can be is well illustrated by the Med-fly crisis of 1981. Before it was over, $100 million had been spent and the local, state, and federal governments were involved in the process. The losses to Santa Clara Valley farmers that year were high as fruit could not be marketed outside the county.

Of Co-ops and Calamities

As the marketing of various fruits in vast amounts became more and more complex, the growers began to see that their interests would be better served if they controlled more of the process, not just growing the produce but marketing and advertising it. The tenor of the conflicts that drove farmers to form cooperative groups is made clear by the following 1872 quote from the California State Board of Agriculture.

The truth is the grain merchants, the hucksters, the middlemen, the shippers, the railroads, the sack makers, the assessors and the tax collectors manage to hold the agricultural classes in a condition of servitude unparalleled in a free country. It has been said that these things always regulate themselves. I question if anything regulates itself. The farmers and fruit growers must combine for their own protection, as the grain dealers and hucksters combine for their own profit—otherwise they will continue to labor for the benefit of those who, however useful as a class, produce nothing.[13]

In the same year, similar sentiments prompted members of the San Jose Farmers Club and Protective Association to band together in a common effort against the railroad's high freight rates and its refusal to provide a night train so that produce could arrive at the market by early morning. Santa Clara Valley farmers arranged for steamers to run to San Francisco from Alviso at 4:00 A.M. The cost of freight dropped from $1.00 per small chest of fruit to $0.60. Quickly the railroad reduced its price and made a night train available.[14]

One of the lasting institutions to come out of the 1870s was the Farmers Union Corporation. The idea that the farmers ought to form a union of their own was a product of the national recession that followed the Civil War. The San Jose firm, with farmers as shareholders, was founded in 1874 and continued until the early 1960s. It was intended as a place for farm families to shop for all their needs, with the exception of clothing. Even financing for crops was available. The historic union buildings, just off Santa Clara Street in San Jose, have been converted to restaurants, offices, and antique shops.

While cooperative groups made efforts to form an effective force against the food processors, shippers, railroad barons,

Frank Martinez, who has worked on the Olson farm in Sunnyvale since 1950, steers our freshly packed cherries to a truck for their journey by air freight to New York, where they will be auctioned within twenty-four hours (1980 photo).

The first braceros (legally admitted Mexican laborers) to arrive in Santa Clara County, 1942. Bracero program (1942–64) was inspired by wartime labor shortages (hence workers' V-for-victory signs) but continued after war. *Photo by Dorothea Lange, Courtesy Oakland Museum*

The Farmers' Union, a co-op with headquarters in San Jose
and branches in valley towns, delivers a wagon of grain in
Campbell, c. 1895. *Courtesy Campbell Historical Museum*

Potential bidders inspect Olson brand, About Town, at the New York Auction, June 18, 1954. *Olson Family Collection*

Seventeen-acre dryyard of Campbell Fruit Growers Union,
organized in 1892, and taken over by Sunsweet in 1917;
workers are scraping dried fruit from trays into boxes. View
south toward Los Gatos gap c. 1900. *Courtesy Campbell Historical
Museum*

Charles S. Barrett (center), first president of the National Farmers Union, posing with officers of its local branch, the Campbell Farmers Union Packing Company, 1911. Left to right: F. M. Righter (president), Earl Morris, Perley B. Payne (manager), John McNaught, Lloyd Gardner, and Arthur Ernst. *Courtesy Sun-Diamond Growers*

Grower's Market, a co-op outlet for produce at wholesale, Seventh and Taylor streets, San Jose, October 1939. Fruit peddler with full truck is Joe "Shorty" La Scola, an Italian immigrant who, like my mother, regularly bought produce there. *Courtesy Joe Ferrari*

These strawberry pickers worked for Naturipe Berry Growers, Inc. Headquartered in San Jose, the Co-op was begun in 1917. This photograph was taken in Gilroy in 1975. *Courtesy* San Jose Mercury

California Prune and Apricot Growers Association, formed in 1917, acquired this older plant on Lincoln Avenue San Jose, for packing dried fruit under its Sunsweet label. Note railroad car between buildings (far right), and farmer (center right) who, having no truck, pulled load behind automobile (1920 photo). *Courtesy California History Center*

"Tenderized" prunes from Sunsweet displayed in Brooklyn, New York, 1935. Low prices—bulk prunes four pounds for 19 cents or a two-pound box for 15 cents—show impact of Depression on Santa Clara Valley. *Courtesy Sun-Diamond Growers*

"You are taking everything but my shirt in taxes, so you might as well take that," is the theme of this 1952 radio broadcast in which Santa Clara Valley Farm Bureau members, all farmers, protest to Washington. *Courtesy* San Jose Mercury News

Ray Perusina (who farms with his brother Dan in the Coyote Valley) explains why he collects farm equipment, like the Caterpillar 30 (shown to the left) which he bought from my father. "It's all there is left of our history."

Paul Mariani, Sr. (right), watching worker pour Blenheim apricots in harvest of 1950. That same year he and my father, along with forty-two other growers, organized a co-op to pool their Royal Ann cherries. *Courtesy* San Jose Mercury News

John Bean spray pump in operation on Butcher family farm,
Santa Clara, c. 1913. Pump required one man to pump while
the other sprayed. *Courtesy Eugene Butcher*

William T. Baer, Cupertino blacksmith, at work in his shop, c. 1920. *Courtesy California History Center*

Between 1918 and 1921 this photo was used in advertisements by the John Bean Company to illustrate the advantages of a Bean six-horsepower Tract-Pull tractor over a team of six horses. Designer of tractor was Alf Johnson. *Courtesy Department of Special Collections, University of California Library, Davis, California*

W. J. Buchser (at wheel) pulling a sprayer he designed for the pea crop of his brother-in-law, Vernon "Doc" Holthouse (standing), September 1942. Crop was on present site of Moffett Field, formerly Chief Yñigo's land. *Courtesy Vernon and Emma Holthouse*

Our neighbor Jack Peters of Hollenbeck Road, Sunnyvale, on his one-cylinder Sampson Sieve Grip tractor, 1909, when there were only some 2,000 tractors in the United States. Sampson was made by Stockton company bought in 1918 by General Motors. *Courtesy Roger Bibb*

and bankers, the early history of the co-ops can best be described as "fits, starts, and quits." In times of short supply, farmers sold to the highest bidders and found they could make a living. In times of overproduction, farmers brought in their crops to the struggling co-ops for marketing. From 1888 right through the depression of the 1890s several co-ops were formed in Santa Clara County. Only a few of these early organizations survived into the twentieth century.

California Fruit Union. The first formal organization to gain some ground for the growers of fresh fruit was the California Fruit Union, an offshoot of the State Horticultural Society. Founded in 1885, the union elected John Z. Anderson, a Santa Clara County pear grower, as its first president.[15] Its achievements were substantial but mostly short-lived. Railroad rates were reduced because it shipped in great quantity (Senator Leland Stanford had a hand in accomplishing this). The auction system was introduced under its guidance. Growers and handlers combined in their efforts for the first time, and by 1889 the union shipped about two-thirds of the "green" (fresh) fruit that left California. The commission of 10 percent was returned to the growers. Due to a variety of causes, the union went out of business by 1894.[16] High railroad freight rates continued to be of major concern to farmers, especially before the opening of the Panama Canal in 1914.

The Grange. Another farmers group that played a part in developing a spirit of cooperation was the National Grange, or Order of Patrons of Husbandry, which was organized nationally in 1867 to act as a support group for farmers. The first San Jose chapter was formed in 1873. From the beginning the California Granges attempted to form a marketing outlet for their members, but the Grangers' Business Association, which was the result, did not survive long. The Grange then moved away from being a social support system for farmers toward national political advocacy. Although efforts to gain

power failed, it was successful on the national level in its support of rural free delivery, land-grant colleges, and agricultural experiment stations. Locally, it provided a forum for farmers to discuss their mutual problems and fostered cooperative efforts, social meetings, and educational programs. Chapters operated in almost every valley town, with membership reaching a peak during 1950 to 1955. Today, the remaining ten chapters are primarily social but Grange booths can still be seen every year at the Santa Clara County Fair.

Co-ops and the Populist Movement. The depression of the 1890s affected agriculture no less than industrial cities. The ordinary citizen, particularly the farmer, saw the common enemy as big business, the railroads, and bankers. The Populist movement, begun in Texas, spread across the United States like wildfire. Suddenly, more agricultural co-ops were organized in order to put control in the hands of the growers.

In California, the part of the Populist platform that called for greater government involvement in economic affairs, including agriculture, bore fruit in the Cooperative Marketing Act, passed by the state legislature in 1895. In 1915 Governor Hiram Johnson, who had come to office on a platform to rid California's government of the political influence of the Southern Pacific Railroad, established the Commission Market Act, headed by Colonel Weinstock. Its original purpose was to put the state into the business of marketing produce, but the idea failed to gain backing among growers or packers. Weinstock was successful, however, in fomenting the cooperative movement, especially in Santa Clara County. Other marketing acts on the state level followed in the depressed 1930s. The most important was the Marketing Act of 1937, which called for special boards to be established to deal with marketing prunes, peaches, plums and pears, among other crops.[17]

While the Populist party failed, its philosophy ultimately triumphed, changing the nature of the national government.[18]

By 1929, under Herbert Hoover, the Federal Marketing Act and the Federal Farm Board were established. This program of aid to agriculture culminated under Franklin D. Roosevelt, whose Federal Marketing Act of 1937 forced the farmers to organize and cooperate in spite of themselves. In the same tradition, the Prune Marketing Act of 1949, in response to the drop in farm prices and the loss of export markets following World War II, established a federal Prune Marketing Committee.[19]

Since this act was passed, the Dried Fruit Association of California (DFA), which still has its headquarters in Santa Clara County, has been the inspecting agency that checks on the quality of dried fruit. The DFA is a cooperative venture, financed by fees based on tonnage, begun by growers and packers in 1908 to monitor quality control themselves. Its organization was inspired by the national Pure Food and Drug Act of 1906, which set higher standards for meat packers, food processors, and canners. Its function is to maintain fruit size and standards, including cleanliness, and to monitor surpluses so that the market is not flooded. The DFA also checks the end product for quality on behalf of the consumer. I well remember the inspectors sent out from this organization to check every batch of prunes we processed for water content, cleanliness, and size.[20] In 1952 the California Prune Advisory Board (now the California Prune Board) was created by the State of California to promote the virtues of prunes and assist those who grow them. It consists of fourteen growers, seven handlers, and one public member who represents the consumer. The efforts of the state and federal governments are coordinated by naming the same two persons as chairman and manager of both the California Prune Board and the Prune Marketing Committee.

Today the federal government is further represented in Santa Clara County by the Agricultural Marketing Service, which regulates the quality of finished products, whether canned, dehydrated (aside from prunes), or frozen, and checks on the sizing by food processors, lest the grower is cheated on the true quality and quantity of what he has brought from his fields. The service monitors the tonnage of the surplus market and promotes research and advertising for specific crops.

Co-ops Before Sunsweet. The 1890s proved to be an important decade for the cooperative movement in Santa Clara County. Among the most successful was the Santa Clara County Fruit Exchange, incorporated in 1892 to handle dried fruit.[21] In 1891, the West Side Fruit Growers Association was formed. It was followed in 1892 by the Campbell Fruit Growers Union, which lasted until 1913. Both were brought into the County Fruit Exchange. In the meantime a national group, the Farmers Cooperative and Educational Union, developed several branches in Santa Clara County. By 1905 this co-op, which fostered education for farmers and packer unions to improve markets, was called the National Farmers Union. A local branch formed in 1909, the Campbell Farmers Union Packing Company, was so successful that the national president, Charles Barrett, came to visit the packing plant in 1911. The California Farmers Cooperative and Educational Union promoted local packing unions as well.

Many improvements came into being as a result of the efforts of these groups. These included a more economical method of drying fruit, standardization of sizes (important in improving the marketing and attractiveness of fruit), and greater collective bargaining power for sellers.[22] Nevertheless, for different reasons, each group failed. The farmers who signed into the County Fruit Exchange, for instance, were not required to sell all their fruit to it, an omission that undercut the effectiveness of its marketing effort. The exchange lasted until 1916.

The first statewide co-op for dried fruit was the California Cured Fruit Association, formed in 1900.[23] One thousand growers gathered together in San Jose in 1900, but their plan to capture the market failed: nature produced a crop so large in 1900 and 1901 that it could not be sold. The association was liquidated in 1903, though not before building a large dried fruit packing house in Santa Clara that later became the home of Rosenberg Brothers. Its breakup gave growers cold feet concerning dried fruit co-ops for several years.

Meanwhile, in another effort to organize the fresh fruit growers the California Fresh Fruit Exchange was created in 1901. As the California Fruit Exchange it is still in existence; its best-quality brand is sold under the label of Blue Anchor. By 1931 it was marketing 22.7 percent of the fresh deciduous-tree fruits and 9.7 percent of the fresh grapes shipped out of the state.[24] This co-op operates on the so-called federated plan by which local exchanges deliver their produce to central shipping points, such as San Francisco. Shipping efforts are then coordinated for the benefit of all. The California Fruit Exchange represents the local chapters as shippers and handlers, marketing the fruit for the total co-op. The exchange goes beyond marketing and buys standing forests to supply farmers with wood for their fruit boxes. Thus the threat of big business has inspired a big-business response—one that works.

The Triumph of Sunsweet. As the state's first market commissioner, Colonel Weinstock gathered sympathetic people around him. One was Aaron Shapiro, an orphan who grew up to be the foremost legal authority on farm cooperatives in the world. Indeed, he was so successful that Henry Ford accused him of masterminding a worldwide Semitic plot to corner the world's food supply. Shapiro sued Ford and won, forcing a retraction and claiming a settlement of one dollar.

During 1915 and 1916 several meetings were held in San Jose on behalf of the dried fruit growers, who were angered because of packers' efforts to control the price of the 1915 crop, even before the blossoms had appeared.[25] The Prune and Apricot Growers Association had begun at a local improve-

ment club in the Cupertino area; it attracted people like R. Vince Garrod, prune grower and co-op supporter, from nearby Saratoga. "It is the belief of the average prune grower," Garrod recalls, "that the only handlers of prunes that have any humanity in them are the producers and the consumers."[26] Colonel Weinstock was there at the mass San Jose meetings and inspired the huge audience to action. Shapiro, whose office was in San Francisco, also attended the meetings. It was he who drew up the legal framework that added so much to the success of what would become Sunsweet.

By 1917, after many efforts on behalf of the dried fruit business had come to nothing, the Prune and Apricot Growers Association, using the brand name Sunsweet, emerged as a viable co-op for the state's dried apricots, peaches, and prunes. From its Santa Clara Valley headquarters it claimed the participation of 75 percent of the state's bearing acres of prunes and apricots. By 1963 Sunsweet had nine packing plants in the county, with the three in San Jose employing between a thousand and twelve hundred workers at the peak of the season. But even this organization failed to hold all the growers all of the time or even to prevent the growth of other co-ops in its own realm.

It was in 1961 that Santa Clara County's prune acreage was exceeded for the first time in history by another area: Sacramento. Sunsweet growers reorganized and moved out of Santa Clara County to Stockton. In the early 1970s the prune cooperative was joined by a walnut co-op and six years later, in 1980, by a raisin-and-fig co-op. They combined to better meet the rising challenge of corporate food conglomerates. They market under the names Sun-Maid Raisins, Diamond Walnuts, Sunweet Prunes, and Blue Ribbon Figs.

To Join or Not to Join? The depression of the 1930s gave rise to several other cooperative efforts. Among them was Orchard Supply Hardware, which retailed goods directly to the farmer and remained a co-op until 1980, when it was sold to the W. R. Grace Company. Then there was the Growers Market Cooperative, which created an outlet on Seventh and Taylor streets in San Jose for local farmers to sell produce directly to local trades. Restaurants, grocery stores, roadside stands (including ours), and fruit-and-vegetable peddlers—an occupation now lost to society—all bought there. At the same location today the privately owned Produce Market allows middlemen to continue the tradition.

A latecomer to this company was the Pear Growers League. Santa Clara County was the pear-growing center of the state. Pears were the county's third largest crop, behind prunes and apricots. The league was begun by twenty-five orchardists from Santa Clara and San Benito counties. While it did not market pears, it encouraged the development of markets, arbitrated disputes between canners and growers, and served to promote pears on the local and national levels. Eventually it boasted twenty-three hundred members who produced, in the 1940s and 1950s, about seventy thousand tons, or half the tonnage in the state. One of the largest pear growing groups in the nation, it was discontinued in 1978, by which time it had dwindled to twenty-two local members. The centers for pears today are Sacramento, Lake, and Mendocino counties.[27]

Another major farm organization that developed during the Depression was the Farm Bureau. Organized nationally in 1919, it began locally in 1933 as part of an effort to bring the Cooperative Extension Service to Santa Clara County, a move that did not succeed until World War II. Today the Farm Bureau is probably the most powerful lobby in Sacramento representing the farmer. Through Farm Pac, its political arm, it seeks to influence legislation in favor of the farmer. But the Farm Bureau also offers insurance coverage and farm labor service (to aid in union labor problems) as well as farm news through its publications, social and educational meetings, and discounts on goods and travel. In the 1950s and 1960s the local chapter was active in promoting legislation to protect farmlands from annexation and helped sponsor the Williamson Act (for which see Chapter 10).

Today the California Cattlemen's Association serves ranchers whose annual income in Santa Clara County in 1983 was over $5 million. Cattle and calf operations are still found scattered over the two hundred thousand or so acres behind Mount Hamilton and the upper reaches of the Santa Cruz Mountains. But the largest single crop in the county occupies only one percent of the available land. Cut flowers, chrysanthemums, roses, and carnations surpassed in value prunes when, in 1960, they were at their dollar peak of $20.3 million.[28] Flower cooperatives are organized along ethnic lines and represent the efforts of Japanese and Chinese American families to work together for their mutual benefit. Not only do these co-ops function as purchasing agents for their members but they are a major focus of each group's social activities. One such co-op is the California Chrysanthemum Growers Association, located in Palo Alto; it began in 1933 among Japanese growers intent on improving their bargaining position in the San Francisco market. Another is the Bay Area Chrysanthemum Growers Cooperative Association, begun by Chinese growers in 1935 and incorporated in 1957. The United Flower Growers Association, formed in 1979, is a splinter group of the latter.

While most farmers belong to such groups as the Farm Bureau, it takes a special mentality to join a co-op. Membership in a co-op involves one's profits as a grower. The quality of independence that characterizes the farmer's mentality runs counter to the concept of cooperative profits and of yielding control to others. This was noted very early by a grower. At the Thirtieth Fruit Growers' Convention in 1904, a Mr. Gordon put forth the rule by which farmers responded to the co-op movement: "You can get one-third of the growers together in an organization; these can get another third to join; but no power outside the Almighty can draw the other one-third in."[29]

Dad belonged chiefly to the last-named group. He joined a co-op in the 1930s, in the depths of the Depression. It was called Drew Canning Company. The secretary-treasurer, L. J. Campodonico, sent him a check dated December 19, 1932, along with the following letter. "We are enclosing herewith our check no. 1729 for $15.21, which represents the total net return on your 1931 Apricot deliveries to us. We regret that the return could not have been more but we believe you understand the conditions which were responsible for the return not being larger." Payment was for eight tons of apricots, or less than $2.00 per ton! Dad never forgot the experience— neither the Depression nor the co-op. The worn, folded letter was taken out of the cubbyhole in his rolltop desk whenever anyone spoke to him about joining a co-op.

But even he could change. During the 1950s he joined and helped to direct a local group of forty-two growers who sold their cherries packed in brine for maraschino. They were able to get a better price than buyers had been offering.[30] He also joined California Canners and Growers, a co-op formed by several formerly prosperous canneries as a means of financial survival. Though it grew to be the largest co-op in the nation, it filed for bankruptcy in 1983, after serious losses from the federal ban on the use of certain artificial sweeteners.[31]

One of the reasons Dad survived in the business was that he was able to establish long-lasting business relationships. As an example, shortly after World War II, through the efforts of its buyer John De Lury, Dad established such a relationship with H. J. Heinz Company. We have continued to sell it prunes for baby food ever since, and John became a close family friend. The moral is that a farmer could survive outside the co-ops. But I never had the feeling, while growing up within the business, that it was easy. The great masters of the farmer were still the weather, the markets, labor, and money. It would be wrong to think the beautiful blossoms reflected only tranquillity. Rather, life seemed a series of conflicts and disasters tempered by endurance, patience, frugality, and hard work.

Even so, the beauty of the landscape and being part of nature's unending cycle were among the highest rewards.

Notes

[1] Janet Lewis, *Against a Darkening Sky* (New York: Doubleday, Doran & Co., 1943), 73. This novel, one of the finest to come from a local author, illustrates the rural values and small-town nature of Santa Clara County before World War II. The lynching in the novel echoes the infamous lynching that actually took place in San Jose in 1933: see articles by Harry Farrell in *San Jose Mercury-News*, Nov. 29 and 30, 1983.

[2] E. J. Wickson, *The California Fruits and How to Grow Them*, 6th ed. (San Francisco: Pacific Rural Press, 1912), 55.

[3] Foote, *Pen Pictures*, 264. Foreign markets were available for certain fruits, particularly pears and grapes, which could withstand the long journey by ship. During World War II, Santa Clara Valley produce was sent to many countries, including England. As soon as the war ended, the English placed an embargo on fresh pear imports to protect their own industry.

[4] The Gould orchards were planted near the site of Santa Clara County's only Mexican War battle, the Battle of the Mustard Stalks, so called because it was so tame. While the orchard was on the corner of Scott Lane and El Camino Real, the battle was just north, halfway between Scott Lane and Lawrence Station Road (now Lawrence Expressway).

[5] J. P. Munro-Fraser, *History of Santa Clara County* (San Francisco: Alley, Bowen & Co., 1881), 528.

[6] "The Experimental-Vineyard Plot at Cupertino," *Bulletin of the Agricultural Experiment Station*, no. 59 (Berkeley: University of California, Nov. 26, 1886).

[7] W. L. Howard and W. T. Horne, "Brown Rot of Apricots," *Bulletin of the Agricultural Experiment Station*, no. 236 (Berkeley: University of California Press, 1921), 71–88.

[8] Lysle D. Leach, "University Plant Pathologist at Davis: Memoir of Lysle D. Leach," interview by A. I. Dickman and F. J. Hill, 1983, Oral History Office, Shields Library, University of California at Davis, 20. Professor Leach states that during the time he was at the Deciduous Fruit Station, in 1928, it was in a small cottage on Settle Avenue in Willow Glen. He also indicates that the Mountain View Station was closed.

[9] Telephone conversation with Peter Lert, agent at the Cooperative Extension service for many years, Dec. 29, 1982; and with Frances King, secretary, Dec. 28, 1982.

[10] Robert W. Harper, "History of Regulatory Entomology in California," *California Department of Agriculture Bulletin* 47, no. 4 (Oct.–Dec. 1959): 202.

[11] Edward M. Ehrhorn, "Santa Clara County," in *Report of State Board of Horticulture* (Sacramento: State Printing Office, 1895–96), 156; Patricia Loomis, "Signposts: Agricultural Agency History," *San Jose Mercury-News*, Mar. 16, 1980.

[12] Interview with Gordon Spencer, Joe Ferrari, and Roger Bibb of the Santa Clara County Department of Agriculture, Dec. 17, 1982.

[13] E. J. Wickson, *Rural California* (New York: Macmillan 1923), 288.

[14] Erich Kraemer, H. E. Erdman, "History of Cooperation in the Marketing of California Fresh Deciduous Fruits," *Bulletin of the Agriculture Experiment Station*, no. 557 (Berkeley: University of California, September 1933), 8.

[15] James, *History of San Jose*, 126. The first president of the State Horticultural Society was E. W. Hilgard of the College of Agriculture at Berkeley; its first secretary was E. J. Wickson, editor of the *Pacific Rural Press* and later dean of the College of Agriculture at Davis. Their participation reflects the close ties between cooperative ventures and the colleges.

[16] Kraemer and Erdman, "History of Cooperation in the Marketing of California Fresh Deciduous Fruits," 23.

[17] California Department of Agriculture, "Division of Marketing," *Thirty-Fourth Annual Report* (Sacramento: State Printing Office, Dec. 31, 1953), 345; ibid., "California Agricultural Marketing Programs," *Bulletin* 45, no. 1 (Jan.–Mar. 1956): 2–7; ibid., "Bureau of Markets," *Bulletin* 50, no. 2 (Apr.–June 1961): 100–105.

[18] For a discussion of the effect of the Populists on federal policy see, Carl N. Degler, *Out of Our Past* (New York: Harper Colophon Books, 1959), 333–37.

[19] For a discussion of the background to this act, see Robert Couchman, *The California Prune Industry and Its Problems*, ed. Carrol K. Hurd, reprint of articles in *San Jose Mercury-News*, Sunday issue, Ranch-Home-Garden sec., as follows: in 1948, Nov. 7, Nov. 14, Dec. 12, Dec. 26; in 1949, Jan. 2, Jan. 9, Feb. 6, Mar. 20, Mar. 27, Apr. 3, May 15, May 22 (San Jose, n.d.).

[20] A special device is manufactured in San Jose that measures the moisture in prunes. Some growers liked to plump up their prunes with water to increase their weight; hence the concern for water content.

[21] James, *History of San Jose*, 134.

[22] Robert Couchman, *The Sunsweet Story* (San Jose: Sunsweet Growers, 1967), 29. Couchman's book is the most complete history of the cooperative movement and the dried fruit industry. See also *San Jose Mercury-News, Sunshine, Fruit and Flowers*, 202.

[23] James, *History of San Jose*, 143; Couchman, *The Sunsweet Story*, 31.

[24] Kraemer and Erdman, "History of Cooperation in the Marketing of California Fresh Deciduous Fruits," 118; for a history of the California Fruit Exchange see: ibid., 44–68. One of the local growers who served as director of the California Fruit Exchange and president of its Santa Clara Valley chapter was Henry G. Stelling (1874–1934), whose family name remains on Stelling Road in Cupertino.

[25] Couchman, *The Sunsweet Story*, 48–53. For a brief history of the co-ops that joined to form the present Sun-Diamond co-op, see "The History of Sun-Diamond Companies," *Sun-Diamond Grower*, June–July, 1981, 28; Aug.–Sept., 1981, 20; Oct.–Nov., 1981, 28.

[26] R. V. Garrod, *Saratoga Story* (Saratoga, Calif.: the author, 1962), 161; for a personal account of the formation of Sunsweet, see 152–66.

[27] Rick Carroll, "How the Pears Got Bulldozed," *San Francisco Chronicle*, Jan. 27, 1978.

[28] Santa Clara County Department of Agriculture, Environmental Management Agency, *Crop Report, 1981* (San Jose, 1982).

[29] Kraemer and Erdman, "History of Cooperation in the Marketing of California Fresh Deciduous Fruits," 120.

[30] "Path to a Future, "*San Jose Mercury News*, July 9, 1950.

[31] "Cal Can Files for Bankruptcy Law Protection," *San Francisco Chronicle*, June 14, 1983, 49.

Other Sources for Chapter 8

For the auction system, see Henry D. Greene, "Auctions— Serving our Greatest Fruit Markets," *The Blue Anchor*, Oct. 1934, 8.

R. V. Garrod, *Confidential Report of Cupertino-Saratoga Prune and Apricot Growers Association*, April 24, 1962, Higgins Collection, Shields Library, University of California at Davis.

Charles Simon Barrett, first president of the National Farmers Union, served from 1906 to 1928. He details his experiences in *The Mission, History and Times of the Farmer's Union* (Nashville: Marshall & Bruce Co., 1909). A good history of populism is Lawrence Goodwyn, *Democratic Promise: The Populist Moment in America* (New York: Oxford University Press, 1976). The 1908 *Articles of Incorporation* of the Dried Fruit Association (author's collection) give an interesting picture of the association's membership and purposes. Information on the Federal Marketing Service in San Jose was gathered from a phone conversation with Salvador Morales, Fruit and Vegetable Division of Processed Agricultural Products, Jan. 22, 1984.

For the Japanese family nursery, see especially Hiroji Kariya, ed., *Kiku Kumiai: Fifty Years* (Palo Alto: California Chrysanthemum Growers Association, 1981), a history of the association that includes photographs of early nurseries as well as personal comments and reminiscences. The comparable Chinese experience is treated in Mike Culbertson, "The Chinese Involvement in the Development of the Flower Industry in Santa Clara County," in *Chinese Argonauts*, ed. Gloria Sun Hom (Los Altos Hills: Foothill Community College, 1971), 46–59.

My father's favorite cherry tree, planted in 1906, blooming in
1979. When these blossoms turned into fruit, the tree, too
heavily laden, blew down in a windstorm.

Michelle, our daughter (1963–1982), at the family fruit stand, 1979.

Eastern foothills of Evergreen district, San Jose, as seen from
Charles Kuhn's ranch, Yerba Buena Road, 1981. At present
these foothills are classified agricultural, but for how long?

We always helped my mother bottle fruit from the orchard at the end of the season, just as our children have helped me (1980 photo).

French prunes ready to enter dehydrator at Bianchi Brothers farm in Berryessa district, 1980. Lack of prune trees in today's district has reduced commercial customers for dehydrator to two.

Eiichi Sakauye, whose family settled in Santa Clara County in 1906, continues to care for pear trees around his house on Trimble Road, San Jose.

Anita Chan of Chan Nurseries in Berryessa district of San Jose
gathers long-stem roses, 1984. Nursery business today
produces largest agricultural crop in Santa Clara County.

Robert T. Butcher stands before plum tree on six acres remaining from original 160-acre farm, in family for one hundred years, at Butcher's Corner, Santa Clara.

Oil painting by E. Standish in 1929 captures the "Valley of
Heart's Delight" when it most fully deserved the title. Painting
was widely reproduced as an inducement to settle in Santa
Clara County. *Courtesy Ralph Rambo*

CHAPTER 9
TECHNOLOGY, RESEARCH, AND FARMING

OUR FARM IS A RELIC. Strewn in and around the buildings, barns, and sheds are artifacts, junk, or scrap metal, depending on your viewpoint. It was because of his conservative nature that my father kept so many pieces of the past. I once asked him what was the worst period of history that he lived through, fully expecting him to respond, The Depression. But I was mistaken. He said, "Right now, this is the worst. In the Depression, when you had a dollar, it was worth something. Today money isn't worth much."[1]

As of most farmers, it was part of him to save, not only cash, but anything that might be useful in the future. Like the biblical Joseph, he stored up through the fat years in order to survive the lean. And he expected the lean years all through his life. He spent little on himself. At the time of his death, his personal possessions amounted to two gold watches he had inherited from his father, his few clothes, and a reputation for being both a good farmer and a good man. Referring to that reputation, he once told me, "It took me a lifetime to build."

It wasn't a case of deferred spending, fulfilling some life's dream in the future. It was a question of living one's dream, as a working farmer. This was the end in itself. Money was for saving against illness and future uncertainties. Land was the solid base with which he, like so many others, hedged his bets: if worst came to worst, you could grow your own food and survive. If this philosophy sounds as if it comes from a different age, it does.

As a result of Dad's thrifty habits, our farm has a collection of "things" that, taken together, summarize a great deal of the farming technology of Santa Clara County. This tendency to save old equipment characterizes almost all the remaining family farms I have visited. In one corner of a barn or behind a building there is the usual pile of leftovers, some from half a century ago. I had seen these objects all my life but never realized what they meant until now. A tour of the farm and its buildings revealed an old oak shaft that had been used to harness a horse and connect it to a buggy, wagon, or imple-

ment. There was a leather horse collar, with reins attached, still on the nail it was hung on when last used. An old wagon that had been converted into an irrigation sprinkler cart stood in a corner, now reduced to its iron wheels. My grandfather's scythe hung on a nail; its sharp blade and oaken snath reminded one of the Grim Reaper. There was a plow whose wooden handles are gone that my father had used originally for plowing close to tomato plants.

I do not remember plow horses, but my sister Jeanette, five years older than I, remembers a workhorse in our barn. Of course, my aunt remembered them only too well and was not sorry that they had passed into history. Within one generation, within a few years, what had been familiar to everyone, had become a relic of another era. Almost all of the implements were made locally. There were many suppliers of plows in the valley; foundries tended to specialize in them. While Robert Knapp had first designed his reversible plow to follow behind a horse (see Chapter 4), he soon adapted it to follow behind a tractor.

These horse-drawn implements remind me of Mr. Joy, the last blacksmith in Sunnyvale. A visit to his shop gave one the feeling that important work was being done, somewhat mysteriously. The old building on Washington Street was always dark. Inside, by the glow of the hot-burning embers, one saw Mr. Joy himself. He was of medium height. He always wore a leather apron and cap, and was smudged with the coals he worked with. A short cigar stuck out from the corner of his mouth; he took it out occasionally in order to spit. The smell of the shop, the long-pronged tools, the white heat, and the dipping of the red-hot metal in water created a respect for his craft.

Like the tinsmith who traveled from house to house with his cart, the blacksmith has become part of our national past. We did have a tinsmith come to the farm. He sharpened knives for my mother and, in earlier days, made pots and pans and utensils to order. While the tinsmith was looked upon with some distrust, since he moved from community to community,

202

the blacksmith was part of the town's backbone. His shop was an institution where people met, exchanged useful information, and communicated their personal news. No farm could go very long without a visit to the blacksmith. Even in my day, after the horses were retired, my father took small metalworking jobs to Mr. Joy.

Farm Technology and Food Machinery Corporation. Probably one of the firms most represented on our farm (we have at least three spray rigs built by it) is Food Machinery Corporation (FMC), which grew to be an international business, but which began as the result of a Yankee farmer-inventor's frustration over the insects in his almond orchard. His story illustrates how many farm problems were solved by the farmer's own inventiveness. It also proves that Santa Clara County was a beehive of research and development long before the electronics revolution and the silicon chip. Indeed, not only was the county a focus of fruit growing and food processing, it was also the center of research in fields relating to every aspect of food, from breeding plants to tilling the soil, from canning food to marketing it through co-ops.

John Bean settled in Los Gatos in 1883. He was from Michigan and Ohio. In the early 1850s he developed the first double-acting force pump—a continuous-flow turbine—for wells. It is still in use throughout the world.[2] In Los Gatos he soon discovered that his orchard, like his neighbors', was infested with San Jose scale, and that the only spray pump available was ineffective. Bean went to work, using the same continuous-flow principle, and developed a high-pressure, air-chamber pump that produced a continuous spray. This small, hand-held pump was patented in 1884. He formed the John Bean Spray Company two years later.

D. C. Crummey, son-in-law of John Bean, took over the business when Bean retired and moved it to San Jose, where he founded a corporation, today the fifty-seventh largest in the world. His son John D. Crummey transformed the small company into Food Machinery Corporation. Its early success re-

sulted from its ability to absorb many other small companies that excelled at specific tasks. For example, the Ostenberg brothers designed a highly successful two-cylinder, four-cycle gasoline engine that was put on the market in 1903 for general farm use. In 1912 Bean bought it out and renamed it the Bean Opposed Engine.[3] He also absorbed the Caton Foundry, which made agricultural implements for valley farms. It was here that my grandfather worked in 1910, riding back and forth between Sunnyvale and San Jose on his bicycle, even in the rain.

Bean's most significant merger was in 1928, when his own company joined Anderson-Barngrover Manufacturing Company to form Food Machinery Corporation. Anderson-Barngrover, formed in San Jose in 1902, made every sort of farm equipment. One of their specialties was a machine that immersed cling peaches in a mild caustic solution, loosening the skin that was then stripped from the fruit in a fresh-water bath. This lye process, in other variations, helped to make cling peaches the primary canned food product of California after 1902.[4]

Another piece of equipment with a place in our collection is a sorter that jogs dried fruit over grates with different-sized holes. It was made by the Smith Manufacturing Company, which also joined the big merger of Food Machinery Corporation in 1928. My father remembered buying it directly from John S. Smith, who made it. Someone offered to buy it from my father, but wasn't willing to pay what my father thought it was worth, so there it sits, in a shed.

The Tractor

In evidence at several locations on our farm are small gasoline engines. They are used for a multitude of purposes, including the running of the fruit graders and sorters, the pumps that bring water up from the wells, the wood saws, and the spray rigs. As their presence shows, the most important innovation

Courtesy Department of Special Collections, University of California Library, Davis

on farms in this century was the change from horsepower to the internal combustion engine. The first replacement of animal power was by steam power. The next major step, internal combustion, opened up new possibilities. Not only the automobile but the gasoline tractor were to change the farmer's life.

While my grandfather did not buy a tractor immediately, he did buy one by the end of World War I. His first spray rig was also bought then. The horses were kept despite the early mechanization; they were cheaper than the new equipment. As the horses went out of use, more land became available for the planting of trees since the farmer no longer needed ten acres to keep his horses in feed. The freeing of these acres helped to boost the number of acres in trees during the 1920s. Also, Prohibition hit the United States in 1920 and existing vineyards in Santa Clara County were being planted with trees

between the rows.[5] These two factors contributed to the jump in orchard lands and the record high of some 125,000 acres in trees during the 1920s.

There are few people today who could tell you anything about the numerous efforts to establish a tractor industry in Santa Clara County. I know because efforts to trace its existence, sparked by a comment my father made to the effect that the Johnson tractor was made in Sunnyvale, proved to be very difficult. But there is no doubt that such an industry existed. Among the individual inventor-engineers was Alf Johnson, who grew weary of cultivating his father's orchards in Woodland, near Sacramento, with a horse and plow and took steps to develop a field tractor especially for tree farming. Alf and his brother got parts from Stockton for the first model, which sold immediately to a waiting farmer. They were among the first to make use of a three-wheeled design, a tricycle, for a tractor. Their machine weighed 2,700 pounds and had a two-cycle motor. It was especially useful for orchard purposes. In 1907 they opened their own company in Sunnyvale, responding to W. E. Crossman's offer of land at good rates for industry. The Johnson Tractor Company was a success: according to their publicity material, orders far outstripped production.[6]

In 1912 the Johnsons' design was bought out by Hendy Iron Works of Sunnyvale, which claimed that "it replaces horses for every farm work." Hendy then sold it to Rumely Products Company of Indiana, which advertised it for several years in an effort to enter the small tractor field. By now it was competing with the crawler tractors put on the market by the Yuba, Best, and Holt companies. The crawler is a track-lay design that works effectively in orchards, even when the ground is slightly wet. Johnson continued to experiment. Several tractors later he developed a one-track machine he sold to the John Bean Company, which promoted it heavily during World War I.[7] Eventually, Bean went out of the tractor business. Alf Johnson remained with the company, which made another attempt to break into the tractor field in the late 1940s, with Johnson in charge of tractor design. In the meantime, FMC concentrated on food processing equipment, farm machinery, fertilizers, and sprays, as well as war materials.

Despite the variety of technological experiments, the main consideration with farmers was price. The most popular tractor was the one that could be bought the most reasonably. That was the Fordson, which sold for only $500. The 1917 model was a 20-horsepower one with 1,000 RPM and four cylinders. Since the frame was made from two pieces of cast iron bolted together, it became a favorite of junk dealers in later years.[8] Eventually the Caterpillar, developed by Holt Company of Stockton and Best Company of Elmhurst, California (they merged in 1925), became the farm tractor that we used almost exclusively. To supply these machines an underground gasoline tank with a hand-turned pump was installed sometime before 1920. The pump is still in use.

New Plant Varieties

While inventors were developing new machinery to aid the farmer in tilling the soil, plant breeders were developing new varieties to improve his chances of successful, salable crops. The university experimental station did a great deal of plant research, but cross-pollination to produce the varieties in question was often done by individuals working on their own in Santa Clara County.

The walnut trees that lined our driveway were developed by George C. Payne, descendant of an early American pioneer to the county. Raised in Campbell on a hundred-acre farm, Payne worked for Luther Burbank for one year budding and grafting. He developed the Payne seedling around the turn of the century, and it is still a standard in California. He is credited with being the first horticulturist in the state to succeed in grafting walnut trees commercially.[9] Another developer of a new walnut was our neighbor, Frank C. Willson, a nurseryman of Sunnyvale, who in 1910 brought out the Willson Wonder Nut, so called because it is the size of a small fist. His orchard, with Pastoria Avenue running through it under lush walnut trees, became a local attraction because of the care he lavished on it. These were successful varieties. Others were tried for a while and then forgotten. John Rock developed the Imperial prune in 1886; it was planted in our prune orchard, among others, but today is largely out of favor. Frank Leib of Wayne Station developed the walnut, Leib Royal, in conjunction with California Nursery in the 1920s. The list could go on.

A major breakthrough in strawberry culture took place in 1945, when U.C. Davis released five new varieties. The parents of those plants were developed at the Deciduous Fruit Field Station in San Jose, where research in strawberry culture is concentrated. Two of the five, the Shasta and the Lassen, took hold commercially, and were grown by local berry growers. James T. Imahara rented land at Dawson Corners (at Wolfe Road and Reed Lane), and three generations of

Imaharas worked the strawberry fields. The Lassen and Shasta were the varieties my mother bought from the Imahara family to sell at our fruit stand. There were many other discoveries at the field station, including controls for disease affecting raspberries, walnut blight, apricot brown rot, and strawberry mites, and a special canning tomato that resisted wilt—no small contribution, considering the size of the tomato canning industry. Important work was also done on root stocks resistant to oak root fungus, olive wilt, and the cultural problems of the pear. Today, along with research on deciduous fruits, the station emphasizes research on minimum irrigation, minimum-maintenance grasses for landscaping, and ornamental trees and shrubs for the urban environment.[10]

The Smudge Pot

Among the most devastating natural disasters that could hit an orchard was early frost. A farmer might lose up to ninety percent of his crop long before the fruit was due to appear on the trees. An air heater known as a "smudge pot" was first used on a large scale in Los Angeles about 1896, to keep the citrus buds, deciduous fruit crops, and vineyards from freezing. The pot was filled with oil, coal, or other fuel, which was then burned, warming the air just enough to prevent ruin. Those of us who experienced the smudge pot are not likely to forget waking in the cold chill of early spring to find a dark soot hanging in the air for miles around.

One of the most popular models of pot in our county was the one designed by J. P. Bolton, a U.S. Weather Bureau official in Fresno. It contained two gallons of fuel which were fired with a torch. The pot was manufactured in San Francisco by J. P. Bolton Company and the torches in Santa Clara Valley by American Can Company. Another essential device was a thermometer that tripped an alarm to wake the weary farmer, usually between two to four in the morning when the temperature dipped to the danger point below 34 degrees Fahrenheit. A difference of two degrees could spell disaster. The exact temperature that would doom the crop depended on whether or not the trees or vines were in bud or blossom, and on the lay of the land; the low places were particularly susceptible.[11]

This process of lighting up open pots of oil had obvious drawbacks. If the housewife put out her laundry and failed to take it in the same day, it was blackened. Stores would find their merchandise sooted over. Efforts to lessen the pollution created new types of smudge pots, including the return-stack-gas heater.[12] Although these reduced the amount of soot in the air, "smudging" was banned in the 1950s, when air quality became a political issue, and newer methods were tried. Our smudge pots were buried after a propeller was installed to circulate the air above the apricot orchard. Some of the oil cans are still in a shed.

Innovations in Dried Fruit Production

The dehydrator was as conspicuous a feature in August and September as the smudge pot had been in February and March. You could hear it as well as smell it. Along with the sweet scent of prunes a droning sound, persistent but not unpleasant, filled the surrounding air. These were the tell-tale indications that a dehydrator was nearby. Ours was just twenty steps from our house, and we went to sleep and woke to its familiar traits. So that the prunes did not overdry, my father or a workman got up in the middle of the night to change the cars, which were on rail tracks embedded in cement. Trays, laden with prunes spread evenly for drying, were stacked on the cars.

As many as 250 million pounds of prunes a year came from Santa Clara County orchards by the 1950s. The small prune farmer with five or ten acres usually sold his crop to a farmer who had built his own dry yard or to an established commercial dryer. Fresh prunes were delivered in boxes by wagons to the yard and weighed. The grower was paid by the pound. Some growers chose to do their own drying and then sell to a dried fruit packing house. If a grower went to the trouble to set up a dry yard, he generally would buy fruit from other growers and pack the dried fruit himself, becoming a processor. This was what my father did in 1938. The new barn—the big one described in Chapter 1—was built that year to accommodate the prunes that he bought fresh, dried himself, packed in wooden boxes or one-hundred-pound sacks, and resold. Some small, family operated plants have grown into much larger enterprises, such as the Rubino family's Valley View Packing Company. There are also some small independant dry yards still in existence, handling as few as 25 tons. At the peak of operations in the 1960s, my father handled 700 tons; the average was more like 300 to 400 tons.

Although sun drying had proved to be more economical and superior to the nineteenth-century version of the dehydrator, the drawback of the sun was that you couldn't assume it wouldn't rain. It did rain in September 1918, for three days, just when the county's huge crop of prunes lay on the ground drying. Charles Forge recorded in his diary for September 12 that the day's rainfall was 3.5 inches! While efforts were made to save the crop, including the enlistment of World War I trainees from Camp Fremont in Menlo Park to stack the trays of fruit, they were of no avail. Someone quipped that, with the rotting fruit lying on the ground, the county smelled like "a distillery in distress."

Shortly thereafter, scientists at U.C. Davis began to research a dehydrator run on gasoline. Professor A. W. Christie of Davis worked with Romolo L. Puccinelli, an independent inventor whose father had a prune orchard in Los Gatos. This Davis team successfully developed a mechanical dehydrator that Puccinelli was allowed to patent and sell successfully throughout the United States and abroad.[13] Henry M. Griffoul, of San Jose, also designed and manufactured dehydrators Our dehydrator, built by Griffoul in 1938, has been abandoned; hundreds of prune boxes, no longer used, are stored on top of it. While the volume of prunes that my father and brother handled decreased, the cost of gasoline rose. The

dehydrator was no longer economical to operate. Since the gasoline crisis of 1976, Olson prunes have been sent to Dominic and Sonny Bianchi in Berryessa, who are among the last small commercial dryers in Santa Clara County. Despite the cost of trucking the prunes about thirty miles each way, it is still cheaper for the Bianchis—now down from serving twenty growers to two—to dry them than for my brother to do it himself.

When dried prunes emerge from the dehydrator, they are tough and need to be boiled or steamed to soften them for eating. In 1933 Sunsweet (then still called the Prune and Apricot Growers Association) placed softened prunes on the market in small, two-pound containers. These "Tenderized" prunes, as Sunsweet advertised them, were received well by the public, and it was not long before the competition developed its own version. In 1937 a scientist with Richmond-Chase Company, Paul Wilbur (he later joined FMC), developed a new thermal method by which the prunes were sterilized, softened, and packaged in airtight paper containers. In the meantime Sunsweet introduced foil-wrapped packaging to keep the prunes moist.

Paul Mariani, Jr., son of my father's one-time business partner, added another step. Paul senior had come to this country from Yugoslavia and worked his way up from dishwasher in San Francisco to cooper in the Napa Valley, then up the farm ladder from hired hand to fruit buyer to landowner to dried fruit processor. He joined Dad in a partnership during the early years of World War II, when the federal government was looking for independent operators to bid on jobs for prunes they bought for the war effort. Paul junior took the family business into the realm of international agribusiness. While studying for his degree in pomology at U.C. Davis in the 1940s, he did work in the food technology department under Professor Emil Mrac. Research was being conducted on food packaging, and Paul introduced a new process that keeps dried fruit moist and soft in see-through packages. Known as "moist pack", the method is standard in the industry today. He also helped develop the modern freeze-dry process to preserve fresh fruit.[14] Yet another innovation to come from Santa Clara County was the pitted prune for commercial sale. John Cantoni of Sunsweet developed a special machine for this purpose, and by 1965 the pitted prune had entered the market.[15] It is not an exaggeration to say that the manner in which the consumer buys dried prunes today reflects Santa Clara County technology.

The Canneries

Similar credit can be given to Santa Clara County's canning firms, which dominated the state's canning industry from before the turn of the century until the 1970s. In order to keep abreast of the competition the major canneries maintained research and development laboratories, and the resulting innovations helped maintain the dominance of the valley's industry. During the 1930s and 1940s the county produced as much as ninety percent of California's output. From 1950 through the end of the 1970s it still produced at least one-third—and California produces more canned goods than any other state. In 1977 the County produced no fewer than sixty million cases of canned fruits and vegetables.

The history of preserving food in pressurized containers can be traced back to the early years of the nineteenth century. The first food packing companies on the West Coast were established during the 1850s in San Francisco, close to the source of produce in the outlying Bay Area counties; they used containers made of glass. Tinplate was imported from the East in 1862; that first box of it cost sixteen dollars in gold. Eventually the word "can" came into use and "canning" became an accepted term for the common practice of preserving foods. Cans were made by hand; fruit or vegetables were stuffed through a hole in the top of the can, which was then sealed and boiled to cook the produce and also to create a vacuum. The hand-soldered can was replaced in 1911 by the more sanitary three-piece can. This innovation introduced the present mechanized process, and, as we shall see, Santa Clara County played an important part in its development.

For home canning the reusable glass jar, developed by John Landis Mason in the 1850s, was a staple of farm and nonfarm families alike. We had dozens that were filled during the summer, emptied in winter, and reused the next season. Canning was officially part of the housewife's province, but in practice the whole family participated. My job was scrubbing the jars in hot, soapy water. My sister helped my mother fill the jars with fruits and my father was there to tighten the screwcap lids.

It was no doubt a family tradition of this kind that resulted in the first commercial canning undertaken in Santa Clara County. Dr. and Mrs. James M. Dawson, who lived at 1370 The Alameda, in San Jose, gathered fruit and vegetables from their neighbors' kitchen gardens and put up three hundred cases in 1871, just two years after the transcontinental railroad. The canning was done on a wood stove in a 12-by-16-foot shed at the back of their modest house.[16] From these beginnings the San Jose Fruit Packing Company developed in 1873. Another company, Golden Gate Canning, was formed in 1875 under the leadership of George M. Bowman. Both canneries specialized in freestone peaches and each employed about three hundred workers, mostly women and children, during the canning season. In the meantime Dr. Dawson retired from San Jose Fruit Packing and, in 1879, opened the J. M. Dawson Packing Company in partnership with his son E. L. Dawson. Dr. Dawson's wife, Eloise Jones Dawson, took his place when he died in 1885. Notable too was the career of Elmer Chase, who rose from hired hand to president of Golden Gate, and went on to become a national leader in the canning industry. So did R. I. Bentley, later president of California Packing Company. Chase joined E. N. Richmond, a prune grower and dried fruit processor who had begun the E. N. Richmond Dried Fruit Company in 1916. Richmond-Chase Company, formed in 1919, became the largest independent dried fruit and canning operation in the United States. During World

Steamboats, scows, and schooners were a main mode of transport for agricultural products to San Francisco until the 1920s. Note the boxes of fruit stacked on the deck of this steamboat, c. 1895. *Courtesy San Jose Historical Museum*

The first cannery in San Jose, J. M. Dawson & Company, was housed here; it became the San Jose Fruit Packing Company in 1875, year of photo. Note fresh fruit arriving on one wagon (left), and canned goods, packed in boxes, emerging from the other. *Courtesy Sourisseau Academy*

Preparation of pears for canning at Schuckl & Co., Sunnyvale, 1930s; despite improvements. much work is still done by hand. Increasing mechanization has steadily reduced number of such jobs. Schuckl shut down in 1983. *Courtesy Fern Ohrt and Sunnyvale Historical Society and Museum Association*

Two-gallon Bolton smudge pots burn in an apricot orchard on
a frosty morning in 1953 to protect the fruit which is still in
blossom. *Courtesy* San Jose Mercury News

Fresh peaches arriving by train at Plant No. 7 of Richmond-Chase cannery, San Jose, 1927. Once largest independent canner in nation, company sold in 1958 to now defunct California Canners and Growers. *Courtesy E. N. Richmond II*

The Anderson-Barngrover Continuous Variable Discharge
Cooker and Cooler, a breakthrough in canning technology,
on display at Panama-Pacific International Exposition, San
Francisco, 1915. *Courtesy California History Center*

Mechanical shaker has replaced hand-held hooks to bring down walnuts (1960 photo). Same machine can shake prunes, which are caught as they fall by a canvas skirt fitted around the tree. *Courtesy* San Jose Mercury News

The effort to mechanize harvesting has resulted in machines like this one for picking field crops. While this is an improvement over stooping in the fields, harvesting is still hard work c. 1970. *Courtesy* San Jose Mercury News

Inside the Anderson-Barngrover plant in San Jose, c. 1915, where the continuous automatic cooker was made which automated the canning industy. *Courtesy FMC Corporation*

The first plane to land on Moffett Field, 1931. Farmer M. H. Holthouse (far right) listens as officials discuss the land deal in which he sold 100 acres to the government for Moffett Field. With this sale the land use changed from farming to one based on high-technology—the wave of the future in the Santa Clara Valley. *Courtesy Emma and Vernon Holthouse*

It takes a bulldozer less than a minute to push down a tree, a common sight in Santa Clara Valley since World War II.
Courtesy Santa Clara County Planning Department

IBM settles into the orchards in 1955 where Cottle Road meets
Monterey Highway and the Southern Pacific Railroad, south of
San Jose. *Courtesy Santa Clara County Planning Department*

Manufacture of silicon chips, here under way at Fairchild plant, San Jose, requires conditions of utmost cleanliness, as particles as small as atoms are implanted with great precision in pure silicon wafers no thicker than half a millimeter. *Courtesy Fairchild, a Schlumberger Company*

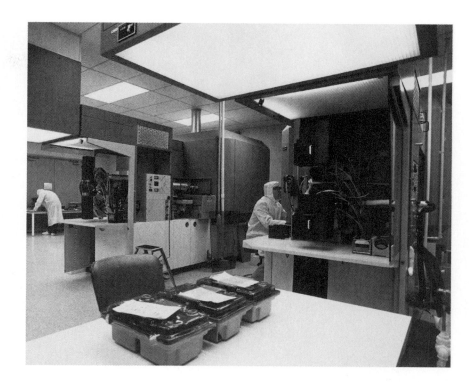

My brother Charles John Olson (right) and his son Charles Norman sort cherries at Olson Fruit Stand, 1980. *Courtesy Peninsula Times Tribune*

Ray Benech, standing in his pear orchard in Almaden Valley, 1982.

Pear orchard of Ray Benech family farm in Almadén Valley,
winter 1982.

Santa Clara Valley from Blossom Hill Road in Los Gatos, 1974.
A remnant of an apricot orchard provides one last place to run.
Courtesy San Jose Mercury News

War II, the company produced K rations for American soldiers under conditions of strict security.

Many other canneries failed or sold out or were absorbed. Some were so short-lived that there is no record of them beside their names on antique can labels. An example is The Woman's Cannery of San Jose. Some believe it may have been connected with Mrs. Dawson, but no evidence one way or the other has yet been uncovered.[17] Other canneries begun with or by women include Empson and Daughter, in Colorado (1887); Mrs. Lovejoy's A. L. Lovejoy and Sons, in Oregon (1880); Mary Ellen, begun by John and Mary Ellen Browning in Berkeley (1915); and Flotill Products, begun by Tillie Lewis in Stockton (1935). Freda Ehmann canned the first olives near Oroville in 1897; the first olive canning operation followed in 1902.

In 1916 five major companies merged. Each had acquired several canneries, many of them in Santa Clara County. The new giant, with sixty-one food processing plants, was called California Packing Corporation (CPC or Cal Pack, and later Calpak, were common names for it). It continues to sell, under the Del Monte label, and still maintains a dried fruit packing house on Bush Steet in San Jose—one of the few remaining links with the heyday of packers.

In some ways the early canneries paralleled the family farm system. They provided a vehicle for an individual to build a company into a family-owned enterprise that very often employed several family members from one or more generations. In many cases the canners either began as growers or later became growers, in order to improve their margin of profit. One such cannery that is still operating is Sun Garden, begun in 1941 by Frank DiNapoli and Joseph Perrucci. They actually developed two businesses, Sun Garden to can fresh fruits and vegetables and Mayfair to handle dried fruits. Today the third generation of each family is involved in both companies.

Out of these family-owned canneries new technology developed. There is Joseph Amori, for instance, who is married to a DiNapoli daughter and helped to found Sun Garden. As a seven-year-old child, his first job was helping to catch the rats that plagued San Jose after the 1906 earthquake; he, along with many others, was paid ten cents for each tail he could produce. He began working in the local canning industry at CPC. His invention, first marketed in 1947, was a machine that cuts and pits apricots. While not the first on the market, it is one of only two models available today. He also developed a similar machine for fresh Italian plums and, at the age of eighty-five, is working on a new processing device for the tomato canning industry.[18] Then there is Joseph Perrelli, one of the founders of Filice and Perrelli Company ("F & P"), who developed a special device that twists the pit out of the cling peach. The trade name "Filper" is still used in the industry to describe this machine, which leaves the center of the peach rough but wastes no fruit.[19]

But the most significant piece of canning equipment to come from Santa Clara County was an invention recognized by the American Society of Mechanical Engineers as a landmark in American technology. It was the Continuous Can Sterilizer, developed between 1912 and 1920 by Anderson-Barngrover and its engineer, Albert Thompson. Called the Sterilmatic, it revolutionized the canning industry by sterilizing, cooking, and cooling the cans in one continuous process. Before it was invented, cans had been moved by hand from one stage to the next. The Sterilmatic not only reduced the number of men required from fifteen to one, it also improved the product by introducing uniformity in cooking. Better flavor resulted as well. While it took some time for the machine to be accepted throughout the industry, it was used widely in the milk industry from the first. The basic principle is still employed in canning food.[20]

After the merger that formed FMC, Thompson became chief engineer. In the mid-1930s FMC developed a pear preparation machine that fed the pear into position, cored, halved, and peeled it—all work previously done by hand. The same company, during the 1940s and 1950s, did extensive research on adapting high thermal processes to canned food—research that has changed the process of canning. In 1983 FMC was given an award from the American Society of Mechanical Engineers for its Whole Fruit Juice Extractor. The research for this device, which squeezes juice from whole oranges, was done in Santa Clara County between 1946 and 1950. The machine was put on the market in 1950 and further refined over the years. Today it is used in thirty countries and has captured seventy percent of the international market.[21]

A partial list of "firsts" in the processed foods and canning industry of Santa Clara County would include the first western cannery to put up tomato paste (Greco Canning Company of San Jose), the first company to develop and market prune juice (Sunsweet), and the first to do the same for fruit nectars made from liquified whole ripe fruits such as pears, apricots, peaches, nectarines, and plums (Richmond-Chase with its Heart's Delight brand, named for the Valley of Heart's Delight). Richmond-Chase also pioneered in diet canned fruits, entering the market in 1945 with Diet Delight, and in techniques for freezing fruits and vegetables (Ed Mitchell, head of the Richmond-Chase laboratories, worked on them before World War II).[22] It was around this time that home freezing began. As a child I remember Dad freezing cherries for family use. We rented a small space at a freezer facility in Mountain View, located along the railroad track, and drove three miles to store or pick up our fruit. To continue the list of firsts, Barron-Gray Packing Company of San Jose, later bought by Hawaiian Pineapple Company, developed the first fruit cocktail in 1930, along with the special equipment needed to dice and mix the fruit. In 1938 it introduced the first commercially canned carrot juice.[23] After 1946 several local Santa Clara County canneries experimented with flash pasteurization, a process that prevented juices from separating and so resulted in the canned fruit juice so common on grocery shelves today.[24]

By 1960 Santa Clara County had a total of 85 canneries, 23 dried fruit plants, 25 frozen food operations and 85 fresh fruit and vegetable packers, plus numerous dehydrators—still the world's largest center for these industries. In 1983 there were only a handful of canneries, a few commercial dryers, and no frozen food operations left. Most of those firms that continue to survive are independent, family-owned businesses. Besides Sun Garden there is Stapleton-Spence Packing Company, Bonner Packing Company, and Wool Packing Company, the oldest cannery left in the valley. Begun in 1903 by F. G. Wool, it cans fruits, including fruit cocktail, and is managed by a third generation of the same family. Also a survivor is Diana Fruit Preserving Company, established in 1921 by a Yugoslavian immigrant, Alexander Diana. He was the first to develop a red dye for Maraschino-type cherries that did not stain the other fruits in fruit salad. While the business is no longer family owned, the founder's grandson Eugene C. Acronico serves as its president.

Only two national corporations, however, continue to be represented: Del Monte, a Reynolds company, and Beech-Nut Baby Food, owned by Nestlé. The high cost of water and energy, the problems of sewage disposal, the distance from the produce, and the decrease in the demand for canned goods have demoralized the local industry.[25]

The Effects of Technology

The mechanization of farming has helped to doom the small family-farm system. Even the family canneries have dwindled in number as they have been forced to cope with expensive new equipment, large-scale competition, and enormous expenses for energy and water. Producing small quantities of high-quality produce, the family farm has proved no match for the industrialized or corporate farm with its huge acreage and computer-controlled planting, harvesting, and marketing. The modern farm is often vertically integrated with a cannery that in turn is integrated with a merchandising outlet. The result is that the entire process of growing food may be controlled by one giant firm, like Tenneco, that even supplies the farmer with fertilizer, spray, and equipment.

226

Of course, mechanization has many advantages. Among them are the ten thousand or so articles the shopper can buy in a supermarket today compared with the three hundred of fifty years ago. Specialization has brought lower food prices relative to earning power. On the other side of the ledger is the fact that certain foods have lost flavor due to a number of factors: early picking to increase shelf life; controlled ripening processes and the use of gas to retard spoilage; concentration on varieties that are easy to harvest but less tasty; and the use of cosmetic materials to give a high gloss to certain fruits. The social health developed by the family-farm system is another price we have had to pay. In very few present-day occupations does an entire family work together for common ends.

Notes

[1] Author's Journal, May 11, 1979.

[2] George G. Bruntz, *History of Los Gatos* (Fresno: Valley Publishers, 1971), 30; F. Hal Higgins, "The Battle of the Bugs," *Pacific Rural Press*, Feb. 20, 1937, 267.

[3] I am indebted to R. D. Hamp of the Early Day Gas Engine & Tractor Association for materials on John Bean, on the Ostenberg Manufacturing Co., and on early tractors from Santa Clara County. Some information was also drawn from publicity material.

[4] Florence R. Cunningham, in *Saratoga's First Hundred Years*, ed. Frances Fox (Fresno: Valley Publishers, 1967), 15.

[5] Charles Sullivan, *Like Modern Edens*, Local History Studies, vol. 28 (Cupertino: California History Center, 1982), 115.

[6] Sunnyvale Chamber of Commerce, *Sunnyvale, the Manufacturing Suburb of San Francisco*, 44.

[7] Much of the information on the tractors, especially the Johnson tractor, comes from material in the Hal Higgins Library, University of California at Davis. Higgins himself wrote at least two articles on the Johnson tractor.

[8] R. B. Gary, comp., *The Agricultural Tractor, 1855-1950* (Saint Joseph, Mich.: American Society of Agricultural Engineers, 1954), 52. Another source of information on local tractors has been our long-time family friend Louis Paviso, who wrote out a series of notes on the subject for me in 1983.

[9] Eugene T. Sawyer, *History of Santa Clara County* (Los Angeles: Historic Record Co., 1922), 1664. Also, telephone conversation with Perley Payne, nephew of George Payne, on Dec. 27, 1982.

[10] Conversation with Alfred Amstutz and Dr. Harold E. Thomas, Jan. 25, 1984; see also "Deciduous Fruit Field Station," *California Agriculture* 19, no. 11 (Nov. 1965): 2–3. Mr. Amstutz, superintendent of the station from 1963 to 1969, sent me notes about its staff and accomplishments during his forty years there. The notes are now in the collection of the California History Center, De Anza College, Cupertino.

[11] Alex G. McAdie, "Notes on Frost," *Farmer's Bulletin*, no. 104 (Washington, D.C.: Government Printing Office, 1917); E. S. Nichols, "The Probability of Certain Minimum Temperatures in the Santa Clara Valley, Calif., in Spring," *Monthly Weather Review* 52 (May 1924): 253–57.

[12] Robert A. Kepner, "Operation of Orchard Heaters," Cal. Exp. Sta. *Bulletin*, Aug. 28, 1940; ibid., *The Principles of Orchard Heating*, Circular no. 400, Nov. 1950. Kepner lists seven different types of orchard heaters used in his experiments.

[13] Sawyer, *History of Santa Clara County*, 1628; W. V. Cruess and A. W. Christie, "Dehydration of Fruits," *Bulletin of the Agriculture Experiment Station*, no. 330. There is a small photo of the Los Gatos installation of the new dehydrator in this bulletin.

[14] Paul Jr. visited my parents, sitting with them at the back of the house and looking into the orchard, just two weeks before his untimely death in 1979, at the age of 59.

[15] "History of Sunsweet," *Sun-Diamond Grower*, Oct.–Nov. 1981, 37.

[16] Audrey D. Dennis, "100 Years of Canning in the West," *Canner and Packer*, Sept. 1958, 17.

[17] A label of The Woman's Cannery is in the private collection of Ralph Rambo, Palo Alto. He mentioned to me that he thought it may have had something to do with Mrs. Dawson. It could have been one of the labels used when she and her son ran the J. M. Dawson Packing Co. after her husband died in 1885.

[18] Phone conversation with Joseph Amori, Jan. 25, 1984.

[19] Conversation with Michael Filice, ibid. He is a grandson of Gennaro Filice, one of the founders of Filice and Perrelli.

[20] Telephone conversation with William J. Adams, formerly of FMC, and John Abbot of FMC, Feb. 5, 1984; American Society of Mechanical Engineers, *The FMC Rotary Pressure Sterilizer* (Madera, Calif.: the society, May 17, 1982).

[21] Discussion with James Hait, Feb. 3, 1984. Mr. Hait was in charge of Central Engineering Lab at FMC after World War II and went on to become corporation president and chairman of the Board. Also, discussion on February 5, 1984, with William Belk, who was project engineer for the Whole Fruit Juice Extractor in Santa Clara County and is

now in Florida with FMC's Citrus Machinery Division.

[22] Conversation with Paul Wilbur of Richmond-Chase and FMC, Feb. 3, 1984; "Perspective, Richmond-Chase Company," *CCG Picture*, 33.

[23] Dennis, "100 Years of Canning in the West," 51. Barron-Gray put out a promotion film called *Rainbow Harvest*, available from film archives, Board of Education, Santa Clara County. Despite the sales pitch, it gave an informative picture of the canning facility and laboratory, the pineapple being grown in Hawaii, and the process by which it and other fruits became fruit cocktail in San Jose.

[24] Dennis, ibid., 59.

[25] Marion G. Hanson, "The DiNapoli Family: Independent Fruit Packers and Canners of Santa Clara Valley," Unpublished manuscript, (California History Center, Cupertino), 8; conversation with Albert De-Franco, president of National Preserve Company, Jan. 23, 1984.

Other Sources for Chapter 9

E. N. Richmond II loaned me the business records of the Richmond-Chase Company for 1932–39. They reveal that in 1938, a government loan of $500,000 saved the company from bankruptcy. World War II brought recovery, but the company again faced financial difficulties in the 1950s, which it solved by conceiving the idea of California Canners and Growers, a co-op that took over its plants.

For the story of the peach canning industry, see Earl Chapin May, *The Canning Clan*, (New York: Macmillan, 1937). An excellent history of Del Monte is William Braznell, *California's Finest*, (San Francisco: Del Monte Corporation, 1982).

Also worth consulting is Robert James Claus, *Fruit and Vegetable Canning in the Santa Clara Valley*, typescript, n. p., Aug. 1966. A copy is on file in the California Room, San Jose Public Library.

CCG Picture, magazine of the now-defunct California Canners and Growers, published from 1966 to 1969 and again from 1973 to 1981, did historical profiles of three firms it absorbed in Santa Clara County: Shuckl (summer 1976), Richmond-Chase and San Jose Cannery (summer 1978); it also absorbed Filice and Perrelli of Gilroy. For Sun Garden, see Erin Mulcahy [granddaughter of Frank DiNapoli], "A Family History," (Unpublished paper, 1975, library of California History Center, De Anza College, Cupertino). Also on file at the center are California League of Food Processors, "Member Profiles," which includes short histories of many Santa Clara County canneries; and Ralph Rambo, "Facts Relating to This Label Collection—1981," which is full of interesting notes on local industry.

CHAPTER 10
SANTA CLARA COUNTY
TODAY

SANTA CLARA COUNTY IS FIGHTING a holding action in the cause of agricultural land reserves. We are a wagon train, besieged by the whooping Indians of urbanization, and waiting prayerfully for the U. S. Cavalry.[1]

The U.S. Cavalry never came. Santa Clara Valley was urbanized and the family farms all but disappeared—within three decades. When there is a death in a family, there is a burial and period of mourning. But how do we grieve for whole communities? It is memory that links us to past generations. To know who we are, we need to know where we came from. The search by adopted children for their biological parents bears witness to this need. But what should we remember about what was? What is of value?

"We thought we would be here forever," said one woman whose family farmed pears for almost one hundred years in Santa Clara County.

"Who would have guessed that this wonderful valley would change in such a way?" said a Chicano farm labor contractor who has lived here since the 1930s.

"I hate the name 'Silicon,'" said my aunt Elsie Olson Kay. "It even sounds awful."

"I will never forget the way it looked in spring. The creamy white cherry blossoms, the yellow mustard for miles and miles," said Louis Paviso, whose family has been in the county since the early part of the century.

Most people who remember the early valley emphasize that it *was* beautiful. The landscape was so fine it left one with a sense of quiet pleasure, an inner well-being. Whether you looked down into the valley, protected by mountains and bounded by the sparkling blue bay, or looked up at the rim of purple hills from the valley floor, you had a sense of vast natural beauty that had been enhanced by human hands. The orchards seemed to fit the level plain exactly. The vineyards clung in just the right proportions to the mountainsides. The dairies scattered alongside San Francisco Bay and in south county seemed to have been tailored to the landscape. The vegetable fields, the berry patches, the ornamental flower shelters—all had the look of being just right.

"We had purpose, the children knew that they had to help; we all worked together," said Catherine Paviso Gasich, Louis Paviso's sister. She spoke from experience, for in the Paviso family the five children worked in the orchards, cutting apricots and picking prunes through the summer in order to help support their widowed mother and themselves through the winter.

Perhaps this aspect of farm life was the most important. Well-known child and family psychologist Bruno Bettelheim, speaking in Santa Clara in 1984, expressed similar sentiments. "Parents and children traditionally worked together in the home and on the farm, where most families lived. . . . Parents served as positive role models for the children, who watched their mothers bear and rear children and run an entire household and watched their father shoe a horse or plow a field. Such a child could not help but respect his parents and honor them."[2] That the life was hard cannot be denied; that it engendered a special relationship between people and the soil, between families and the natural world, was equally true. Add to this the honesty in human relations, the concern for those around you, and you had a place where there were few if any anonymous people.

The End of the Family Farms

In the 1950s the population of Santa Clara County was just under 300,000. In 1980 the U.S. Census listed it as 1,289,550. With the influx of newcomers, our way of life has altered dramatically. The farm families remain in small pockets scattered like so many pieces of confetti waiting to be swept up. There is little to suggest that once this area was covered in trees. I did see an apricot tree that had struggled up between

230

the sidewalk and the pavement of a local gasoline station. The valiant tree had survived long enough to bear fruit, something an ungrafted tree is not supposed to do.

Two questions seem essential to this story: Why did the family farms die out and what, if anything, was done to save the valley's farmlands? In answering the first question, we need to begin with the character of the farmer himself. If this life, so in tune with nature's cycles, was fulfilling for some, it was not for everyone. My father looked down the line at his seven grandchildren and remarked, "I don't see a farmer among them!" He died before our eldest child declared her major in earth sciences at California Polytechnic State University, San Luis Obispo. To our eternal grief she died from injuries sustained in an auto accident before she had her chance.

My mother, who dislikes housework, was revived every spring when my father would bring her a twig with the first cherry blossoms from the orchard. Then came the branch showing the first red on the pale fruit. At that she was ready to go down to her fruit stand eager for the work ahead—much like her granddaughter Debbie Olson, who runs the fruitstand today, from mid-May through the summer months. One of the problems of continuing the family-farm tradition is that younger members of families are drawn to other areas of work.

This trend reflects changes in American culture. We have moved from a producer to a consumer society. Americans turn their backs on manual labor. White shirts for men and high heels for women are the norm in the workplace, and a person who gets his hands dirty and sweats in the noonday sun has to have a strong commitment to farming to carry on. The average age of the remaining farmers in Santa Clara County is fifty-seven.

Several economic factors have contributed to the breakup of the small family farms. If land has been passed down through several generations, parcels become too small to farm individually. In many cases the farmer's decision to sell precious land has been forced by harsh economic realities; in-creased costs of labor, fuel, water, fertilizer, sprays, equipment, and taxes, costs that have not been matched by increased profits. Also, farm services have moved away, making repairs more expensive and more difficult to obtain. Even the local markets, like the canneries, have shrunk to a mere handful. Many farmers soon reached the point at which their land became more valuable as real estate than as farmland. For the dedicated farmer it was easier to sell an acre here and buy three acres for the same price elsewhere in California, where the farmer could work in peace. The serious farmer and the marginal farmer were the ones to sell first.

It was a way of life whose time had passed, whose potential had been realized, and now it was coming to an end. It happened not just in Santa Clara County but across the nation.[3] The small family farms near urban centers began to disappear—and will continue to do so. It is estimated that 50,000 acres of farmland are converted to nonfarm purposes in California every year. Nationwide the figures indicate that 12 square miles of agricultural land go out of production every day. Each year, 100,000 farms close down or are absorbed by more successful operations.

History, too, has taken its toll. In the late 1930s the county still had 100,000 acres in orchards and an additional 20,000 acres in vegetables. The war changed everything. It brought thousands of military personnel to the West Coast on the way to the Pacific and helped speed the country's westward movement of population. While California itself was considered, from the 1870s onward, to be one of the ten largest urban states, it was also one of the most significant agriculturally. Amid the large farms were pockets of small farms, as in Orange and Santa Clara counties. It was to be expected that these two flat areas, so close to Los Angeles and San Francisco, would be among the first to be overwhelmed by the rapid postwar urbanization. After the war Santa Clara County led the state with an increase in population at a rate double the growth of California itself. It also became a major center for

231

high-technology research, development, and production. San Jose boasted in 1970: "Two decades of growth have established metropolitan San Jose as one of the nation's four fastest-growing markets and the unquestioned leader in Northern California."[4]

Efforts to Save Farms

When the history of farmland preservation in the United States is written, it will begin with Santa Clara County. Heroic efforts to preserve farmland were originated by the farmers themselves. Farmers served on local and countywide planning boards such as the Santa Clara County Planning Commission, created in 1931, and one of the first of its kind in the United States. Its members, who serve without pay, are appointed by the county supervisors, and the interests of agriculture have usually been represented on it. Weller Curtner, whose family had been ranching in the Calaveras area for over one hundred years, and Will B. Weston, Santa Clara pear grower, served from the commission's beginning through 1959. Charles B. Kuhn, an Evergreen district rancher, Will Lester, a Santa Clara orchardist, and George Milias, Jr., a Gilroy pear grower and rancher, were commissioners, as was Robert C. Kirkwood, another pear grower who later went to Sacramento as a Santa Clara County assemblyman and was later elected state controller.

An early executive director of the commission, Nestor Barrett, was succeeded in 1952 by Karl J. Belser, a professional planner with a deep, almost spiritual commitment to the continuation of agriculture in Santa Clara Valley. As head of the County Planning Department, he did all one person could do to alert the public to the threat of urbanization and the problems it would cause. Will Weston, a scholar as well as a farmer, subscribed to an English journal, *The Countryman*, from which he learned of the English system, known as greenbelting, in which land is retained around an urban center for nonurban use, like a belt of green. Belser had become aware of green-

belting when he studied in Europe. In the early 1950s the two men promoted and developed the concept for Santa Clara County—possibly its first use on the West Coast.

One example of the thinking of Belser, Weston, and the Planning Commission is the greenbelt idea for Berryessa, a community east of San Jose.[5] On paper the plan looked perfect for the circumstances. It recognized that this area was prime, class I soil, perfect for fruit growing, that should remain agricultural through greenbelting. In 1962 the Eastside General Plan was published; it called for gradual development, and projected that by 1985 there would still be almost 3,500 acres of farmland left in the area. Today, the number of acres in farmland on the eastside is so small—about one hundred, according to the growers I have consulted—that the fifteen-acre farm of Dominic and Sonny Bianchi on North Capitol Avenue is surrounded by chain-link fence to protect it from its urban neighbors.

While planning departments could make recommendations, they could not enforce them, and when farmers were offered increasingly high prices for their land, they sold. Old orchards of ten to twenty acres whose yields had declined were the first to go. Diseases, a natural problem of orchards, began to take their toll. The smaller farmers sold out.

There were also forces within the county itself that were looking for new industry for Santa Clara County, and with good reason. San Jose's Chamber of Commerce had long sought to broaden the community's economic base. In response to the Depression, the Chamber sought aggressively to bring new companies to the county. As it was, there were several thousand workers who were employed seasonally in the fruit orchards or canneries. For four or five months of a year these workers were idle. In 1944 the Chamber of Commerce actively sought funds from the San Jose City Council and the Board of Supervisors. With $35,000 in hand it launched a campaign to attract new industry and hired a representative to visit companies interested in moving west. In 1946 Chicago's large International Minerals and Chemical

232

Corporation built a plant for manufacturing Ac'cent just south of downtown San Jose. Eventually Ford Motor (1953) and General Motors (1956) settled nearby. Before the end of the 1950s, General Electric and IBM were also welcomed into San Jose's sphere.[6]

Annexation Battles and the Olson Family. San Jose was not alone in its effort to be part of the coming bonanza. Since our property is on El Camino Real, it was a natural for incorporation into the expanding boundaries of the city of Sunnyvale, which developed an aggressive annexation policy following World War II. One of the main reasons farmers do not want to be included in cities is because of the added city property taxes and the regulations that city government brings. This was another reason so many small farmers sold to builders during this period. On ten or twenty acres, the margin of profit was too small to afford the higher city taxes, which were based on the land's potential value as urban real estate.

The battles of the 1950s and 1960s that we waged as a family parallel the experiences of other farm families across the valley. The city of Sunnyvale eyed our property covetously. My father, along with many other like-minded farmers, and with the backing of the farm-oriented County Planning Commission and Department, petitioned the County Board of Supervisors to create a designation of land for agricultural purposes that could not be annexed.

Since the Board of Supervisors also had farmers sitting on it at the time, the legislation was passed in 1953. Called "type A," this classification of greenbelt may have been the first such effort in the United States to preserve agricultural land.[7] It provided a protection for farmers from city annexation—a significant step, if one considers that in the early 1950s Santa Clara County was still one of the leading agricultural counties in the United States.[8] The cities reacted by using loopholes in state annexation laws to grab as much farmland as possible. My father developed ulcers as he manned the telephone with other worried farmers and helped to devise schemes to counterattack the cities' drive to annex. One such scheme entailed incorporating Cupertino, then still an unincorporated village, which would then annex all the county territory, including ours, between Santa Clara and Sunnyvale. This idea backfired (land prices soared when the plan was leaked), but, eventually, the same leaders of that movement formed the drive to incorporate the city of Cupertino as an effort by the farmers to keep the area agricultural.

A cartoon of the 1955 incorporation battle shows Cupertino embraced by several octopuses, namely, San Jose, Santa Clara, Sunnyvale, and Los Altos. In October of that year Cupertino incorporated as Santa Clara County's thirteenth city. Its primary purpose was to preserve the rural atmosphere of the community and to allow farmers to operate at minimum tax rates while industrial forces from neighboring communities were kept out. In an effort to increase its tax base, San Jose began to annex farmlands, creating a patchwork of boundary lines and isolated islands of development that were expensive and impractical to service.[9] But each city practiced the same method of grabbing land. This patchwork development, or "leapfrogging," was to have the worst effect on agricultural lands by creating pressure on all sides for the few remaining farmers to sell out to development, even if they didn't want to.[10] By 1955 nearly 30,000 acres of prime farmland had been lost. By 1965 there were 52,000 acres left in fruit, nuts and berries; a decade later the number was down to 23,000. Seventy-seven thousand acres were urbanized within thirty years![11]

Development was not only uneven but inequitable. North county—Palo Alto, Mountain View and Sunnyvale, Santa Clara—garnered the most lucrative firms, leaving San Jose and points south to deal with the less attractive housing market. This created an imbalance in the county tax base.[12] Despite its early efforts to attract industry, San Jose began to fill the need for affordable housing for the new influx of people. The orchard lands of south county became more and more desirable for this purpose, and subdivisions began to appear even in

233

areas designated in the county's general plan as agricultural preserve. Land in such areas had proved to be nothing but land waiting for development.

The cities have another technique at their disposal to deal with land which is deemed necessary to the public welfare: eminent domain, the condemnation of private property for public use. The first major loss of our land was a ten-acre piece of cherry orchard, part of the original Spalding-Caulkins tract, which yielded our very best cherries. This orchard was in the middle of the path between Old San Francisco Road and El Camino Real. In extending Fairoaks Avenue between them the city of Sunnyvale was responding to a need for handling increased traffic. By so doing it opened up this section of prime cherry land to development. Here was a classic case of the rights of private ownership versus the welfare of the community. Something had to give.

Several property owners were involved because the city wanted to widen Fairoaks at the same time that the avenue was pushed through our property. Along with others Dad helped organize the Fairoaks Citizens Committee, which fought the city because it intended to assess the property owners for "improving" their land. The wrangling went on for several months until August of 1958, when the city forced a sale by eminent domain. Not only did my father lose the land, but he was assessed $17,199 in additional property taxes. It was argued that, since the road would improve the land, the owners should pay for improvement. The day the bulldozers arrived my father stood at the edge of his orchard and wept. It took less than a minute to pull out each tree that had taken my father and other farmers before him a lifetime to grow.

Then El Camino Real, which passes in front of the home ranch, needed to be widened. More land was sliced away. Next Mathilda Avenue, suddenly carrying so much traffic from Lockheed and other industries, needed to be extended— unfortunately, right through our orchard. The battle flared into a full-scale war that can be traced in detail through the local press from as early as 1962 until October 1965. An editorial of October 20, 1965, in the *Sunnyvale Daily Standard* claimed, "At Long Last, Mathilda Extension Deadlock Appears to Be Broken." During those years my father was portrayed in the newspaper as impeding progress, preferring to be left alone with his cherry orchard. It wasn't too far from the truth. He also insisted that he be paid a fair market value for his land and be given zoning that could enable him to develop if the necessity arose. The newspapers reported that the city felt he asked too much, and that he was unreasonable. Since 1966, when the two and a half acres were bulldozed, there has been a busy six-lane road with divider running through the orchard.

In the meantime Sunnyvale grew tenfold, from 9,829 in 1950 to 95,480 in 1970. In 1980 its population was 106,618. Its land size increased from 6.1 square miles in 1950 to its present size of 24 square miles. Today Sunnyvale claims the highest concentration of high-tech firms of any city in the county and calls itself "the heart of Silicon Valley."

State Farmland Legislation. Many farmers recognized the threat to their way of life and they exerted pressure on Sacramento. Based largely on what had been done in Santa Clara County, an Agricultural Exclusion Act was passed in 1955. It infuriated the cities even more. In the ninety days between the closing of the legislature and the effective date of the law, the cities set about widely extending their boundaries. At one time the city of San Jose had a boundary over 200 miles in length enclosing less than 20 square miles of land.[13] By that time many Santa Clara Valley farmers had indicated their desire to stay in business. The first 744 acres to become part of the 1953 County Exclusive Agriculture Zone belonged to the pear growers near Agnew. Will Weston and his brother Sam, the Brown family, and thirteen other families signed their land into greenbelt in April 1954.[14] The zone grew to 40,000 acres by 1958. But the legislation enacted by the state, though helpful, only slowed the pace of urbanization; it could not stop it.

234

In the meantime the County Planning Department under Karl Belser drafted a proposal to buy development rights from farmers in order to make these agricultural lands a permanent part of the county's future.[15] Belser saw agricultural land as a national resource that should be preserved in the same way as national parks. His department's proposal called for a pilot program that would plan in advance to save the 40,000 acres remaining in the county's agricultural reserve by making them farmland in perpetuity. The idea called for the public to buy the development rights to farmland while the farmer retained mineral, water, trespass, and aerial privacy rights. In this plan the county was to have greenbelts gracefully buffering its urban areas. While nothing came of this plan in terms of agricultural preservation, the idea was communicated to a growing number of people concerned about the environment of Santa Clara County. Belser attended meetings with Wallace Stegner and Lois Hogle, who would later help to organize the Committee for Green Foothills.

The farmers organized again. John Leonard and his son Burrel, Will Lester, and Norman Nathanson, all four from Cupertino, my father, and many others backed Senator John Williamson of Kern County, who presented a plan to the state legislature to aid in the preservation of farm lands. Our local assemblyman Bruce Allen, who had grown up on a prune farm in Santa Clara, ushered the bill through the assembly on behalf of John Williamson. By 1965 the Williamson Act was passed, mainly at the instigation of Santa Clara Valley farmers. Included in its provisions are tax benefits to the farmer, whose land is taxed at a farm rate rather than a commercial rate—in other words, in relation to his actual income from it rather than its value as real estate. The farmer signing into the Williamson Act does so for ten-year periods, and if he wants out is obligated to pay back taxes.

My father was one of the many to sign up as the city of Sunnyvale stood by helpless to thwart him. The city changed its attitude as it began to choke on the wealth progress had brought. When my father died, fifteen years after placing his property under the act and thereby ending his struggle with the city, he was widely acclaimed for his efforts to save his land from the bulldozer.

Even with local agricultural zoning laws, state laws, and the designation of agricultural preserves, the cities quickly found they could get around the restrictions. The general plan for Santa Clara County, published in 1982, summarizes the situation. "Instead of concentrating their annexation activity in a compact area, cities have stretched long tentacles out to connect to territory far from their urban core. These have been described as 'cherry stem' annexations. The shape of certain cities defies description and creates serious obstacles to efficient public service provision."[16]

Where Did the Farmers Go?

Many of our neighbors, being committed to farming, sold their land and went to other parts of California. Some continue to farm in places such as Winters, Yuba City, Marysville, and Gustine. Others sold their land and thought their sudden wealth would last forever. It didn't. Still others sold and invested the money in the new high-tech companies. Finally, a number of families, such as the Pavlinas, the Tikvicas, the Vidovichs and the Sakauyes, retained their land and developed it.

In 1962 seventeen families in Cupertino, in an effort to move with the changing times, banded together and formed Vallco Park, 200 acres zoned for industrial and commercial use. Heading the group of farmers-turned-developers were Will Lester, who continues to farm in partnership with his sons in Winters, and Burrel Leonard, whose family was among the early farm settlers of the county, and who retains five acres of property where the old Leonard packing house still stands, amid the shopping center and industrial buildings.[17]

Farmers will be farmers, but the style varies. Lou and Jack Mariani saw the future well in advance and began to buy land for farming in other parts of the state as early as 1953.[18] Today their family-farm enterprise is one of the largest walnut-growing concerns in the state. Bob and Audrey Butcher, on the other hand, whose families reach back over one hundred years in Santa Clara County history, farm their remaining six acres not because it pays them to do so, but, as Bob said to me, because they enjoy the opportunity to work outside in a productive job, helping, along with the soil, sun, and rain, to make the trees grow and bear fruit. An example of how farming is being eased out of the county is that of Lee and Ray Lester, cousins of Will Lester. They farm in south county in the Coyote Valley on land belonging to IBM. Originally, they worked the land, mostly prune orchard, on a sharecrop basis. The farm had formerly been part of the 310-acre Ole Christopher ranch. Every year their acres dwindle as the big corporation extends its buildings. They are down to the last 140 acres and now, because of the increased costs of farming, IBM pays them to farm the land.

Some order was introduced into the chaos of uncontrolled growth in Santa Clara County when it undertook to avail itself of a state-created board, the Local Agency Formation Commission (LAFCO). Created by law in 1963, the agency was not used in Santa Clara County until 1970, when it formed a commission here. The commission mapped out the guidelines by which the county and the cities divided responsibility for territory under their respective control. By 1973 it was accepted that urban development should be allowed only in incorporated areas, not on county land. Cities also were required to designate "urban service areas" where development would be allowed; all other land was reserved for nonurban use, such as agriculture.

As of 1982 there were just over 20,000 acres of land left in agriculture (fruits, nuts, berries, and vegetables) on the valley floor. Most of these acres were in south county, around Morgan Hill and south and east of Gilroy.[19] County agriculture still produced an impressive dollar figure; the total value, including cattle and field crops such as hay and grain was $124

million per year. The orchards that had covered 125,000 acres of prime valley land in the 1920s covered only 8,000 acres. Of tree crops, only apricots were listed among the top ten items of agricultural return. The county's number one crop today is cut flowers, accounting for some twenty percent of total income. Chrysanthemums top the list of flowers. Next come mushrooms and third is nursery stock, which includes Christmas trees. The high value of land has resulted in the introduction of an intensive agriculture that is more compatible with an urban environment. We can look forward to an even greater concentration of horticulture—greenhouse farming similar to the type that exists in Los Angeles and other highly urbanized settings. There is also a trend toward part-time farming. The increase in the number of farms—from 1,427 in 1978 to 1,518 in 1982—that has been recorded by the Commerce Department, Census of Agriculture, is a further sign of urbanization, since the additional "farms" are actually "ranchettes" of 1 to 9 acres. Their owners pursue urban vocations but qualify as farmers under the current census definition (1978, 1982) because they also raise at least $1,000 worth of produce a year.

Why High-Tech?

What or who is responsible for the electronics industry's major growth in our community? In 1933, as a result of intense local political effort, the federal government established a military base at Moffett Field, the former land of Chief Yñigo. In 1940 Ames Research Center, later a mainstay of the U.S. guided-missile and space program, was established in nearby Mountain View to supply the military with basic research into aerodynamics. Lockheed Missiles and Space Company followed in 1956. In many ways the county was an established base of research and development long before today's high technology became a factor. The area of technology for which we are known as Silicon Valley is electronics. That area was the province of Dr. Fredrick Terman (1900–1982), who came to Stanford University in 1926 as an engineering professor and became head of the engineering department. William Hewlett, a student of Terman's, developed an audio oscillator in 1938. Terman saw the commercial potential and found grant money to help Hewlett. David Packard, another Stanford graduate student, was asked to join. Just as the canning industry began in a backyard building the new electronic industry was born in Packard's garage. Their first eight oscillators were sold to Walt Disney for use in the movie *Fantasia*. They formed a company, and today Hewlett-Packard employs over sixty thousand people worldwide—fifteen thousand in Santa Clara County alone.

Meanwhile, major investments in building and hiring have made Stanford a major university, while the combination of Stanford's land use policies with the presence of major research institutions has resulted in a unique environment for high-tech development. The Stanford Industrial Park, developed in the 1950s, represented the wave of the future for industries without smokestacks. The Varian brothers, Russell and Sigurd, had developed the klystron tube while working within the Stanford Department of Physics in 1937. They created Varian Associates in 1948 and moved their company from San Carlos to the Stanford Industrial Park when it opened in 1952. Then the county's first suburban shopping center came into being on Stanford land. In this way new revenues were brought into the university coffers at the same time that the university-linked companies extended Stanford's prestige.

Another stride in the development of Silicon Valley was the return of William Shockley, the "father of the transistor," to his hometown of Palo Alto in 1955; a job at Stanford had been arranged for him by Terman. At the same time, Shockley established Shockley Transistor Corporation, employing several bright engineers and a physicist, Robert Noyce. In 1957 seven members of this group, dubbed the Traitorous Seven by Shockley, broke away and found financial backing in New York from a high-technology company that had developed

out of World War II, Fairchild Camera and Instrument Corporation. Calling themselves Fairchild Semiconductor, they were headed by Robert Noyce, who became traitor number eight from Shockley's chosen few. Noyce had developed the transistorized chip, producing it on silicon wafers instead of germanium.

Thanks in part to Noyce, today's Santa Clara County has a reputation for egalitarian management. He has been credited with establishing the style that is the hallmark of the new corporate culture: open shirts, casual clothes, interaction on a first-name basis. He has also helped to show the way for employees to become owners very much as farm laborers used to become landed farmers. No less than fifty spinoffs, including Noyce's own Intel Corporation, followed from Fairchild, and the decade of the 1970s was one of tremendous expansion in Silicon Valley.

The New American Dream

While the Indians altered the landscape of the Santa Clara Valley by burning to promote growth, and the Spanish cut down its trees and dammed its streams, no change in its environment has been as complete as the one since World War II. Social change, though more peacefully accomplished than in those earlier periods, has been no less pervasive, for the result has been a new scale of community.

We know what we have lost by change, but what have we gained? Those who have little appreciation for the glitz of megabucks have come away calling our new culture "smug." Yet others have called it "soulless." One analyst, trying to explain why someone in Silicon Valley should sell military secrets to the Russians, said: "What you've got in the valley is a very aggressive group of overachievers. It's a highly motivated, fast-track, materialistic environment; most people live beyond their means; there are more Ferraris and Mercedeses in this area than anywhere in the world."[20] At the same time the creativity, the risk taking, the competitive spirit that brings many nationalities together makes for an exciting situation. It is the Gold Rush all over again, with some of its rewards and most of its hazards.

Living in this new society has its own set of problems. New jobs were created by the thousands. One out of three jobs in the valley is related to high-tech industry. These jobs were created faster than houses for workers. From 1971 to 1979 the median price of a new home increased from $24,300 to $83,600, or 244 percent. Median household income rose only 69 percent.[21] The system of building high-tech firms at one end of the county and houses at the other depends on the automobile and cheap gasoline. Traffic to and from work has created a commuter's nightmare as bad as any in the United States; air pollution is a major problem. Responding to the cries of overcrowding, cities have begun to change their tune about development. At the beginning of the 1980s Sunnyvale was the first town to slap a hold on any further business expansion because of housing shortages and traffic jams.[22] Palo Alto followed. Other cities around the Bay have instituted similar holds. Sunnyvale lifted one but reinstated another in 1982, because the sewage capacity of the city had been reached.

On the other hand, the lure of new firms to bring in more money has remained strong, as was demonstrated in 1983 in the case of Coyote Valley, the last 5,000-acre parcel on the valley floor within the boundaries of the city of San Jose. The city, faced with little revenue, increased cutbacks in services, and a school system about to declare bankruptcy, could do nothing else but agree to develop what had been designated as agricultural preserve.

Other problems have appeared in this new version of the American dream. Once again Santa Clara County's water resources are in the news, not because of its extraordinary artesian wells, but because the aquifer itself is being poisoned by industrial chemicals. While the industry in question is without smokestacks, some companies use as many as six thousand different chemical substances. A major effort to keep waste products out of the water system is under way.[23] A sharp rise in the crime rate has resulted in a shortage of prison space for criminals. Roads in the county need repair.

Coming to Terms with Change

Some efforts to save lands for public use have been successful. Locally, the Committee for Green Foothills, founded 1962, was one of the factors behind the formation of the Mid-peninsula Open Space District, formed by the voters in 1972 to buy land outright with public money to create a greenbelt zone. Several thousand acres have been purchased in Santa Clara and San Mateo counties to preserve some vestige of our natural heritage, along the foothills and the bay.

While such measures have addressed the question of greenbelting, they have offered no solution to the conversion of farmlands. It is possible that the time will come when some balance between continued development and farmland conservation at the state or even the national level will be worked out. Trusts are being established to buy farmlands in various parts of the United States. But it is too late for this valley. At present the need for jobs, the lack of tax money to improve services, the belief in progress and development work against a long-term commitment to preserving farmlands. The high productivity of California farming also makes the problem of disappearing farmlands seem less real. If we cannot preserve the farmlands, we can at least preserve something from the farming past. What, in that past, is of value today?

For Japanese poets the drifting cherry blossom, especially the single blossoms of the orchard tree, symbolizes the transitory nature of life. Like the blossom, life is beautiful but also fragile and brief. Those of us who lived among orchards have had no little opportunity to observe this floating of blossoms to the ground. When the breeze comes up, the petals drift gently, covering the ground with snow-like white. At the same time in April great billowy clouds move over the valley from the Pacific Ocean like a caravan of tall ships, riding so high

238

that the fluffy mass sails right over the Coast Ranges. The sky, so vast, blue, and empty, is suddenly filled. Drifting blossoms, drifting clouds, white on bright blue . . . the effect causes one to be still.

In coming to terms with change I cannot but look to the cherry tree itself for a way of understanding. Yes, the blossoms drop, but they are followed by fruit, fulfillment of the blossoms' promise and equally breathtaking. And that is not all. To illustrate what I mean, I must turn to an example that grows out of something that irritated my father. He particularly disliked the unthinking people who stole fruit from the orchard. These were not the gleaners of the Bible, who come after the crop has been harvested to pick the fruit that remains. These were the people who came with shopping bags in the middle of the harvest and took as much as they could get away with. To add to the insult, they normally broke limbs and branches in the process. Whenever my father encountered one of these thieves he delivered his lecture, picking up the trampled branch and showing the offender that not only was he or she stealing this year's crop but destroying next year's. He would show the spur that lies in the joint between the leaf stem and the branch—the spur that, no more than a red nodule, is already in place, the beginning of next year's growth. To me the spur implies ongoing change and continuity.

While change can transform the landscape, robbing us of the familiar, it is integral to the ongoing cycle of life. One generation begets another; one community succeeds another. But amid the rush of the present and the excitement of the future it is well to remember the past. The thread that binds us to that past is fragile. Its basis is memory, the combined and proven memory of individuals. The past is important because it can lead us back to ourselves and to what is of value in our lives. Perhaps we can never recapture the exact human scale, the intimacy of a community where there were very few anonymous people. But the ideal should be in front of our eyes. The values of a closely knit community that fosters independence and meaningful purpose, one in which concern for one another is of prime importance, should never be forgotten. These values must endure in any society that calls itself human.

Notes

[1] Santa Clara County Planning Department, *Green Gold, A Proposal for a Pilot Experiment in the Conservation of Agricultural Open Space* (San Jose: the department, 1958), unpaginated (hereafter cited as *Green Gold*).

[2] Quoted in Barbara Wood, "Reasons behind Conflicts between Parents, Children," *Peninsula Times Tribune*, Feb. 10, 1984, B-1.

[3] Rebecca Conard, "Slurbanizing the Valley of the Heart's Delight: Origins of Agricultural Land Protection in California" (Submitted to Sourisseau Academy, San Jose State University, in fulfillment of grant stipulation, 1983), 26. This study is one of the first to attempt a history of land preservation in Santa Clara County. Page 26 includes a chart on relation of farm size to money earned on farms in the county from 1945 through 1964.

[4] *San Jose Mercury News, Facts about Metropolitan San Jose* (San Jose, June 1969). Included in this collection of data on the county are all the ways in which it can be shown how affluent, successful, and prestigious the county has become.

[5] Santa Clara County Planning Department, *Conservation of Agricultural Lands in the Berryessa Area* (San Jose: the department, Oct. 6, 1955); Conard, "Slurbanizing the Valley of the Heart's Delight," 25.

[6] Taped interview with Duncan Oneal, president of San Jose Chamber of Commerce in 1944, Oct. 15, 1982.

[7] See *Green Gold* for details of the Agricultural Exclusion Act.

[8] U.S. Department of Commerce, Bureau of the Census, *Census of Agriculture, 1950 Agriculture: Ranking Agricultural Counties, 1950* (Washington, D.C.: Government Printing Office, 1952), tables 46, 49, 50, 51, 52, 54. For example, we were the sixth leading county in growing fruits, berries, and other small fruits and nuts, including cherries; first in plums and prunes; and third in pears.

[9] "The Independent City," in *Cupertino Chronicle*, ed. Seonaid McArthur and David W. Fuller, (Cupertino: California History Center, 1975), 130–135; "Farmers Prepare for Last Stand," *Sunnyvale Standard*, Feb. 11, 1955.

[10] Howard F. Gregor, "Urban Pressures on California Land," *California: Its People, Its Problems, Its Prospects* (Palo Alto: National Press Books, 1971), 145. This map originated with Karl Belser. It illustrates patchwork or leapfrog annexation, also called strip annexation, in Santa Clara County in 1955.

[11] Santa Clara County Department of Agriculture, *Agricultural Crop Report, 1974,* (San Jose: the department, 1975), 11.

[12] Pacific Studies Center, *Silicon Valley: Paradise or Paradox, the Impact of High Technology Industry on Santa Clara County* (Mountain View: the center, Sept. 1977). Palo Alto's refusal to address its need for affordable housing continues to be a hot issue in town politics. An ongoing example in 1983 was the squabble over new development on Stanford property that abuts Menlo Park.

[13] Karl Belser, "The Making of Slurban America," *Cry California, The Journal of California Tomorrow,* Fall 1970, 1.

[14] Stanley Waldorf, "Santa Clara 'Green Belt' Plan Voted," *San Francisco Examiner,* Apr. 7, 1954.

[15] A major effort has been made to institute a similar concept in Santa Clara County by which developers would buy development rights from farmers in an area that would remain farmland, and would receive in exchange the right to build in another "receiving" area. See *Transfer of Development Credits as an Open Space Preservation Tool for Santa Clara County* (Santa Cruz: Harbinger Communications, Nov. 1983).

[16] Santa Clara County Planning Department, *General Plan, Santa Clara County* (San Jose: the department, Aug. 1980), 18.

[17] *Cupertino Chronicle,* 135–138; see also Burrel Leonard, comp., *An Old Time Picnic* (pamphlet written for First Annual Vallco Park Employees' Family Picnic, July 12, 1982, photocopy), on file at California History Center, Cupertino.

[18] Taped interview with Lou Mariani, Dec. 17, 1980.

[19] Santa Clara County Environmental Management Agency, Department of Agriculture, *Crop Report from Santa Clara County Agricultural Commissioner [1982]* (San Jose: the department, Feb. 28, 1983) 7.

[20] *Peninsula Times Tribune,* Oct. 30, 1983, E-2.

[21] *General Plan, Santa Clara County,* 35.

[22] "Permits Quietly Granted, but Lockheed Plan Spurs Furor," *Sunnyvale Journal,* Jan. 9, 1980.

[23] "Huge lawsuit against Fairchild over health hazard from spills," *San Francisco Examiner,* Jan. 21, 1983, B-10.

Other Sources for Chapter 10

For a complete summary of the various ideas current in the area of farmland preservation, see Eleanor M. Cohen, ed., *The Farmlands Project* (Claremont: California Institute of Public Affairs, 1983); see page 28 for a brief overview by the author on Santa Clara County. This study was underwritten by the California State Legislature and is based on a conference held in Fresno in April 1983. The California Farmlands Project has also published several papers, among them Eleanor M. Cohen and Dennis Castrillo, *Local Farmlands Projection in California: Studies of Problems, Programs, and Policies in Seven Counties* (ibid., 1983).

An early study of urbanization in the valley is Richard Rowe, "Agricultural Land and Open Space in Santa Clara County and Its Preservation" (Ph.D. diss., Stanford University, 1962). Several County Planning Department studies on greenbelting are on file at Stanford. They include *From Roadside Towns to Greenbelt City: A General Plan for Santa Clara County* (San Jose: the department, 1958).

Dirk Hanson, *The New Alchemists: Silicon Valley and the Microelectronics Revolution* (Boston: Little, Brown & Co., 1982) is a history of high-technology.

Conservation and planning groups have contributed to our awareness of open space problems. See especially Larry Ormon, project director, *Endangered Harvest: The Future of Bay Area Farmlands* (San Francisco: People for Open Space, 1980); *The California Land: Planning for People,* Report of the California Land-Use Task Force (Los Altos: William Kaufmann, Inc., 1975).

And there came a time when the farmer stopped caring for his orchard and left it abandoned. "Orchard near Stanford", 1940. *Photograph by and courtesy of Ansel Adams*

INDEX

To ripen these Pears to best advantage, keep in original wrapper at living room temperature of approximately 70° Fr. until slightly soft around stem. To retard ripening hold in refrigerator.

Old Orchard

WILL B. WESTON
Santa Clara, California

PRODUCE OF U.S.A.

Worswick's

FULL WEIGHT

CHERRIES

SAN JOSE   CALIFORNIA

COLOPHON

Text design by James Chadwick.
Photo spreads designed by James Chadwick and James Petersen.
Cover design by David Mike Hamilton.
Jacket design by Gary Head.
Composed in Weiss and Weiss Italic
by Jonathan Peck Typographer, Ltd., Santa Cruz.
Printed offset on Warren's Patina and Warren's Old Style
by Publisher's Press, Salt Lake City.
Bound by Hiller Industries, Salt Lake City.